Understanding Phenomenal Consciousness

William S. Robinson has written insightfully about the mind–body problem for many years. In *Understanding Phenomenal Consciousness* he focuses on sensory qualities such as pain, color, and sound and argues for Qualitative Event Realism, a dualistic theory of consciousness that opposes currently dominant materialist views. The theory is developed with attention both to contemporary philosophical arguments and to recent developments in psychology and the brain sciences.

This provocative book will appeal not only to those who approach the mind through traditional philosophy, but also to those in many disciplines who have been working toward the development of a science of consciousness.

William S. Robinson is Professor of Philosophy at Iowa State University.

CAMBRIDGE STUDIES IN PHILOSOPHY

General Editor ERNEST SOSA (Brown University)

Advisory Editors:
JONATHAN DANCY (University of Reading)
JOHN HALDANE (University of St. Andrews)
GILBERT HARMAN (Princeton University)
FRANK JACKSON (Australian National University)
WILLIAM G. LYCAN (University of North Carolina at Chapel Hill)
SYDNEY SHOEMAKER (Cornell University)
JUDITH J. THOMSON (Massachusetts Institute of Technology)

Recent Titles:

Understanding Phenomenal Consciousness

WILLIAM S. ROBINSON

Iowa State University

PUBLISHED BY THE PRESS SYNDICATE OF THE UNIVERSITY OF CAMBRIDGE
The Pitt Building, Trumpington Street, Cambridge, United Kingdom

CAMBRIDGE UNIVERSITY PRESS
The Edinburgh Building, Cambridge CB2 2RU, UK
40 West 20th Street, New York, NY 10011-4211, USA
477 Williamstown Road, Port Melbourne, VIC 3207, Australia
Ruiz de Alarcón 13, 28014 Madrid, Spain
Dock House, The Waterfront, Cape Town 8001, South Africa

http://www.cambridge.org

First published 2004

Printed in the United States of America

Typeface Bembo 10.5/13 pt.   *System* LaTeX 2$_\varepsilon$ [TB]

A catalog record for this book is available from the British Library.

Library of Congress Cataloging in Publication Data

Robinson, William S. (William Spencer), 1940–
Understanding phenomenal consciousness / William S. Robinson.
p.   cm. – (Cambridge studies in philosophy)
Includes bibliographical references and index.
ISBN 0-521-83463-5
1. Consciousness.   I. Title.   II. Series.
B808.9.R63   2004
126–dc22   2003059539

ISBN 0 521 83463 5 hardback

Contents

Acknowledgments

Much of the work on this book was done while on a Faculty Improvement Leave from Iowa State University. Equally necessary for its completion was a grant from the Center for Consciousness Studies at the University of Arizona. I would like to thank both of these institutions for their support.

Richard Epstein, Bill Lycan, Bill Seager, Leo Stubenberg, Brad Thompson, and an anonymous reviewer have read versions of the entire manuscript and provided enormously helpful comments. Veronica Dark helped shape the discussion of the latter two-thirds of Chapter 7 by providing a psychologist's point of view on attention, unconscious perception, and monitoring. David Chalmers provided editorial direction that has significantly improved the book. I am grateful to all these people for their help. I am, of course, solely responsible for the responses I have made to the many suggestions I have received and for any shortcomings that remain.

In one section of Chapter 9, I have drawn heavily on my "Orwell, Stalin and Determinate Qualia", *Pacific Philosophical Quarterly* (1994) 75:151–164, and I thank Blackwell Publishers for their kind permission to do so. Several sections expand on themes developed in a 1999 article, "Qualia Realism and Neural Activation Patterns", that appeared in the *Journal of Consciousness Studies* 6:65–80. I thank the journal's editors for permission to use some of the material from that article, including the diagram that appears here as Figure 1 of Chapter 12. Compurons and compusyns, which are discussed in Chapter 12, were introduced in the *AISB Quarterly*, No. 99:13–18, in an article titled "Could a Robot Be Qualitatively Conscious?" I thank the editors of this journal for permission to repeat some of the formulations that introduce these thought-experimental objects.

Some of the views in this book have been presented to conferences in Bremen (ASSC-2, 1998), Brussels (ASSC-4, 2000), and Tucson (II, 1996; III, 1998; IV, 2000). I thank the members of the audiences at these conferences for their comments. I also thank my fellow members of the Advanced Reasoning Forum for their responses to my presentations of "Consciousness, Materialism, and Ideology" in Humor, Romania, in 2000, and "Deep Experience" in Berkeley, California, in 2001.

The conviction that I should write a book on the topics here included crystallized during my participation in a 1995 NEH Summer Seminar directed by Bill Lycan. Research on what eventually became a 1997 *Erkenntnis* article, and then the basis for much of Chapter 4, began at that time, and I thank the NEH for its support of this work. Administrative duties made it impossible to begin a book-length project for several years, but work on papers related to the seminar continued during the interval. I would like to thank the other participants in the seminar for their critical reactions to several position papers I circulated. Above all, I would like to thank Bill Lycan, an extraordinary teacher, who, despite our divergence of philosophical views, has been unfailing in his encouragement of my efforts.

Finally, I would like to thank Maureen Ogle for her creation of unique and satisfying history – as much in her living and being as in her wonderful books.

Part I

1

Introduction

The central problem of this book can be introduced by thinking about even the simplest cases of phenomenal consciousness. Let us, therefore, begin with afterimages, and let us fix our ideas by reference to a novelty item that some readers may have encountered. This item is similar to an American flag, only it is printed in green, black, and yellow. A caption instructs users to stare at the oddly printed flag for 10 seconds, in good light, and then to look at a white wall or a white piece of paper. The predicted, and actual, result is that one will then see an American flag in its correct colors.

The principle behind this novelty item is that afterimages brought about by brightly colored things will have the complementary colors of the objects that cause them. This principle can easily be verified by staring at some brightly colored thing in strong light, then looking at a white surface. Red or green will each produce the other, as will blue or yellow. This little experiment will also demonstrate that the distance of the afterimage will be the same as the distance of the surface upon which one's eyes are focused.

I want to know how red comes into the situation we are in when we have stopped looking at the printed "flag" and are having an afterimage in which we see red. The reason for puzzlement here is that there isn't anything red in front of me, where a flag appears to be. Unless I have some strange disease, there isn't anything red in my brain, either. (Well, there is oxygenated blood; but this is always present, and so its color has nothing special to do with the redness in my afterimage, i.e., nothing that it doesn't equally have to do with green or blue afterimages.) But to say that there is nothing red at all anywhere in the situation would seem to deny an obvious fact, and to make it difficult to give an account of the difference between the redness of the stripes in the afterimage and the blueness of its upper-left-hand corner.

There are, of course, differences among the neural events that cause our afterimages. Color stimuli increase the activity in some of our cells, and different stimuli increase the activity in different sets of cells. Increase of activity in some cells results in inhibition of other cells and, when a stimulus is removed, there can be a "rebound" effect in the inhibited cells – an effect that "overshoots" the neutral state for a short time and thus produces a reverse color impression. These neural activations, however, are not something of which we are ordinarily conscious. For example, Aristotle knew about afterimages almost as well as we do, but he had no knowledge whatever about cells in our visual systems.[1] If we confine ourselves to the neuroscience of how afterimages are produced, we will never have any reason to use color words, and thus we will not have a full answer to our question of how colors come into the afterimages that neural activations bring about.

It would be natural to say, at this point, that having an afterimage of the stripes in the American flag is a situation in which it *looks like* there is something red before us. This is surely correct, but it leads to the further questions "What exactly is *looking like*?" and "What is the difference between its looking like there is something red before us, when there isn't, and its looking like there is something blue before us, when there isn't?" One can give a short answer, that the difference is the difference between red and blue; but as there need be no red or blue things present, this answer just returns us to the question of how colors come into situations in which we have afterimages.

In this book, I shall consider several answers to this surprisingly complex question. This question, however, is only one, readily understood, member of a family of related questions. For example, other senses could have been considered. Removing a tight hat can leave us with what we may call an "afterfeel" of pressure along a circle around the head. Some foods, or medicines taken by mouth, can leave an aftertaste. I want to know how these sensory qualities come into the situations described. I want to know what is happening that is different when (due to different hats) afterfeels are in different places on the head, and what constitutes the taste difference between two aftertastes.

---

1 Aristotle, *De Somniis* (*On Dreams*). I say "almost", because Aristotle seems to have missed the fact that afterimages often have colors complementary to those of their external causes.

4

Bodily sensations, e.g., pain, itch, sexual pleasantness, or nausea, do not present "aftersensations", but they do lead to questions similar to those about afterimages. For example, pain is caused by tissue damage, and our neurons have to be working in order for us to feel pain. But having pains does not give us knowledge about cells or about the neural causes of our painful feelings. Thus, we can sensibly wonder just how we should describe the way in which painfulness comes into a situation in which we are suffering. Similar remarks hold for a wide variety of feelings that are associated with emotions, e.g., fear, the feeling of butterflies in the stomach, the feeling one has when angry, and so on.[2]

Visual images (not afterimages) can be formed by most people upon request. For example, one can be asked to imagine a pink elephant or the face of some famous actor. Auditory images are likewise familiar – imagine, for example, the sound of some sinister remark by Darth Vader. Imagery of this kind is not the most typical example of the occurrences to which the arguments of this book are intended to apply, and there are many aspects of imagery that will not be investigated here. Nonetheless, the views to be considered have some bearing on the question of what kind of difference occurs when, on one occasion, we have an auditory image of, say, "red" and on another occasion we have an auditory image of "blue".

PERCEPTION AND OUR BASIC QUESTION

Some years ago, while lost in thought, I happened to stare out through a window with a venetian blind for a considerable time without moving. When I did move, my eyes chanced to fall on my trouser leg, where, to my surprise, I saw that the brown fabric had a pin stripe in it that I had never noticed before. Or did it? How could I have never previously noticed such a thing? Yet, there it was. It was at least 15 seconds before I was able to convince myself that the unnoticed pin stripe was in fact merely the afterimage of the bright spaces between the slats of the blinds.

This anecdote indicates a close relation between what happens in cases of afterimaging and cases of ordinary perception; namely, they are so alike

---

2 Besides *feelings*, emotions often include a cognitive component. For example, to be remorse-ful, one not only has to have a certain sort of bad feeling, one also has to believe that one has failed to live up to a standard one accepts. To be embarrassed, one must believe that one has done something socially unacceptable. This book will not attempt a theory of emotions; they are mentioned here only because the feelings involved in them are examples of phenomenal consciousness.

that one may be mistaken for the other. My puzzlement about afterimages is thus naturally entwined with the question of how colors come into our ordinary perceptions of colored things. To pursue this question, and to fully understand the motivation behind it, it will be essential to have an account of some basic facts about how we see. Fortunately, these facts are very familiar, and not controversial until the end of the account, so a brief and sketchy overview will be sufficient. As it will be helpful to consider a particular example, let us begin by telling the story of what happens when Eve sees a ripe, red apple.

Eve will not see anything if it is pitch dark, so let there be light, and let us assume it is sunlight. The light must strike the apple if Eve is to see it, and that light must be reflected into at least one of Eve's eyes. At the point of reflection, that is, on the surface of the apple, something distinctive must happen – something that transpires differently, depending on whether the reflecting surface is red, green, or some other color. This difference arises because of the particular molecular structure of the surface of the skin of the apple, which results in some of the wavelengths present in sunlight being reflected more efficiently than other wavelengths. The light reaching Eve's eye from the direction of the apple thus has a composition different from sunlight, that is, the ratios of the amounts of light at various wavelengths differ from the ratios found in sunlight.

The propensity to make this difference in the wavelength composition of arriving light and reflected light is a property of the apple's surface that it acquires when it becomes ripe and that remains with it for a good while (that is, until it spoils). It is convenient to have a name for this property, and we shall use "reflectance profile". The apple has its particular reflectance profile because of its molecular structure; but things with a different molecular structure might have the same reflectance profile, so we should count the molecular structure and the reflectance profile as two properties that the apple possesses.

Let us resume our story at the point where reflected light is traveling toward one of Eve's eyes. This light enters her eye, becomes focused by her lens, and falls on the cells that compose her retina. Some of these cells (the cone cells) contain chemicals that change their state when light falls on them. There are several of these chemicals, and they differ in the wavelength of light that is most likely to cause them to change their state. Suppose that a collection of cone cells is illuminated by light reflected from the apple, and suppose that this same set of cone cells is illuminated on another occasion by light reflected from a daffodil bloom. The reflectance profile of the daffodil bloom is different from that of the apple, so the wavelength composition of the light entering Eve's eye from the daffodil bloom will be different from that of the light that enters her eye from the apple. The result will be that the chemical changes in the set of cone cells will be different in the two cases.

Cone cells, like neural cells, can be regarded as having an input end and an output end. We can take the chemical changes to be the inputs. The outputs are releases of molecules called "neurotransmitters". Releases of neurotransmitters, in turn, raise the probability that other cells, namely neurons, will undergo a certain kind of change. This change commonly goes by two names, "action potential" and "firing". What these terms refer to is a process that results in a cell releasing neurotransmitters from its output end.

Our story now becomes exceedingly complex and fascinating in detail, but, fortunately, it admits of a simple summary if we take a somewhat abstract point of view. Neurotransmitters from cone cells cross the tiny spaces that separate cone cells from neurons, called "synapses". Neurons receive these neurotransmitters and, under certain conditions, undergo internal changes that lead to the release of neurotransmitters at their output ends. These neurotransmitters cross synapses and are received by other neurons, which again may undergo internal changes that lead to their release of neurotransmitters. This story is repeated again and again; in general, millions of neurons in the brain may have their activity altered as a result of the light reflected from the apple falling on Eve's retina.

In due course, Eve may respond to the presence of the apple. Perhaps she will utter the words "What a nice red apple!" or perhaps she will reach for it. In such cases, more neurons will undergo changes, release neurotransmitters, and raise the probability of other neurons firing and releasing neurotransmitters. At the end of this process, some of the released substances will encounter muscle cells instead of neurons. In this case, the muscle cells will contract, and this contraction will result in the movement of Eve's lips and tongue or her arm.

The foregoing account has been selected and emphasized for philo-sophical purposes, but it is the account that, so far as it goes, can be found in any introductory psychology textbook. At this point, however, further questions arise that do not have noncontroversial, textbook an-swers in either psychology or philosophy. We can see how they arise by quickly listing the elements we have mentioned: wavelength composition of sunlight, reflection, altered wavelength composition of the reflected light, lens, retina, chemical changes, neurotransmitters, synapses, neural activities, neurotransmitters, synapses, neural activities, neurotransmitters, synapses, neural activities . . . muscle-stimulating substances, muscle contractions, movements. Nowhere in this list do we find red or any other color. But Eve sees *red*. The apple she sees is red, and if conditions are normal, it looks red to her. How or where, we may ask, does Eve's experience of red come into our account at all? How is what normally happens when Eve sees a red apple like, or not like, what happens when she has a red afterimage? It will be convenient to summarize these questions into one general formulation, which will serve as a Basic Question in the early stages of our discussion.

(BQ) How does color come into a full accounting of what normally happens when a person sees a red apple?

The theories to be considered in the next few chapters do not all approach this question from the same angle, nor do they accord it equal prominence. They would differ in their ways of making the question more specific. Despite these differences, they all imply answers to the Basic Question as just formulated, and considering these answers will provide a way of comparing the commitments and success of several important theories.

The Basic Question is most easily discussed by reference to particular examples, but there is nothing special about the color red or the sensory modality of vision. The label (BQ) or the phrase "Basic Question" may thus stand indifferently for the preceding formulation or for a still more general formulation. To give the more general formulation, we will have to have a term that will cover qualities of all the kinds we have mentioned, such as colors, pitches, tastes, smells, degrees of pressure and warmth, shapes (e.g., of afterimages or apples), pain qualities, itches, sexual pleasantness, nausea, and other qualities like these. This term is "phenomenal qualities". The resulting general formulation of (BQ) is "How do phenomenal qualities come into a full accounting of what happens when a person is having a perceptual experience or sensation?" Since some philosophers have special understandings of the terms used in this general formulation, I stipulate that it is to be understood simply as a way of encompassing the example given and others that are like it in the way the items on this list are alike:

How does flavor come into a full accounting of tasting a spoonful of honey?
How does sound come into a full accounting of hearing a harp string?
How does warmth come into a full accounting of feeling the brow of a fevered patient?

How does pain(fulness) come into a full accounting of what happens when
someone stubs a toe?

How does red come into a full accounting of what happens after staring at a
flag printed in the complementaries of its usual colors?

We can see red things that, like heated metals, fireflies, and the sun,
emit light rather than reflect it. We can also see colors contributed by
transmitting media, such as stained glass windows, or ice cubes made
from pink lemonade, and colors produced by refraction, as in rainbows,
diamonds, and oil slicks. Differences among these cases, however, will
not make any substantive difference in the arguments to follow. I shall
thus avoid the tedium of repeating these other possibilities and conduct
the discussion of visual examples almost entirely in terms of objects that
reflect light.

ORGANIZATION OF THIS BOOK

Let us imagine one answer that might be given to (BQ). This answer,
which I will call "Minimalism", begins by noting that we learn to apply
the word "red" to a large set of objects that have a variety of reflectance
profiles. Because of the structure of normal human perceptual and cognitive systems, normally sighted and normally trained English speakers
almost always agree about when "red" should be applied to things they
have never previously seen. According to Minimalism, the class of red
things is the class of things that normally sighted people who have had
the training typical of English speakers call "red". (Of course, nonnative
speakers can learn the English habit. Further, many languages have a word
that is applied to all and only the same things to which "red" is applied
by normal English speakers. So, despite some circularity, Minimalists may
also say that the red things are those that normal English speakers call
"red" and that speakers of other languages call by their term that trans-
lates as "red".) The property red that a thing may have, according to
this way of thinking, is the property of being such that normally sighted
and trained English speakers would call it "red" in normal conditions of
seeing if they are being sincere and are not incapacitated by drugs or disease. And, according to Minimalism, the way in which red enters into
a full accounting of what normally happens when Eve sees a red apple
is exactly this: the apple that Eve is seeing has the property red (i.e., the
property red as understood by Minimalism).

We may put this claim as the view that Eve is seeing an apple that is M-red, i.e., that has the property red as that property is understood by Minimalism. But a Minimalist holds that there is no other property red, no other redness in any sense anywhere to be found in the full accounting of what normally happens when Eve sees a red apple. So, Minimalists have no reason to add a special flag to their uses of the word "red"; for them, M-red just is red.

Most philosophers are not Minimalists. But if something needs to be added to what Minimalism provides, there are still many questions about what kind of addition should be made. This book will argue for a particular kind of addition. To anticipate, it will be argued that an adequate answer to the Basic Question requires us to recognize that there are nonmaterial events that consist in occurrences of phenomenal qualities, and that such occurrences are nothing more or less than episodes of phenomenal consciousness. I call this view "Qualitative Event Realism" (QER, for short), and I will begin to explain what this label means in the next section. Chapter 2 will begin the substantive argument for the view.

QER shares its dualism (i.e., its commitment to nonmaterial events) and its focus upon phenomenal qualities with many other theories. Thus, part of what is to be done in this book is to justify the particular version of dualism presented here. Since there are several distinctive aspects of QER, this is a task that will continue throughout the book. Some of my initial efforts to motivate QER will support a variety of views, but many of the arguments to come are reasons for adding certain specific commitments to a view that begins by accepting the cogency of the initial motivations. The overall aim will be to support dualism by articulating the most defensible form of it and arguing for that.

In Chapter 3, I will explain why dualism cannot be demonstratively established in a simple and direct way. This fact entails that QER can be accepted only if it proves to be the best theory of phenomenal consciousness, all things considered. This conclusion, in turn, forces the argument for QER to have a certain structure: not only must its virtues be identified, the inadequacies of its rivals must also be shown. That is why several of the chapters that follow are devoted to the discussion of alternatives to QER.

The alternatives to QER that we must consider fall into two kinds, which can be roughly characterized as the partially sympathetic and the downright hostile. The latter are versions of materialism, and these are considered in several places, mostly in Part I. While the ultimate conclusion of these discussions is negative, it should be borne in mind that these views have been very thoroughly worked out. Many ideas that we must understand in order to understand phenomenal consciousness are either parts of the materialist views we will examine or are most easily understood in the context of explaining their inadequacies.

Part II has a somewhat different character. If nonmaterial qualitative events are recognized, their relation to the neural events that cause them must be investigated. Chapter 11 contains discussions of two views that appear to have some promise but are not adopted here. Chapter 12 presents the distinctive answer of this book, namely, that patterns (probably of neural activation) are the causes of qualitative events. This proposal naturally leads to a number of objections, and the view is developed in reference to these in Chapter 13. This chapter is necessarily speculative, but goes as far as seems possible toward envisaging a future unified, intellectually satisfying perspective on the problem of understanding phenomenal consciousness.

A NOTE ON TERMINOLOGY

"Phenomenal quality" was introduced earlier as a general term for qualities that enter in some way into perceptual situations, bodily sensations, emotions, and imagery. This is the meaning that this phrase will have throughout this book. In the works of some of the authors to be discussed, we will also encounter another term that has much the same use, namely, "qualia" (singular: "quale").[3]

One example of a phenomenal quality is pain. This is a general property, of which shooting pain, dull pain, pain in the left leg, and so on are species. Besides having species, however, the property pain has particular *occurrences*. "I have a shooting pain in my left leg" says that an event of a certain kind is occurring, and the *kind* in question is shooting pain in the left leg. I could have other occurrences of the same kind on other occasions, and in each case I would be correctly said to have *a pain*. "A pain" *can*, of course, also be used to indicate a species of pain; for example,

---

3 The term "quale" goes back to Peirce's work in the 1890s (see Peirce, 1935), where it is introduced in connection with a number of difficult doctrines. The root meaning of contemporary usage is best understood by reference to C. I. Lewis. "There *are* recognizable characters of the given, which may be repeated in different experiences, and are thus a sort of universals: I call these 'qualia.' But although such qualia are universals, in the sense of being recognized from one to another experience, they must be distinguished from properties of objects" (Lewis, 1929, p. 121; emphasis in the original). Lewis's examples in nearby text were red, blue, round, and loud.

arthritic pain is a pain and headache is another. But in one of its standard uses, "a pain" indicates a certain kind of occurrence, which has a time of onset and lasts for some particular duration.

There is no term in common use that unambiguously functions like "a pain" but can be used in a general way for an occurrence of any phenomenal quality. "A quale" might serve, by analogy with "a pain", but the term seems so wedded to its use as a genus of properties that confusion would probably result. It seems best, therefore, to coin a term for the explicit purpose of indicating occurrences of phenomenal qualities, and this is the meaning of the term "qualitative event".

Just as one can ask whether a pain is identical with an event in some part of one's brain, so one can ask whether qualitative events are identical with events in brain parts. But we should note that an answer to the first question cannot be gotten out of the grammar of "a pain" alone. A pain has to be an occurrence of (some specific) pain property, but whatever else may truly be said of it has to be argued for. Analogously, a qualitative event has to be an occurrence of a phenomenal quality, but the grammar of the term alone neither includes nor excludes further characterization.

By contrast, the *theory* that this book will offer will make substantive claims about qualitative events that do not follow merely from the meaning of the term. According to this theory, qualitative events are caused by, but not identical with, some brain events, namely, occurrences of patterns of activity (most likely, of neurons). Many other claims will be made that need some preparation for their understanding. These substantive claims must be (and will be) argued for and defended.

The name of the theory to be offered is, as noted previously, "qualitative event realism" (or QER). Now, one could think that qualitative events are real, and even real and nonmaterial, and still not accept other parts of the theory of this book. Thus, strictly, this book offers a particular version of QER – QER plus a number of distinctive, specifying theses. However, at present, neither the term "qualitative event" nor the phrase "qualitative event realism" is in use. I will thus use "qualitative event realism" as the name of the particular theory, with all its specifying theses, that I present in this book.

The occurrences to which "qualitative event" is intended to refer go by many names, of which "experiences" and (episodes of) "phenomenal consciousness" are the most familiar. To maintain connection with the thought of others, I shall often use these terms, and it is to be understood that the theory of qualitative events presented here is a theory of what experiences, episodes of phenomenal consciousness, etc. actually are.

It will be convenient to have a term that indicates acceptance of qualitative events without taking a position on certain specific, additional theses of QER. I shall use "experiential realism" for this purpose. QER is to be understood as one among several species of experiential realism. Some of the arguments for QER will be arguments for experiential realism in many forms. Others will be concerned to support QER as the best form of experiential realism, to the exclusion of other species.

It remains to say something about "consciousness". It is likely that every reader will have some idea of what is meant by this term, and that this idea will not be completely off the mark. Moreover, it is likely that most will agree that rocks and trees are never conscious, that normal, awake people are conscious, and that it is a lot more plausible that dogs are conscious than that bacteria are conscious. "Consciousness" ought to be whatever it is that we are thinking of as making the difference between these classifications with respect to being conscious.

Beyond this understanding it is not possible to go in a preliminary, definitional, noncontentious way. The work to follow, however, is most assuredly relevant to further understanding of consciousness. As was briefly indicated earlier, QER holds that qualitative events are episodes of consciousness; in clarifying our understanding of qualitative events, therefore, we are furthering our understanding of consciousness. Moreover, the speculative unification of thought attempted in Chapters 12 and 13 provides us with a glimpse of how intellectual satisfaction about consciousness and its relation to events in the brain might one day be achieved. At present, however, these claims can only be regarded as oracular and contentious; clarification and argument are promised.[4]

---

4 The structure of the phrase "phenomenal consciousness" may suggest a contrast with some other kind of consciousness. From the point of view of QER, however, "phenomenal consciousness" is almost redundant; what is phenomenal is always conscious, and where there is consciousness, there are phenomenal qualities. There is, however, no point in giving a preliminary argument for this statement, as it will become evident, if the argument of the rest of the book is accepted. For an interesting and completely different route to a similar conclusion, see Lormand (1996).

2

Qualitative Event Realism

The main outlines of QER can be set out in the following response to our Basic Question.

Besides the reflectance profiles, light waves, retinal changes, neural events, and behavioral responses reviewed in Chapter 1, normal cases in which a person sees a red apple will involve the apple's looking red to that person. An apple's looking red requires a distinctive kind of conscious occurrence – a red experience – that is something in its own right, and not reducible to behavioral responses, or dispositions to behavioral responses, or brain state bases of such dispositions. Experiences are caused by neural events, but are not identical to or reducible to them or to any other material events. Experiences are constituted by phenomenal qualities; indeed, phenomenal qualities occur only in experiences and are the essence of consciousness in the most fundamental sense of that term.

An initial motivation for realism about experiences should already be evident and can be summarized as follows. *Something* is happening in afterimage cases, and that something is very similar to part of what goes on in seeing. "Experiences", and "ways in which things look (or, appear)", are more or less well-established ways of talking about this kind of *something*. Differences among experiences cannot consist simply in how experiences are related to different kinds of perceived things, for there are various kinds of experiences in afterimaging, illusions, and dreams but no perceived things to which they stand in the right relations.[1] Experiences are therefore naturally taken to be occurrences that are of different kinds

1 "Relations" in this paragraph means "real relations", i.e., it does not include the pseudorelation that a thought may have to its intentional object. Thus, representationalists should agree that there is a prima facie motivation for realism. Naturally, we shall consider their case for overruling this motivation, but that must wait until Chapter 4.

in virtue of what they *are*, as contrasted with what they may be related to. This much realism leaves open many questions about how, exactly, we should think about experiences, but it recognizes them as realities for which we must find some place in our total view of what there is.

Plausible though these remarks may seem, there are materialist views that are in conflict with almost every aspect of them. These views will be discussed in due course. In this chapter, I will be more concerned with those aspects of QER that may be surprising even to those who are firmly persuaded of some kind of realism about experiences. I need to argue not only for realism, but also for certain specific commitments within realism. It will be convenient to begin with three fairly brief clarifications.

THREE CLARIFICATIONS

Red Experiences?

It will be suggested that the phrase "red experience" is misguided and potentially confusing, and that if it is to be used at all, it must be regarded as elliptical for "experience of the kind that normal people have when viewing red things in normal conditions". It is therefore important to say in the plainest fashion possible that, according to QER, experiences literally are constituted by phenomenal qualities, and that the phrase "red experience" is to be understood as doing exactly what it appears to be doing, namely, predicating "red" of experiences. According to QER, experiences are real occurrences that resemble and differ from each other not only as to who has them, or when they are had, but in qualitative kind; and the plain nature of these similarities and differences is similarity and difference in colors, timbres, flavors, bodily sensation qualities, and so on.

QER does not deny that a person's red experience is an experience of a kind that that person will have when looking at red things in normal conditions. But to say this leaves one with the phrase "experience of a kind" and thus leads to the question "What kind, for example?" QER answers "Red, for example; and, in general, any phenomenal kind." (Evidently, there are other answers to the question of what differentiates one experience from another, and we shall be looking at these in later chapters.)

The view that experiences are phenomenally qualitied is perhaps easiest to understand if we think of bodily sensations. According to QER, a pain is an experience of one kind and an itch is an experience of a different

15

kind. It is true that a pain is the kind of experience that one is apt to have if one has bodily damage, and that an itch is the kind of experience that one is apt to have after being bitten by certain insects. But if we want to say what kinds of experiences one has on these occasions, the obvious, and only natural, thing to say is that one is a pain and the other is an itch.

Although there are some differences between bodily sensations and experiences associated with the external senses, it is an essential point of QER that pains are, in the respect we have been emphasizing, a good model for experiences in general. Pains are experiences, and the quality of being painful is what makes a pain a pain. Analogously, QER claims that a case of something's looking red to someone involves a visual experience, in particular a red visual experience, and the quality of being red is what makes that experience the distinctive kind of experience that it is.

This claim may be resisted with the following argument. "Red" is surely correctly predicated of some apples. But, equally surely, no experience can have the same color property as an apple. Therefore, experiences are not red.

Let us compare this argument with the following one. "Unhealthy" is surely correctly predicated of cigarettes. But, equally surely, no person can have the same state property as a cigarette. Therefore, people are not unhealthy.

The lesson I draw from this comparison is that "red" as predicated of experiences and "red" as predicated of apples is not the same term, but neither is it simply equivocal. Strictly speaking, there are two senses of "red", but they are intimately related – so intimately that it is no more incorrect to say that experiences are red than it is to say that a person is unhealthy.

Some philosophers who would balk at *red experiences* are quite happy to say that experiences can have *phenomenal red*, or that experiences are *red-ish*, or that they are *red**. It is also widely agreed both that (a) red things are those that produce phenomenally red experiences (or red-ish, or red* experiences) and that (b) the remark in (a) is asymmetrical, i.e., the more basic concept is phenomenal red: it is the redness of things that is being explained in terms of the phenomenal redness of experiences, and not the other way around. Now, if we put these views together, the result is that phenomenal redness is more basic to our understanding of red than is the redness of red things. Or, as QER says, experiences are red – red in a fundamental way – and red things are things that cause experiences of that kind.

It will be helpful to have a definite way of referring to some relevant properties of red material objects. To define them, we may first define the set **R** as the set of objects (or the set of surfaces or parts of surfaces of objects) that normally sighted, normally trained English speakers would, under normal conditions, classify as red – that is, they would *say* "This is red", "That's a red one", and so on if they made any color classification at all. Several properties of objects (or of their surfaces) may then be defined in terms of **R** as follows:

RP-red   The property of having a Reflectance Profile that is in the set **RP(R)**, where a reflectance profile is in **RP(R)** just in case it is possessed by some object in the set **R**.

MS-red   The property of having a Molecular Structure on which a reflectance profile that is in **RP(R)** supervenes.

D-red   The property of having a Disposition to cause normally sighted people to place an object (or surface) in the set **R**.

Although it is important to recognize that there are distinct physical properties that are closely associated with red things, the differences among the properties just defined will not be of much concern to us. For this reason, I will most usually speak of "P-red" or "physical red". These terms stand indifferently for any of the preceding properties.[2]

Inversion

I now turn to an objection that denies that phenomenal red – or any property that an experience could literally have – is really entitled to be counted as genuine redness of any sort. For, at least as far as anything we have mentioned goes, it might be that people have spectra that are inverted or rotated with respect to each other. Perhaps Jones's experience when looking at fresh blood is like mine when I look at summer lawns, and perhaps Smith's experience when looking at fresh blood is like mine when I look at autumn pumpkins. If such inversions and rotations were sufficiently common, there might be *no* quality of experience that is normally brought about in all or even most normal perceivers by red

---

2 For other theorists, the differences among P-reds can be more significant. Physicalists must decide just *which* physical property should be counted as being (the same property as) red. For an easily accessible discussion of some of these issues, see Tye (2000). For discussion of several views and defense of one more congenial to the present account, see Boghossian and Velleman (1989). For general background, see Hardin (1988) and papers in Byrne and Hilbert (1997).

things. But if such cases are allowed to be possible, it may seem that "red" can never be properly predicated of experiences, but only of the objects that everyone agrees are properly to be called "red".[3]

The solution to this objection is to make explicit the fact that our discussion has been relativized to individual persons. Red things cause experiences in me that have a certain phenomenal quality, and red things cause experiences in you that have a certain phenomenal quality.[4] Perhaps these qualities are the same, perhaps they are not. In either case, each quality goes, in its owner, with viewing (in normal conditions) things that we have all learned to call "red". Each of us will naturally apply the word "red" to our experiences. For example, we may see a new white golf ball placed under a strong red light, and, if asked what it looks like, we may both say "red", knowing full well that we are describing only how it looks.[5] Whether we are mutually spectrum inverted does not enter into the appropriateness of our responses; and, for the same reason, whether we are mutually spectrum inverted does not affect the appropriateness of our each using "red" to refer to the quality of experience that, in us, is distinctive of occasions on which we see red things in normal conditions.

It may seem that this solution falls afoul of something that Wittgenstein might be supposed to have shown.[6] To the contrary, however, our account of phenomenal qualities is fully compatible with all that we ought to accept from Wittgenstein's reflections. Wittgenstein was right in holding (as I interpret him) that it is foundational to "red" having the kind of meaning that it does, that normally sighted people normally agree about the material things to which they apply or refuse to apply the term. The fundamental character of this kind of agreement does not imply that people do not have experiences of different kinds or that, once they have learned

---

3 See Lycan (1996, pp. 110–111). Lycan's argument applies to what he calls "Strange Qualia", which are not our qualitative events. Nonetheless, the argument can easily be reformulated so that it would seem to be an objection to QER.

4 The discussion is still restricted to normal observers, and so this sentence assumes that "you" are not color blind with respect to red. But "normal observer" does not mean "observer who has the same phenomenal quality that most others do under normal conditions". It means, rather, "observer who can make normal discriminations, and can learn to apply predicates like 'red' in the recognitional way characteristic of normally able and normally trained speakers of languages that contain color predicates".

5 Circumstances are crucial: we *may* say that it looks like a white golf ball in red light. So, the key assertion is really that *there are* cases where we will both describe the look of a thing with the same color predicate in the full knowledge that we are describing only the way a thing looks.

6 The relevant paragraphs are to be found in those leading up to the discussion of the beetle in the box in sect. 293 of Wittgenstein (1953).

to use words like "red", they cannot then use them to talk about the qualities of their experiences. It implies only that the connection between the word "red" and the quality of experiences that occur in particular people is a derivative connection, and is not the most fundamental fact in the account of how the word can have the meaning it does.[7]

Error

It may be objected that on the account I have been giving, people may be making wholesale errors whenever they say that an ordinary thing has this or that color. These errors arise because no ordinary thing can have strictly the same property as the property of an experience. So, if people are thinking of phenomenal red when they say that apples or cardinals are red, they are attributing to those things a property that they do not in fact have.

It seems to me likely that (a) ordinary color remarks by ordinary people (i.e., nonphilosophers) really make no commitment on the issue just

---

7   Although my account is compatible with what I take to be Wittgenstein's fundamental argument, Wittgenstein himself rejected it in Wittgenstein (1953), sects. 273 and 274. From 273: "What am I to say about the word "red"? – that it means something 'confronting us all' and that everyone should really have another word, besides this one, to mean his *own* sensation of red? Or is it like this: the word "red" means something known to everyone; and in addition, for each person, it means something known only to him?" From 274: "It is as if when I uttered the word I cast a sidelong glance at the private sensation, as it were in order to say to myself: I know all right what I mean by it."

I take the last remark here to be intended as disparagement of the idea it expresses. That disparagement is fully deserved *if* the view is that there is a word (public or private) that derives its meaning from the "sidelong glance", i.e., that derives its meaning from a supposed unmediated association between word and phenomenal quality. But that is neither a claim nor a consequence of QER. QER countenances one public word, "red", which requires agreement in its application to ordinary things by normal speakers in order to have the meaning it does; and it says that once this meaning is established, normal speakers can also use it to refer to their own phenomenal quality. (It may be helpful here to note that normal, nonphilosophical speakers know nothing of reflectance profiles or other P-red properties. "Red" in its fundamental role is a classifier of *things*, and surfaces are P-red only in a sense that is parasitic on that fundamental role.)

Wittgenstein is right to think that the argument based on the beetle in the box (sect. 293) shows that phenomenal qualities are not the foundation of the meaning of words like "red". We can accept this point without accepting skepticism about either the existence of phenomenal qualities or their constancy within individual subjects in normal conditions. As we shall see later on, QER holds that phenomenal qualitied events have causes (most likely neural events). It would be correct to infer differences in phenomenal effects (in different individuals or in one individual at different times) if and only if there were reason to suppose that there were differences in the relevant causes.

raised. Most of the time people just apply the word in a way that agrees with the applications of the same word by others. But it also seems to me likely that (b) when people first begin to reflect on the questions we are discussing, they are prone to accept that colors are "on the objects", and that their thinking may involve some confusion. Students often express puzzlement and a sense that they need to revise their thinking when they are first exposed to the psychology textbook account of visual perception (see Chapter 1).

It is essential to note that the foregoing account implies that there are facts closely related to the essential function of color words, about which ordinary speakers are *not* in error. For example, it is mostly true that if someone says something is red, that thing is P-red. Most of the time, if someone takes a thing such as a book or a fruit to be red, the surface of that thing has a molecular structure that supports a reflectance profile that would cause normal speakers in normal conditions to classify it as red. It is also true that, for a given individual, the kind of experience had on such occasions will normally be the same as the kind of experience that is typically caused in that individual by the things that normally sighted English speakers call "red" in normal circumstances.

Sometimes, of course, people make mistakes about the colors of things. A red car may be taken for a black one at night, or a blue tie may be taken for a green one in a store with old-fashioned fluorescent lighting. These are *ordinary* errors; the intended contrast is with the *theoretical* error of failing to locate phenomenal red correctly in a philosophical account of perception. One is susceptible to ordinary error when the kind of experience one is having is not of the same kind that one normally has when exposed in normal conditions to the object being viewed. (I say "susceptible", because other knowledge might forestall actual mistaken judgment. For example, a red car may look black, but its owner may know it's red by remembering where it was parked.)

The relevance of these observations to QER is this. (a) QER is compatible with one kind of claim that we are mostly right in our color judgments about things. It is compatible, namely, with the claim that ordinary errors about colors of things we are looking at are comparatively rare. So (b) even though QER is a species of (theoretical) "error theory", it does not say that people are systematically making ordinary errors. But attribution of wholesale error would be an objection only if it were ordinary errors that were being widely attributed. Attribution of theoretical error, which QER does make, is in accord with the facts, and is thus not an objection to but a strength of the view.

Some readers will now want to ask a further question: if phenomenal red is not actually out there on the surface of things, why is it so natural for us to think of red as "on the objects"? This is an important question, but its answer requires some preparation. We shall return to it in the section on structure and location.

AFTERIMAGES AND EVENTS

Some aspects of afterimages reinforce the remarks I have been making about the color qualities of experiences. For example, the discussions of the American flag novelty item and my difficulty about the russet pin stripe were easy to follow, and likely did not produce a sense that I was misusing words, in particular color words.[8] But, after all, I was attributing colors to afterimages; and these were cases where the afterimages were known to be afterimages, i.e., where it was known that there was nothing relevant to the visual goings-on that was P-red.

There are, however, aspects of afterimages that seem to conflict with QER and, in particular, with its claim that experiences are *events* that are constituted by their phenomenal qualities. It will be thought that, if one is going to accept phenomenal qualities as properties of something other than physical things at all, one must at least attribute them to afterimages and then distinguish between afterimages and the experiencing of them. Perhaps the experiencing of an afterimage is an event, but the afterimage of which it is an experience is at best a region of some peculiar sort and not an event.[9]

This way of thinking is deeply entrenched – so much so that the view I mean to propose may fail to be recognized as a considered view rather than an inadvertent infelicity of formulation. So let me state in the plainest terms that I reject the splitting of a case of afterimaging into *an afterimage* and *the experiencing* of *the afterimage*. What QER says is that an afterimage *is* an experience, experiences *are* events, and therefore afterimages *are* events. Like pains, afterimages are events (or occurrences, or episodes) that are entirely constituted by the phenomenal properties they have.

In the long run, this view must earn its keep by contributing to a satisfying account of phenomenal consciousness. As a first installment

8 Readers of earlier drafts of this book have raised objections to many of my claims, but none have expressed any hesitation over the remarks about afterimages in Chapter 1.

9 At worst, an afterimage is simply nothing at all. This view is a species of representationalism, which will be discussed in Chapter 4.

toward exhibiting this contribution, I observe that the alternative way of thinking – i.e., the way of thinking that splits afterimaging into an afterimage and an experience of it – multiplies our difficulties. We have an afterimage that has a color but is not any ordinary physical thing, and we have an experience that is also not any ordinary physical thing. Regarding the latter, we must say either that experiences are of various kinds that vary systematically with the kinds of afterimage that are experienced, or we must say that experiences are the same in every case, or we must take afterimages to be parts of experiences (so that differences of qualities of afterimages can themselves constitute differences in kinds of experiences). None of these alternatives seems attractive: the first just doubles the number of nonordinary things, the second postulates a thing with hardly any qualities at all, and the third contradicts the common philosophical understanding of "experience of" and leads to the question of what the other parts of an experience might be. Now, QER does not multiply problems in this way and gives us a coherent conception of the nature of experience.[10]

Further clarifications of the view that experiences are phenomenal qualitied events are needed. One of these concerns the distinction between instantaneous events and events that have duration. Examples of the first kind are onsets and offsets; they occur *at* a time. Other events – sporting events, for example – have durations of various lengths; they last for a time. They are datable, but the date is an interval, not a moment. Now, in saying that experiences are events, I am not saying they are instantaneous, or punctate. They are, instead, occurrences that have some duration. Some durations, e.g., that of a sharp pain due to a pin prick, are quite short, though still not instantaneous; others, e.g., an afterimaging of a flag, last for times on the order of several seconds.

Events are often taken to be specified by a triple of a time, a quality, and a thing.[11] The events of QER, however, are constituted by times and phenomenal qualities. They are occurrences, during a stretch of time, of phenomenal qualities; that is all there is to them. According to QER, they have no hidden nature. The phenomenal qualities constitute experiences; they are not properties of or in something else. There is no "mind stuff" or mental substance *in* which the redness of an afterimage occurs; an

---

10 It will become increasingly clear as we proceed that I reject adverbialism, and that my references to qualitative events are not to be conflated with adverbialists' talk of "ways of sensing". But even at this stage, we can see a clear difference between QER and adverbialism, namely, the realist stance that QER takes toward the qualities of qualitative events.

11 See, e.g., Goldman (1971) and Kim (1973, 1976).

afterimage *is* an occurrence of redness (for example). In short, QER is not a substance theory.[12]

It may be suggested that consciousness is the substrate in which phenomenal qualities occur. According to QER, this is a mistake. Phenomenal consciousness is not a substrate or a substance. It is a genus, the species of which are occurrences that are afterimages, pains, sounds (*sounds*, not the vibrations that cause those experiences), tastes, lookings-red, and, in general, occurrences of phenomenal qualities. Being in pain is *a way of being conscious*; it is one kind of phenomenal consciousness. Having an afterimage, or an aftertaste, or having something look red to one are other ways of being phenomenally conscious.

This last sentence uses the phrase "having an afterimage". Is this *experiencing* an afterimage? No. Having an afterimage, according to QER, like having something look red to one, is a property of a perceiving subject. Such a subject, S, has an afterimage (or an experience) when a part of S's body is causing that experience. Having is a relation between a person and an experience, not a relation between an experience and what an experience is allegedly *of*.

I hope it will be well understood that the last few paragraphs are not intended as arguments for QER. Although I have tried to present the view so that its coherence will be evident, the main point has been to get some key ideas stated so that evaluation of the view can proceed intelligently. The next thing I shall do is to consider an argument against the stated way of thinking, in the belief that doing so will both clarify and offer some reason to accept qualitative event realism.

The argument is due to Moore (1903/1922). Moore held that a sensation of green and a sensation of blue differed in the respect denoted by "green" and "blue" but shared something, namely, consciousness, because they were both sensations. The shared item had to be different from the items that accounted for the difference. Thus consciousness or, as Moore also said, awareness was one element in a sensation of blue, and blue was a distinct element. These two elements were related; the name of the relation was, confusingly enough, awareness, or being aware of. This relation was held to be an *external* relation, meaning that it was not necessary to the existence of either term that it stand in that relation. If we symbolize the "awareness" term by "aw", the relation of awareness by "— A —", and the property *blue* by "B", we can depict Moore's conception of an

---

12 Dennett (1991, pp. 33–37) pokes fun at mindstuff. But the substantialism of his intended target is imposed on it by no one but himself.

awareness of blue in the following diagram:

(1)   aw — A — B

This conception led Moore to a serious problem. Since he claimed to know about this structure, it seemed he must know what an awareness is. It would not seem plausible to hold that one's knowledge of the awareness term was any less direct than one's knowledge of blue – after all, one must know both if one knows that one is in the situation depicted in (1). But even Moore could hardly stomach the idea that he was aware of an awareness, i.e., that he was ever in a situation that might be depicted as (2).

(2) aw_2 — A — aw_1

I hasten to add that Moore did not use diagrams like (1) and (2) and, I believe, did not realize quite how puzzling his view was. Instead, he let himself get by with clearly inadequate statements to the effect that awareness itself is "as if it were diaphanous".

There is worse to come. It is, perhaps, not so odd to hold that blue can exist without anything's being aware of it. But Moore's making the awareness relation external implies that an awareness can exist that is not an awareness of anything; and that seems as absurd a consequence as any to which philosophers have been driven.

Despite the influence that Moore's argument had upon early analytic philosophy, these difficulties should make us suspect that it has a serious flaw. Indeed, it is easy to see that it is invalid. Compare the following: "In any case where there is a bounded region of green and a bounded region of blue, there is something that distinguishes the regions – namely an element corresponding to green and an element corresponding to blue – and a common element that makes them both regions. Therefore, besides the colors, there must be, in each case, an *expanse* that is externally related to the colors; that is, the colors can exist without being in an expanse, and an expanse can exist without being colored." If we ever find anyone who accepts this line of reasoning, we may well expect that the (in itself colorless) expanse element will be thought to be very special, hard to fix, and as it were diaphanous.[13] But there is clearly no reason to accept such

13 In a 1952 footnote, Moore (1953/1966, p. 30) indicates a change from his earlier view and explicitly recognizes *patches* as distinct from their qualities, e.g., their colors, sizes, and shapes. Moore's reason for introducing patches, however, appears to be that the qualities need a bearer. This reason is quite different from the argument imagined in our text, which parallels Moore's 1903 argument for recognizing the distinction between awarenesses and qualities. Thus, neither "regions" nor "expanses" in our imagined argument are to be

a view, for there is no reason to accept that the commonality indicated by the common occurrence of "region" is the commonality of an *element*, that is to say, an individual, and an externally related one at that. We may, for example, express the commonality in the region cases by saying that each of the colors has the same *property*, namely, the property of *having some (closed, bounded) shape or other*. Analogously, we may say that unless we are surrounded by a red fog, phenomenal red has the property of having some shape or other and that its occurrences are conscious events. These remarks do not commit us to expanses or consciousnesses as elements of red experiences.

In a more positive vein, we may say that QER follows Moore in accepting sensations as realities in their own right that involve phenomenal qualities in some way while avoiding the mistake in his famous argument. This recognition and avoidance of error provide some motivation in favor of QER.

Separating an experience and what it is of permits one to avoid speaking of red events, and this might be thought to be an advantage of a view like Moore's on the ground that "red event" does not make grammatical sense. To the contrary, however, ringings of bells and foghorn blasts are events, and words for pitches and timbres are applied to them without any sense of engaging in special terminologies. The afterglow of an electric heating element fades from red to black when the current is turned off. Lightning flashes are white or yellow, firefly flashes are yellow, signal flashes can be any color; and all are events. These examples are, of course, not experiences, although they may cause experiences. They serve here only to make a grammatical point, namely, that it is not incorrect, but merely unusual, for color qualities to be attributed to events. These cases may thus serve as grammatical models that should help us understand how it can be that experiences are, quite literally, red, green, oreganoish, pungent, painful, and so on. Experiences – the qualitative events of QER – are occurrences in which phenomenal qualities fill time for short, but noticeably nonpunctate, durations.

STRUCTURE AND LOCATION

The qualitative events caused by the striking of a bell or the blowing of a foghorn are qualitatively complex in that they have both pitch and timbre.

---

confused with Moore's later "patches". We have already seen that QER rejects the need for "bearers" of phenomenal qualities, and we will be reinforcing this point as we proceed.

25

Similarly, afterimages typically have a hue, a saturation, and a shape. I cannot rule out the possibility that some qualitative events have simple properties, and perhaps some smells would qualify as examples. For the most part, however, qualitative events are events in which complexes of phenomenal qualities occur.[14] Now, this complexity raises some questions that may appear to be problems for QER as so far stated.

Suppose that we look at two very similar light bulbs and as a result have two after-spots that are qualitatively identical. Is this two afterimages or one? Is it two qualitative events or one? It seems that one could adopt either way of speaking. However, no matter what terminology we might adopt, we would have to recognize that there is a relation between the two spots. It is not that there is simply and solely spot A and spot B; instead, there is spot A and spot B and some relation between them. For example, depending on the angle of our head relative to the alignment of the bulbs, A might be to the left of B or A might be above B. To help keep this significant phenomenological fact in mind, it seems best to think of the indicated case as a single complex afterimage, a single event that contains two color patches. This suggestion may draw the objection that it violates a principle of uniform instantiation, i.e., the principle that two particulars cannot have the same property if they are of fundamentally different kinds. That is, one may object that the proposed way of thinking takes orange (for example) to qualify both a qualitative event and a patch, and that this is impossible. We may avoid such an objection, however, by denying that patches are genuine exemplifiers of colors. If a color occurs in a qualitative event at all, it must have some extent or other. If this extent is bounded on all sides, then the color will extend to fill some shape or other. From this point of view, the shape is a (second order) property of the color, and "patch" is a convenient abbreviation for "color that is bounded by some definite boundary or other". The upshot of these ways of looking at the matter is that there is only one genuine exemplifier of color, namely, the qualitative, conscious event.

Suppose, now, that two people each look at a light bulb and that, as a result, they have afterimages of the same shape, size, hue, saturation, and intensity in the same parts of their visual fields. Let us suppose that they have them at the same time. What individuates the two afterimages? The answer is that there are two brains at work in this case and thus two sets of neural causes. Since causes are themselves generally regarded as

14   I am counting intensities as properties of (first level) properties rather than as properties of the qualitative events that are occurrences of the first level properties.

events, this answer evidently does not provide a general theory of the individuation of events. The task of providing such a general theory may, however, safely be left to others. Whatever the best account of events should be taken to be, all things considered, it does not seem remotely likely that any crucial difficulty attends the individuation of neural events. Thus, the dependence of individuation of qualitatively conscious events upon individuation of neural events does not plausibly present a potential threat to our ability to make progress in understanding consciousness.[15]

We may describe a certain kind of pain, e.g., intense stabbing pain in the left shin. We may have such a pain once, and two years later we may have another occurrence of the same kind. We need to have a way of referring to the two separate occurrences; relative to the kind, they are particular occurrences. There is, however, nothing in this reference to particular occurrences that requires the additional introduction of an individual in the sense of a "thing".

Let us return to the afterimage of two light bulbs. Yellow-orange is one property that constitutes this occurrence, but since there are two yellow-orange spots, there is some other color that separates them. There are boundaries between the different colors and, in this case, two of the boundaries are closed, i.e., there are two circular yellow-orange spots.

These remarks show that if one begins with admitting colors in afterimages and maintains connection with evident phenomenological facts, one must also allow other properties to have the same status – for example, having a boundary and having a shape (e.g., circular). Thus, a consistent qualitative event realism also allows that differences of boundaries between areas of various colors and differences of shape are also ways in which conscious events can differ.

These facts raise a problem that some may regard as a reductio ad absurdum of QER. We can state the problem, in brief though somewhat old-fashioned terminology, in this way: shape requires extension; consciousness is not extended; therefore, shape cannot (literally) occur in

15   What should we say of a case in which one experiences two images of a light bulb because of drunkenness or pressure on one of one's eyeballs? In the latter case, the two patches can be traced to two sets of neural causes. Must we therefore say that they are two consciousnesses rather than one complex afterimage (as we suggested would be preferable in the preceding paragraph)? No. In both cases, though the neural causes are unusual, the two images are related to each other (e.g., as left and right) within the same experience, and for this reason should be counted as elements of the same complex image.

More will be said about causes of qualitative events in later chapters, especially Chapter 12.

consciousness. A correspondingly brief response to this argument can be given in the same old-fashioned terms. Descartes claimed that extension was the essence of the material world, but he was wrong. What is essential to materiality is *mass*. Once we give up Descartes' inadequate physics, there is no obstacle to recognizing that phenomenal colors are literally spread out in a spatial way in consciousness.[16]

We can give a somewhat more enlightening response by reminding ourselves of Sellars's (1963, 1971, 1981) concern with *homogeneity*. Homogeneity is the spread-outness that is characteristic of colors – their continuity (or at least apparent continuity) over expanses, and the through-and-through-colored character of pink ice cubes. Homogeneity will play a significant role in later developments in this book, but for the moment, let us just observe that the notion of a color *point* (or, the color of a point) makes no evident sense, unless it is analyzed as a point that lies within a color expanse that extends for some nonzero neighborhood around the point. Color, by its nature, fills area. Area, in turn, brings with it the possibility of change of color across an area, rapid change across some part of an area, and thus boundaries. Boundaries, in turn, bring with them the possibility of closed boundaries and thus shapes. Shapes entail spatial relations, e.g., size difference, adjacency, and inclusion. Finally, shapes entail the possibility of plurality of shapes, and therewith number of shapes of specified kinds.

Some tactile qualities also fill areas of bodily surface – think of the difference between the feel of a low-backed chair and a higher-backed chair. Itches and pains likewise may occur in small regions, or extend over larger parts of the skin surface or region of the body. Other qualities, most obviously those of smell, lack spatial homogeneity. They do, however, have temporal homogeneity, that is, they are spread out continuously over a period of time. Here too, boundaries and relations characterize our consciousness. For example, smells can change rapidly or not so rapidly, and a stretch of sound, e.g., the throaty bray of a foghorn, may include or fail to include the sound of the clapping of a bell.

These observations on the complexity of conscious events should help us to understand a very significant further property of consciousness to

---

16 The inadequate and, indeed, somewhat bizarre character of Descartes' physics can be clearly seen in the discussion of density in Descartes (1644). Descartes was able to do as well as he did because, in a restricted set of cases in which mass is uniformly distributed, difference of volume covaries with difference of mass, and therefore there are some cases in which volume can be a proxy for mass.

which we now turn. To wit: the colors of our visual consciousness do not merely fill an area; they also occur in three-dimensional space. In general, they do not have thickness, although this is possible, as in the case of Sellars's pink ice cubes. Opaque surfaces, however, typically have distance. For example, when I said that the lines of the afterimage caused by looking out a window with venetian blinds seemed to be in the fabric of my trousers, I was not drawing a conclusion: I was not *inferring* their location from the facts that I was having an afterimage and that I was looking at my trousers. No, the fabric was where the lines looked to be. This was not a merely judgmental looking, i.e., it was not a case that is fully described as being a tentative judging that the trousers were where the lines actually were. For, although for some moments I was tempted to make that judgment, when I finally and firmly rejected it, the lines still *looked* to be where the fabric was. The locational aspect of the lines was as much a character of that kind of experience as was their color.[17]

Hangover from the Cartesian association of three-dimensionality with materiality may make it difficult to recognize distance as a property that occurs within conscious events themselves. We can, perhaps, appreciate the problem by reflecting on Berkeley's remark that distance is a line turned endwise to the eye.[18] Berkeley evidently felt that distance was a problem; but why should he have thought so? After all, there is no more practical difficulty in measuring the distance of ordinary objects from us than there is in measuring how far to the left one thing is from another. It seems that Berkeley could only have thought there was a problem if he thought that distance, or "outness", would have committed him (or, at least, been thought by some to commit him) to the reality of three-dimensional space and, therewith, material objects in that space. But even this would not have been a problem for Berkeley if he had not accepted that there was distance that needed somehow to be accounted for.[19] If the remarks of the preceding paragraph are correct, we can see why he

17 In Chapter 9, I will come to terms with the view that judgment, or proto-judgment, is all there is to looking. For the present, I can only issue a promissory note that further investigation will not lead to a need to revise the view expressed in this section.
18 See Berkeley (1734/1948, p. 202).
19 Berkeley's text is intriguing here. At first he appears to argue that distance, being a line turned endwise to the eye, cannot be properly and immediately perceived by sight. (Judgments of distance would, in that case, have to be arrived at by inference.) But, having secured Hylas's agreement, he goes on to say (in the person of Philonous): "But allowing that distance was truly and immediately perceived by the mind, yet it would not thence follow it existed out of the mind. For whatever is immediately perceived is an idea: and can any *idea* exist out of the mind?" (Berkeley, 1734/1948, p. 202). I take this passage as a backhanded recognition

should have accepted that there is distance – namely, because distance is a feature that literally occurs within experience itself.

It may be useful here to contrast smell with visual experience. We can, of course, locate smells. It smells musty *in here*, that is, in the attic, but not in the kitchen. You can enjoy the aroma of honeysuckle if you go *over there*, where the honeysuckle bushes are. But these locations are inferential, that is, the smell is where smellers (or their noses) have to be in order to experience a certain odor quality. The locations are not within the smell itself; they are not the locations of odors, but only of the sources of odors. By contrast, afterimages we have when our eyes are open typically have a distance aspect. This aspect can be removed by closing our eyes. The contrasts between smells and afterimages with the eyes closed, on the one hand, and afterimages with the eyes open, on the other, cannot provide a formal argument for the claim that distance is a property contained within conscious events themselves. Nonetheless, these contrasts do help to clarify the sense of the claim that distance is a noninferred, intrinsic feature of the kind of experience we are having; and once thus clarified, the claim is warranted by our experience.[20]

When we turn to touch and bodily sensations, we find events that evidently and saliently involve location of tactile and painful (for example) qualities. If we are not imposed upon by a Cartesian hangover, we will be able to recognize these locational aspects as analogous to the visual depth of our color qualities. Warmth can fill a region of our bodies or all of our bodies; or it may fill most of our bodies, while cold, for example, fills our feet. The point, in this latter case, is not that our feet are where we have to touch in order to find something cold (although that may also be true); rather, the coldness itself has the property of being there, in one's feet. The ache due to our (ordinary, alcoholic) hangover may occupy a

on Berkeley's part that it is just not phenomenologically correct to deny that distance is a feature in experience itself.

20 For excellent discussions that have independently arrived at the same conclusion, readers are referred to Clark (2000) and to chapter 6 of Velmans (2000). Clark's work is particularly interesting here, because some of his further views (e.g., his acceptance of identity theory) are sharply at odds with the theory of this book.

There are anticipations of the intrinsic spatiality of experience in the talk by Russell, Schlick, Broad, and others of private or psychological spaces (as opposed to a constructed public or physical space). These views are, however, not so widely discussed today, and may be thought to be inextricably bound up with commitments to the existence of sense data and to other questionable views. It is thus important to be explicit here about what the best form of qualitative event realism says about the spatial and locational character of experiences and about just what reasoning leads to inclusion of that character.

sizable region of our head; the sharper pain of a migraine may lie along a line stretching from eye to neck.

Let me add that location is also an aspect of sound consciousness. Unlike colors, pitches and timbres do not have area. Like pains, they have location, but unlike pains, this location is usually outside the body.[21]

Earlier in this chapter, I discussed a view put forward by G. E. Moore and summarized it in a diagram. It may be helpful to summarize some of what has been said in this section in a similarly diagrammatic way. To this end, let us represent qualitative events by "[P, t]", where P is a time-filling property and t is a (greater or lesser) duration. Let "S(P)" symbolize P's exemplifying a (second order) property, S. Relevant candidates for S are, e.g., shapes, locations, and intensities. In general, properties in consciousness will have many properties; for example, the yellow–orange of an afterimage when the eyes are open will almost always have some shape, some location, and some intensity. Let us therefore use "$\mathbf{S}(P)$" to symbolize P's exemplifying a set of properties, and let us require that the set be nonempty. With these understandings, we may diagram an occurrence of consciousness as in (3).

$$(3) \qquad\qquad [P, t] + \mathbf{S}(P)$$

This diagram, however, represents a very simple case that perhaps never occurs. For, in general, a conscious event will have several conscious, first order properties. Using $\mathbf{P}$ for a set of conscious properties, of which P1, P2, . . . are members, a more realistic diagram of typical conscious events would be

$$(4) \qquad\qquad [\mathbf{P}, t] + \mathbf{S}(P1) + \mathbf{S}'(P2) + \ldots$$

If there are several color properties in the set $\mathbf{P}$, and at least one closed shape, in a visual experience, then there will be some number of closed shapes of a particular color. Thus, an occurrence of an event of the kind depicted in (4) will often be a sufficient condition of the occurrence of another fact, which might be diagrammed as in (5).

$$(5) \qquad\qquad \mathcal{N}(S; P)$$

Diagram (5) represents the determination of a number by the shape property and the color property. If S is allowed to be the determinable "has

---

21 For what little an anecdote may be worth, I was once inside a house that was struck by lightning, which fused the top of a fish tank to its frame and made holes where there were nails in the drywall. The loud report accompanying this event was located inside my head.

a closed shape", a form of the kind in (5) will represent the number of spots of the color P; if P is allowed to be the determinable "some color or other", then (5) will represent the number of spots of whatever color that have the shape S.

One might worry that these diagrams will lead to an implausibly inhibited logic. For example, we should be able to say that an afterimage is oval and green, and we surely want to be able to infer the occurrence of a green afterimage from the occurrence of an oval green afterimage. Familiar habits will suggest "Oa & Ga" as a representation of an afterimage's being oval and green, and the inference to a green afterimage as a case of simplification. But the form "Fx" does not occur in the preceding diagrams; thus, one may worry that the suggested way of diagramming occurrences of conscious events is incompatible with preservation of even the simplest reasoning about them.

There is, however, no such unfortunate consequence. We can certainly write "Oa & Ga" and read it in the customary way as "a is oval and a is green". The only point we need to attend to is that if "a" is supposed to be a part of an afterimage, it cannot be taken to refer to an "individual" (bare or otherwise) or even a collection of properties other than O and G. "a" in this case would be nothing but the event of green's being bounded ovally (together with whatever other properties, e.g., intensity, may be required by green's being bounded ovally).

WHAT IS CONSCIOUSNESS?

According to the view developed here, the color that seems to us to be "on an object" is in fact a kind of consciousness; it is one of the qualities such that for it to be instantiated is for a conscious event to occur. Those who think that *that* very property occurs in the skin of a tomato, or is a property that a tomato might have all by itself, are mistaken, according to QER.[22] It is not clear that many people do think that way, although it seems likely that many people lack a set of beliefs that would rule it out. For the most part, it seems that people just do not think about such matters at all, unless they find themselves in a class in philosophy or the psychology of perception. But even if some people do make such a mistake, they need not be making any *ordinary* mistake in the sense

---

22 Strictly, they are mistaken unless they can establish that the skin of a ripe tomato is itself a sufficient cause of red conscious events. So far as I know, no one – not even any panpsychist – has ever held such a view.

described earlier. For example, it does not follow from being mistaken in the way just described that people are speaking unjustifiably when they say that these apples are red or those apples are green.

Let us return to Moore's claim that awareness is "as if it were diaphanous" and "extremely difficult to fix".[23] From the point of view of QER, this is certainly wrong. Kinds of conscious events are green, red, painful, itchy, warm, pitched (in the auditory sense), putrid, and so on. There is, of course, a theoretical question about how conscious events are related to knowledge, and I will consider this question in Chapter 10. But we can say that *what* is known, when you know that you have a green experience, is a property that is essentially conscious, i.e., cannot occur except in a conscious event. What you are knowing about when you know you are having a green experience is an occurrence of consciousness of a particular kind. Perhaps some will now complain that they are never conscious of consciousness as such, i.e., of consciousness without its being consciousness of some kind or other. This is true, but it is no complaint. We should regard it in the same light as we might regard the "complaint" of a person who says that he is never conscious of color as such, i.e., of color without its being color of some shade or other. This is true, but it is not a reason to conclude that color is diaphanous, hard to fix, or otherwise mysterious in any way.

A further consequence of QER is that asking what produces consciousness is nothing other than asking what produces colors, pitches, odors, flavors, and so on – all understood as properties of conscious events rather than as any of the P-red properties of the physical objects that, in normal circumstances, cause conscious events in us. Another way of putting the same point is this: the "hard problem" of consciousness – why there is consciousness at all – is equivalent to the problem of why there are phenomenal qualities.

Suppose, now, that we imagine someone asking "But what is the intrinsic nature of *consciousness*?" On one interpretation, this question has already been answered. Occurrences of colors, pitches, odors, flavors, warmth, painfulness, and so on are what occurrences of consciousness are. If this answer does not satisfy the questioner, it may be that what is being asked for is some additional intrinsic nature of consciousness by itself. In this case, we should reply that there is no additional intrinsic nature. For here, "intrinsic" cannot be read as opposed to "extrinsic",

23 Moore (1903/1922), p. 25 and p. 20, respectively.

i.e., to *relational*; it must mean, instead, "hidden" or "behind the (merely) surface properties listed in the answer already given". It is a presupposition of the question that there is such a hidden nature; but that is a false presupposition, according to QER. There is, however, a third interpretation of the question, namely, "What is common to all phenomenal qualities?" Scents do not fill space, in the relevant sense, and some sounds lack a spatial aspect. The same can be said of certain phenomenal aspects of rage or jealousy. Thus, filling space does not seem essential to phenomenal properties, even though many properties, e.g., visual and bodily sensation properties, do so. But all phenomenal qualities fill time. Thus, while time and space have many parallels, time is more fundamental. Finally, besides being able to fill time, properties of experiences are properties that other things may appear as, but that themselves do not appear *as*. The grammar of appearing requires a thing that appears, which contributes causally to an appearance. The properties of conscious events are the properties of the appearances caused by what appears; they are not, in turn, causes of (yet further) appearances.[24]

THE STATE OF THE ARGUMENT SO FAR

In this chapter I have been primarily concerned to *state* QER. Because it is difficult to make arguments clear when the sense of the conclusion is not yet fully understood, I have had to put some points forward without fully explaining the reasons for affirming them. Naturally, I expect the attraction of the view to grow as we see how QER fares against the claims of other theories that we shall be discussing.

Some arguments have, however, been given, and it will be useful to divide these into initial motivations and intrarealism supports. The initial motivations spring from the evident inadequacy of Minimalism, the reality of afterimaging, and the similarity of afterimaging and seeing. When we look at an apple or a pin stripe in a piece of fabric, there is a way it looks. Light is reflected from surfaces with some molecular structure, and we are able to apply words in a way that agrees with other

---

24 I realize that it is contentious merely to assume that there is a sense of "appearance" (or "seeming") that is not reducible to judgments or proto-judgments (i.e., occurrences that are like judgments in every respect except that they fail to make it into the "accepted, all things considered" category). I shall defend this assumption in due course (see Chapter 9). Until then, let us remember that I am partly concerned about getting a qualitative event realist view clearly stated; and it is fair to give its answer to the question at hand even if part of the defense of this answer is to come later.

normally sighted, normally trained English speakers. But besides all those causes and all that behavior, it is at least enormously plausible to say there is something else, something that philosophers have long recognized and called by such terms as "experience". QER is, first and foremost, a realism. It begins with the obvious, namely, that there are experiences, experiences are realities of some kind in their own right, they are similar and different in certain ways, they occur when we look at things, and sometimes they occur as afterimages, aftertastes, and so on.

One can agree to the reality of experiences without agreeing to much else that we have said. Intrarealist arguments are reasons for adopting one or another account of experiences once having agreed to their reality. In this chapter, I have argued that the customary division of, e.g., an afterimage into an image and an experience of that image is a mistake. I have tried, then, to work out a realism that does not make this mistake. In doing so, I have said several things that are unfamiliar, and that may strike readers as obviously incorrect or even not strictly grammatical. I have, in effect, argued that the claims of QER are merely unusual and do not actually offend correct speech. In some cases, I have pointed out that some aspects of quite ordinary speech are very like the usage required by my statement of QER. In other cases, I have tried to resolve problems that may seem to beset the proposed theory. In the course of stating and resolving these problems, I have said several things about the actual character of experience.

There are many things I have not done in this chapter. I have neither described nor argued against many alternative views that in some sense accept the reality of experiences but give completely different accounts of them. I have not argued against a radical denial of realism with regard to experiences. I have not developed the conflict between QER and materialism. I have not said much about the causes of qualitative events or about how they should be thought to fit into our theory of the physical universe. All these things will have to be done before I can responsibly claim that QER is the best theory of phenomenal consciousness.

3

Dualism

Are qualitative events material? Or should we hold that our conscious, qualitative events are something over and above the events that take place in the physical world? My answer to these questions will be developed over several chapters, but a rough guiding statement of it can be given: if one is willing to make "materialism" a sufficiently empty view, then it cannot be refuted, and qualitative events can be supposed to be material without self-contradiction. If, however, one wants one's philosophical views to be more than purely defensive stances, then dualism should be regarded as the more reasonable view to hold (even though it cannot be demonstrated with certainty).

To begin to clarify these rather compressed pronouncements, it will be helpful to go back to Descartes and consider the fate of an argument that is suggested by some of his formulations.[1]

(D1) I am certain that I exist.
(D2) I am not certain that anything bodily exists.
(D3) I cannot be certain and uncertain of the same thing at the same time.

---

1 Descartes never states a premise corresponding to (D3) or (D3a), stated subsequently, and I introduce them only because they are necessary formally to arrive at (D4) or (D4a). The first two premises are suggested by these Second Meditation statements. "But it is very certain that the knowledge of my existence taken in its precise significance does not depend on things whose existence is not yet known to me. . . . But I already know for certain that I am, and that it may be that all these images, and, speaking generally, all things that relate to the nature of body are nothing but dreams [and chimeras]. . . . And, thus, I know for certain that nothing of all that I can understand by means of my imagination belongs to this knowledge which I have of myself" (Descartes, 1641. Translations are from E. S. Haldane and G. R. T. Ross, 1931, vol. 1, p. 152.) Shortly after this last quotation, Descartes explicitly asks what he is, and concludes that he is a thing which thinks.

Therefore,

(D4) I am not the same thing as any bodily thing.

Perhaps the most difficult premise in this argument is (D3). Its force may be a little clearer if we consider the following reformulation of the argument.

(D1a) I have the property of being a thing of whose existence I am certain.
(D2a) No bodily thing has the property of being a thing of whose existence I am certain.
(D3a) For every x and y, if x and y are identical, then every property that x has is a property that y has, and conversely.

Therefore,

(D4a) I am not identical with any bodily thing.

This argument is plainly fallacious in either formulation, and it is well understood what is wrong with it. Ordinary rules governing inferences with identity cannot be applied where psychological verbs (and certain other contexts) are present. For example, what would we make of a beginner in geometry who argues in this way?

I am certain that I am reasoning about right-angled triangles. But I am not certain that I am reasoning about a figure to which the Pythagorean Theorem applies. I cannot be certain and uncertain of the same thing at the same time. Therefore, right-angled triangles are not the same as figures to which the Pythagorean Theorem applies.

Or consider a detective who reasons thus:

John Jones has the property of being certainly known by me to be sitting before me. But the thief I am looking for does not have the property of being certainly known by me to be sitting before me. Identicals must share all their properties. Therefore, the thief I am looking for is not identical with John Jones. I'd better let him go.

Here, surely, is a candidate for quick demotion.

I have made somewhat light of the quasi-Cartesian (D) argument, but I now want to suggest that there is an addition that can be made to it that yields a somewhat more serious argument. In the examples just given, there are *modes of presentation* of the items involved. John Jones is presented *as* a person sitting before me but is not presented *as* a thief. The fallacy is to reason from *is not presented as F* to *is not F*. Likewise, there is more to a right-angled triangle than the property through which it is first

37

presented to the beginner in geometry. Again, it is fallacious to reason from *is not presented as satisfying the Pythagorean Theorem* to *does not satisfy the Pythagorean Theorem*.

These observations may suggest that both thoughts and qualitative events are nothing but modes of presentation. Other things may *have* modes of presentation, which is to say that they are presented *as F*; but it seems very suspicious (not to mention suggestive of regress) to suppose that modes of presentation themselves have modes of presentation (which would be to say that they are presented *as F*). A mode of presentation would seem to be the sort of thing that has nothing to it but the property that something (i.e., what it is a mode of presentation *of*) is presented *as* having.[2] If that is correct, however, then there may be an argument that is analogous to the one I have been abusing but that avoids fallacy by being restricted to modes of presentation. For, within such a restriction, one would, in effect, be reasoning only from "Something is presented as *F* and not as *G*" to "The mode of presentation through which something is being presented *is F* and *is not G*".

Before casting these reflections in a somewhat more formal way, let us note that the same result can be reached through a less technical approach. One infrequent but still quite ordinary and readily intelligible type of remark is that something presents a misleading appearance. In some simple cases where such a remark applies, a misleading appearance can be taken to be what a qualitative event realist would count as a qualitative event. For example, honey may appear bitter to people with hepatitis. In this case, it is natural to say that, because of their disease, honey presents a bitter appearance, or a bitter taste. Now, in this way of speaking, it would be clearly wrong to suggest that appearances appear. The bitter taste does not *appear* bitter; the honey appears bitter and the taste itself *is* bitter. The grammar of (simple) misleading appearances is: *S* is misled about *O* because *O* is the kind of thing that normally appears *F* but in this case is causing a *G* appearance, where *F* is not *G*. The misleading appearance in such a case *is* G – it is not something that appears *as* G. In short, just as modes of presentation are what they are, but are not presented under a mode, so appearances do not appear *F*; they *are* F.

The intuitions developed in the last two paragraphs may be given a more formal statement, which I will call the Restricted Argument for

---

2 "X has nothing to it but Y" means "X is Y and nothing but Y". Thus, for example, the Hesperus mode of presentation of Venus does not *have* the property *first heavenly body to appear in the evening*; rather, the Hesperus mode of presentation of Venus *is* that property.

Dualism. In stating this argument, it will be convenient to introduce a way of referring to certain properties, namely, those properties *F* for which it is true that

Something now appears *F* to *S*.

I shall call such properties "appearance-constituting properties". Grammatical variants of this phrase will be useful and are easily understood; for example, "*S* has an appearance constituted by *F*" means the same as "*F* is an appearance-constituting property of one of *S*'s appearances", and this will be true just in case something now appears *F* to *S*.

"Something now appears *F* to *S*" is not to be confused with "something now appears the way things of kind *F* normally appear". White is the way dry salt normally appears to us, and white is an appearance-constituting property. Salt is a chemical compound, but when *S* is faced with dry salt, it will not generally be true that something appears chemically compound to *S*, even though appearing white to *S* is the way that a compound of this kind normally appears to *S*. Or, as we may also say, when *S* is faced with dry salt, the salt does not appear *as* chemically compound, even though it does appear in the way (namely, white) that the compound that is salt normally appears. Thus, *chemically compound* is not an appearance-constituting property.

It is a substantive question whether appearances may *have* properties other than those that *constitute* them, i.e., whether it can be true that *S* has an appearance that *is* G when it is false that something now appears G to *S*. This question is not begged by the special use of "constituting property". To the contrary, this terminology is introduced to help make the question clear and explicit. The third premise in the following argument takes a position on this question, and we will subsequently see what can be said for or against this position.

The Restricted Argument for Dualism (i.e., dualism restricted to appearances) can now be stated as follows.

(RAD1) *S* now has an appearance that is constituted by *F*.
(RAD2) *S* does not now have an appearance that is constituted by *G*.
(RAD3) Appearances actually *have* the properties by which they are *constituted*, but they *do not have* any nonrelational or nondifferentiating properties other than those by which they are constituted.

Therefore,

(RAD4) *S* does not now have an appearance that is *G*.

Appearances may have relational properties that do not appear; for example, an appearance may occur at 7:37 GMT without there being anything that appears as occurring at a time. Limiting (RAD3) to nonrelational properties ensures that cases of this kind are not counterexamples to it. Appearances are also temporal and conscious, and they exist. But all appearances have these properties (if, indeed, existence is a property at all), i.e., no appearance is differentiated from any other by these properties; thus, the second limitation in (RAD3) ensures that these cases are also not counterexamples to it.

The force of (RAD) can be illustrated by imagining someone who holds that appearances of particular kinds (e.g., red) are identical with neural events of particular kinds (say, a neural event of type 42, or NE 42). A proponent of (RAD) will first note that at least nothing appears *as* an NE 42, i.e., the premise (RAD2) is satisfied when we substitute "NE 42" for "G". The conclusion will then be drawn that S does not now have an appearance that has the property of being an NE 42. But if S has a red appearance (i.e., if [RAD1] is satisfied when we substitute "red" for "F"), and does not have an appearance that has the property of being an NE 42, then a red appearance cannot *be* an NE 42. Moreover, if S's red appearance had the generic property of being a physical event, it would have to be of some specific physical event type, and this specific type would be a differentiating property. Since the argument just given would apply to each specific type of physical event, we cannot say that appearances might be physical – i.e., we cannot appeal to the idea that "physical" is a nondifferentiating property of appearances. Nor can we defeat the application of (RAD3) by viewing association with NE 42 as a merely relational property of S's red appearance. Qualitative event realists will readily agree that red appearances are caused by neural events. Something much stronger than mere relatedness is required if we are to have a view that qualifies as a "materialism" on contemporary understandings of that term.[3]

---

3 Is (RAD) a Cartesian argument? Evidently, it gives up the substantialist flavor of Descartes' statements in terms of "I" and "myself". It resonates well, however, with the many Cartesian texts that exclude everything from "himself" except what appears to him. For example, "I am the same who feels, that is to say, who perceives certain things, as by the organs of sense, since in truth I see light, I hear noise, I feel heat. But it will be said that these phenomena are false and that I am dreaming. Let it be so; still it is at least quite certain that it seems to me that I see light, that I hear noise and that I feel heat. That cannot be false; properly speaking it is what is in me called feeling" (Descartes, 1641. Translation from E. S. Haldane and G. R. T. Ross, 1931, p. 153.)

(RAD) is an improvement on the (D) argument. But is it good enough to pass for a proof of dualism? No. The reason is that the fact that we are only aware of a mode of presentation (or an appearance) as a mode of presentation (or appearance) does not *show* that it has no other, nonpresented properties. We do not conceive of it as having any further properties, but that is not the same as knowing that there are no other properties. It is not the same as knowing that there are no other properties of an appearance that are necessarily connected with those that constitute it, or even that there are no other descriptions of the same properties that are not aspects under which those properties are presented. If, however, there are any further properties, or descriptions, of a mode of presentation (appearance), then, unsavory as it seems to allow it, we must say that a mode of presentation is presented under a mode of presentation (or that an appearance appears *as F*, for some *F*). If there are unapparent properties of modes of presentation (appearances), we would not need to allow that the mode of presentation (appearance) could be false or misleading (i.e., about its *own* nature); but we would have to allow that it was only partial, and therefore that the mode of presentation (appearance) was appearing under only one of its actual properties or descriptions.

In somewhat more formal terms, the limitation of the restricted argument for dualism is that the negative half of (RAD3) may be denied without self-contradiction. Such a denial may be thought of in two ways. (a) It may be held that an appearance can have a hidden nature in the sense that it may in fact *be G*, where *G* is a property that is distinct from any property that constitutes the appearance (i.e., where nothing is appearing *as G*). (b) It may be held that the property *F* may be identical with the property *G*, even though *F* constitutes an appearance and *G* does not constitute that appearance. In the first case, an opponent of (RAD) can say that (RAD3) is a premise to which we are not entitled. In the second case, an opponent of (RAD) will regard (RAD3) as strictly true, but can say that we do not know that the inference to (RAD4) is a valid one.[4]

There are many ways of formulating Descartes' arguments for dualism, and consequently many ways of formulating objections to them. However, all the versions of which I am aware have limited force for essentially the

---

4 Our discussion may appear to diverge from Chalmers' (1996) results. In fact, however, the only possibility that has been said not to be excludable is the same one that Chalmers recognizes under his term "Don't-have-a-clue-materialism" (Chalmers, 1996, p. 162). This view is also not ruled out by Chalmers' arguments, although he rightly regards it as having to give way to something more substantive if materialism is to become a satisfactory view.

reasons I have tried to make clear in the foregoing discussion. Nor do I know of any other way of arguing that qualitative events *cannot* have a hidden nature.

This result is the reason materialism (applied to qualitative events) can be held without self-contradiction. But we should notice that the result we have reached is an unremittingly negative one. We *cannot prove* that there is no hidden material nature possessed by qualitative events; but the way we have arrived at this conclusion provides no positive suggestion whatsoever as to what such a nature might be, how it could be possessed by qualitative events or by phenomenal qualities, or even how such a nature could be discovered. We have no explanation of how or why a red experience or a pain could be the same thing as a neural event or any other kind of material event. The negation of the second half of (RAD3) may not be formally self-contradictory, but this fact provides no explanation either of how an appearance could have a nonconstituting property or of how a nonconstituting property could be identical with a constituting one. If the impossibility of disproving materialism has to rest on the unexplained claim that the negation of the second half of (RAD3) might be true, then it is an empty view that provides no enlightenment. It may seem verbally attractive to assert it, because in other areas, supporting materialism means showing how difficult questions can be brought within the purview of science. But a materialism that rests on rejection of (RAD3) utterly fails to do that.

Contemporary philosophical literature is replete with special terminologies and complex arguments concerning the debate between dualism and materialism. In my view, the actual upshot of these discussions is always exactly equivalent to the position at which we have now arrived. Dualists cannot give a demonstrative proof that appearances have no hidden material nature and therefore cannot conclusively refute materialism. But, in one terminology or another, materialists must make a substantive claim that is equivalent to the claim that appearances do have a hidden (material) nature. And they must make this claim in the face of the fact that they have no understanding of how it can be possible that appearances appear, i.e., that appearances should really be what they do not appear as being.

In this situation, agnosticism would not be an unreasonable position to take. But in my view, despite the nondemonstrability of either materialism or dualism, they are asymmetrical positions, and, in the end, dualism is the more reasonable one to adopt. The asymmetry can be made clearly visible by putting the matter in terms of conceivability. Assertion of dualism requires affirmation of a difference that one can conceive but not prove. Assertion of materialism requires affirmation of an identity that one cannot conceive and cannot prove.[5] This asymmetry already provides some reason to prefer dualism, but the full case for dualism requires developing the view and responding to the many objections that will be made to it. Crucially, it also requires examining the arguments of many materialists who would not agree that their view is as empty as I have made it out to be. In the remainder of this chapter, I will consider some relatively simple arguments of this kind. Later chapters will take up versions of materialism that require a more extended discussion.

REDUCTION AND SCIENTIFIC PROGRESS

Materialism would not be an empty view if we could explain how phenomenally conscious events could be reduced to neural events, in some suitable sense of "reduction". "Suitable sense" here requires more than explaining how a single *thing* could have both physical properties and phenomenal properties. There is, to take an analogy, no problem in understanding how a single thing could be both a musical instrument and a piece of visual art, and painted or finely carved harpsichords are actual examples. Reductive claims in the field of phenomenal consciousness, however, do not merely claim that two properties, e.g., a phenomenal quality and a neural event property, are had by the same occurrences. To be interesting as an alternative to dualism, the property connection must be much tighter; one must claim that one property reduces to the "other" or that the "two" are really one property that merely has two descriptions.

Materialists sometimes suggest that possible models for a suitably tight connection can be found in reductions that are familiar from science, e.g., the reduction of light to electromagnetic radiation, heat to kinetic energy, or burning to oxidation.[6] Reductions of this kind are explanatorily satisfying because they enable us to construct, in thought, the

---

5   Evidently, I am appealing to a notion of conceivability that requires appearance of possibility but not proof of possibility. Others may have different notions. For discussion of several conceivability concepts, see Yablo (1993).

6   These examples occur in P. S. Churchland (1998). Searle (1992, pp. 101–102) argues for the same view by reference to the reduction of liquidity to behavior of H_2O molecules, and the biological account of life.

   Churchland's view (and, as we shall see, its failure) is particularly interesting because it is given in the face of clear recognition of the strength of the required reduction. She describes the view to which she purports to offer a solution in terms very like those of our previous section, namely, as the view that "in the case of consciousness, the appearance *is*

reduced properties from the reducing properties. The thermal motion in a warm body is communicated to adjacent bodies, thus changing their temperature and therewith their volume. The combining of oxygen with other atoms releases heat and results in new compounds found in the resulting ash. The identification of properties apparent to observation with constellations of properties that are not thus apparent results in constructive explanations of why the observable properties are present.

Materialism that *actually* provided an explanatory reduction of phenomenal qualities to neural activations would decisively answer the charge of emptiness of materialism. It would overcome dualism by showing how occurrences of phenomenal qualities can be constructed from neural events, i.e., how there would necessarily have to be occurrences of phenomenal qualities, given that neural events of such and such kinds occur. As things stand, however, materialism can offer no such explanatory reduction. The *entire actual* offering of a materialism that takes reductions in science as its model is a model that has worked in other areas of science, and an unsupported hope that this model can be extended to work for phenomenal qualities.

The now voluminous literature concerning the "explanatory gap" has, however, shown why such a hope is extremely likely to be forlorn.[7] The outline of the project for such reduction has been well known for over 300 years, and some actual examples of the kind of reduction in science described earlier have been available for over 200 years. In that time, we have not only had no successful explanatory reduction of phenomenal

---

the reality. . . . Feeling the pain is all the reality there is to pain" (Churchland, 1998, p. 117; emphasis in the original). A key part of her response to this view is stated as follows.

What is troublesome is the idea that all the reality there is to a sensation is available through sheerly having it. How could you possibly know that? I suggest, instead, a rather simple alternative: A sensation of pain is real, but not *everything* about the nature of pain is revealed in introspection – its neural substrate, for example, is not so revealed. (Churchland, 1998, p. 117; emphasis in the original)

"Neural substrate" here does not mean "neural cause"; if it did, there would be no disagreement between Churchland's view and QER. Its meaning can be gathered from the following.

Commonly, science discovers ways of taking us beyond the manifest or superficial properties of some phenomenon. Light is refracted in water – that is observable. Light turns out to be electromagnetic radiation, a property not straightforwardly observable. Does the observable property – refraction – cease to be real . . . when we discover one of light's unobservable properties? No. (Churchland, 1998, pp. 117–118)

7   See, e.g., Levine (1983), Chalmers (1996), and Robinson (1982, 1996a).

qualities; we have not had any theories that were attractive but proved unworkable. We do not have any promising ideas for a reductive strategy that will explain to us why neural activations of such and such kinds must be accompanied by, e.g., pains (or, if one prefers, why those neural activations must compose pains). In light of these facts, a materialism that draws upon the idea of explanatory reduction for phenomenal qualities is a materialism that draws upon what is now actually nonexistent, and so it is now actually as empty as I have made it out to be.[8]

Considerations of the kind just reviewed are sometimes met by reminders of the glorious progress of science, along with the implication that doubters that science will provide an explanatory reduction of phenomenal qualities are persons with stunted imaginations. Science, however, has not usually taken its major steps forward by following general lines of development that were well laid out in advance of significant insights. Thus, the premise that science will progress is no support whatsoever for the view that it will progress *by* eventually finding a reductive explanation of phenomenal qualities. To the contrary, the fact that the project has been well understood for so long with no plausible suggestions for its accomplishment is inductive evidence against expecting success in that particular direction. Expectation of explanatory reduction of the kind illustrated by heat/mean kinetic energy is thus not only a blind faith, but one that runs counter to the principle of induction on which much of science rests.

It is also sometimes suggested that materialism should be preferred by those who respect science, on the ground that materialism is simpler — it has one kind of entity to dualism's two — and science follows Occam's principle that simpler is better. If we cannot demonstratively prove either view, should we not prefer materialism as more economical?

But science does not follow an unrestricted principle that simpler is better.[9] Simpler *explanations* are better than more complex explanations that have the same explanatory range. But materialism about qualitative events provides no explanation; and simplicity of explanation is, in any case, not always measurable by merely counting the number of entities required.[10]

---

8 The weakness of analogizing from successful explanations to future reductions should be evident to contemporary philosophers who, presumably, have studied Hume's (1748) chapter, "Of a Particular Providence and of a Future State".

9 Nor did Occam, who held that one should not multiply entities *beyond necessity*.

10 Copernican astronomy is better science than Ptolemaic astronomy, but it does not reduce the number of things to be accounted for.

It may be suggested further that science has progressed by assuming materialism and that, therefore, so long as we cannot give a demonstrative argument for dualism we ought to be materialists. The thought is that we would be departing from the scientific spirit if we were to reject materialism; we would be allying ourselves with those who would have frustrated the advance of science because we would be promoting satisfaction with ghostly interventions or occult powers.

But in fact it is not the assumption of materialism that has furthered science. The scientific spirit favors the search for genuine explanations and rejects appeals to nonexplanatory entities or forces, no matter how conveniently they may fit with prevailing ideologies. Where there is independent reason to think that explanations can be found that rely only on the action of material things, the search for explanations will, of course, be a search among material things. But once it is seen that materialism regarding qualitative events is an empty view, its positive assertion belongs not on the side of science, but on the side of ideology that is contrary to the scientific spirit.

Having said that, I hasten to recognize that I have gotten somewhat ahead of my argument. Many materialists will not yet agree that the view must remain empty. That is one reason it will be necessary to continue to explore many attempts to give it genuine content.

PROPERTY IDENTITY WITHOUT EXPLANATORY REDUCTION

Some materialists who propose that phenomenal qualities are identical with neural properties agree that there will never be an explanatory reduction of the first to the second. They find this position palatable because they believe they have an explanation of why there can be no such reduction, despite the identity. There are two forms that this idea may take, and this section and the next will consider them.

Let us return to the example of the musical instrument that is also a work of visual art. It is evident that there is no support in this example for the idea that the property of being a musical instrument is the same property as the property of being a work of visual art. Bringing this point back into the arena of phenomenal consciousness, we may say that even if one held that a single event could be both a qualitative event of a certain kind (e.g., red) and a neural event of a certain kind (e.g., a certain pattern of neural activation), that would not be to say that phenomenal redness is the *same property as* the property of being a certain pattern of neural activation.

While some things appear red, nothing normally appears to us as a set of neurons firing in some way. Perhaps a cerebroscope could be made to drive a monitor display that would look like a bunch of neurons pulsing away at various rates; but that would be the way a brain appeared (in very special circumstances), and it would not (except accidentally) appear red. In the sense in which ordinary appearances are sometimes constituted by redness, no nonlaboratory appearance is constituted by the property of being neurons firing in such and such a manner. Holding the properties to be different explains this obvious fact. Conversely, if redness is just the same property as a neural firing property, it would seem that we could not explain how the one property is the way something appears and the "other" is not.

There is, however, a way in which a materialist might seek to undercut this point, and affirm an identity, not only between events, but also between a phenomenal quality and a neural event *property*. Namely, one might seek to drive a wedge between a property and the *concept* of that property. To do this, one might point to differences in the way we learn certain concepts. Thus, concepts of phenomenal qualities are acquired in contexts of observation (of, e.g., red things) or sensation (e.g., of pain). Others see our circumstances of observation, or our injuries and behavior, and teach us the appropriate words. But concepts of neural event kinds are learned in an entirely different way. Acquisition of such concepts depends on work in the neurophysiological laboratory or, at least, instruction that is based on such work. Because the concepts are acquired in such different ways, a materialist might hold, it is not surprising that we should come to regard the properties of which they are concepts as different. But the difference in concept acquisition would be there even if the properties are the same, and so the difference of concepts does not undercut the materialist claim that phenomenal properties are neural event properties.[11]

---

11 The most carefully articulated version of this view of which I am aware is that of Hill (1991, chap. 4). Hill is replying to a formulation of the argument I have given that is due to Shaffer (1968). Hill objects that arguments like Shaffer's rest on

> the following presupposition: If qualitative characteristics were identical with neurological characteristics, then the experiences that lead us to subsume events under our concepts of qualitative characteristics would partially or entirely coincide with the experiences that lead us to subsume events under our concepts of neurological characteristics. As far as I can tell, there is no reason to believe that this presupposition is true. (Hill, 1991, p. 97)

This argument is ingenious, but it should not persuade us that materialism predicts the fact that appearances are constituted by phenomenal qualities but not by neural event properties. For, according to the present version of materialism, phenomenal qualities *are* neural event properties. This version of materialism thus does not explain how it is possible that the same property could appear as what it is (namely, red or pain) when it is being had, and yet not appear as what it equally is (namely, a neural event property) when it is being had.[12]

This counterargument cannot be turned into a *disproof* of the present version of materialism. The attempt to do so would produce this argument: *Pain* has the property *F* (namely, the property of appearing as what it is when it is being had); *Neural event type 328* does not have *F*; "two" properties are identical only if they have all their (second order) properties in common; therefore, pain is not the same property as being a neural event of type 328. But this argument may be like the (D) argument, i.e., it may be argued that "appears as what it is when it is being had" is a psychological context of the kind that leads to failure of substitutivity even of certifiably genuine identicals. In that case, the attempted argument is just as fallacious as the reasoning of our imagined detective or beginner at geometry.

We must say "may be like the (D) argument" rather than "is like the (D) argument" because the contexts in the (D) argument are cognitive, that is, they involve such concepts as belief, knowledge, or certainty. "Appearing as what it is when it is being had" is undoubtedly psychological, but it is not cognitive. Thus, strictly speaking, we do not know that the argument of the preceding paragraph fails for the same reason as the (D) argument; we know only that it *may* involve a context that does not permit unfallacious substitution of identicals.

Scott Sturgeon (2000, sects 2.3 and 2.4) also focuses on concepts. His argument, however, is different from the one considered in this section. It is an alternative way of reaching a conclusion very like the agnosticism considered earlier in this chapter.

12 William Seager has drawn my attention to the fact that a thing may be classified under a determinate concept without the classifier being able to apply a corresponding determinable. For example, someone may apply the concept "bear" without being able to apply the concept "mammal". This case, however, is triply disanalogous to the one under discussion. (a) No one claims that "bear" and "mammal" are the same property. (b) No one claims that "pain" (for example) is a determinate of the determinable "C-fiber stimulation" (or whatever neural event kind one might propose to be identical with pain). (Such a claim must, of course, be distinguished from the true claim that a particular kind of pain is caused by [or is correlated with] a particular kind of neural event.) (c) There is no apparent explanatory gap concerning determinates and determinables.

While the counterargument has not led us to a disproof of the present version of materialism, our discussion of it does lead to a conclusion that ought to be almost equally distressing for a materialist. Lacking an explanation of how neural event properties can fail to appear as they are, the claim of their identity with phenomenal qualities is an empty claim, a bare assertion of a consequence of materialism that provides no understanding of how it *could* be true. In this respect, QER is a preferable view: in proposing that phenomenal qualities and neural properties are different properties, it provides a natural explanation of why these properties do not appear to be the same.

A variant of the foregoing materialist view makes a distinction between the properties that neural events have and the properties *through which* we become aware of neural event properties. We cannot directly observe neural event properties; we come to know of them through inferences based on examination of stained tissue samples, images produced by scanning, recordings from implanted electrodes, and the like. Let us call the properties of tissue samples, images, recordings, and so on "O properties", while the neural event properties we infer from them are "N properties". Now, it is consistent to hold that (a) phenomenal qualities are identical to N properties while allowing that (b) phenomenal qualities are distinct from O properties. All that one has to do is to allow what seems evident enough, namely, that (c) N properties are also distinct from O properties.[13]

This variant is a genuine attempt to explain how we might come to think that phenomenal qualities could not be neural event properties, even though that is what they are. It proposes a plausible confusion between denying identity of phenomenal qualities and O properties, and denying identity of phenomenal qualities and N properties. But the explanation is not adequate. Although N properties are inferred, they are not unknown. Like knowledge of protons, knowledge of N properties *depends on* knowledge of properties of our instrumental records; but, again like knowledge of protons, knowledge of N properties is not the same thing as knowledge of properties of our instrumental records. As a result of theorizing, we know something about the neural activations that cause our instrumental records. In particular, we know enough about neural event properties to know that, although ordinary things appear red to us, they do not appear neural-activation-set-of-such-and-such-type to us. Alternatively

---

13 It is again Hill (1991) who explains this view most thoroughly. In this case, he is replying to a formulation due to White (1986).

stated, phenomenal qualities are often constitutive of appearances, but N properties never are.

Once again, this conclusion cannot provide a conclusive reason for dualism. But that is only because a materialist of the sort we have been considering can hold that there is some explanation of the asymmetry between phenomenal qualities and N properties that we have not yet thought of. Such a possibility cannot be disproved. However, a materialism that rests on this impossibility of disproof remains an empty view. Despite extensive use of science in the background of such a materialism, affirming it would express a profoundly unscientific attitude; for it would require commitment where there is emptiness of content and nothing by way of explanation.

OUR LIMITED MINDS

A natural response to the conclusion we have reached would be to hold that our minds are simply incapable of understanding the nature of the relation between phenomenal qualities and N properties.[14] This view would do nothing to relieve the emptiness of materialism, but it might make that emptiness more palatable by assuring us of its inevitability. We cannot be blamed for holding an empty view if our minds are constitutionally incapable of removing that emptiness.

Let us concede at the outset that it is *possible* that the intractability of the mind–body problem is due to our mental limitations. Allowing this possibility, however, does not make it reasonable to affirm that we are actually in this position, and, in fact, it does not seem that we ought to make such an affirmation. This claim is a consequence of a general point about the conduct of science: barring actual proof of impossibility of a project, it is not reasonable to suppose that we are incapable of carrying it out.

A model for this point can be gleaned from Gödel's proof of the incompleteness of arithmetic. It may be possible that there are some truths of arithmetic that cannot be proved by any chain of reasoning that mathematicians would recognize as meeting the standards of their discipline. Despite this, no mathematician is, or should be, prepared to declare, with respect to some particular T, that T is a proposition that mathematicians

---

14 The leading proponent of this view is McGinn (1991), who holds that "we are cut off by our very cognitive constitution from achieving a conception of that natural property of the brain (or of consciousness) that accounts for the psychophysical link" (p. 2).

will never prove, and that attempts in that direction should thus be abandoned.[15]

It might be argued, to the contrary, that our concepts are either concepts of phenomenal qualities, or concepts of observable things, or concepts that are derived from these materials by various kinds of compounding or analysis. And it might be further held that our attempts to solve the mind–body problem have shown us that no kind of compounding, analysis, and recombining of elements of our concepts can ever provide materials with which we can achieve satisfaction about the relation of phenomenal consciousness to events in our brains. There are, however, two points to be made against this suggestion. First, it seems profoundly unhistorical. Quantum mechanics is full of ideas that could hardly have been conceived 200 years ago. We might say that the progress of science is misunderstood if it is conceived of as the progressive elimination of false starts from a list that is antecedently given. Instead, advances in science broaden the range of possibilities of which we can conceive. Science teaches us more about what is possible even as it acquires evidence that closes off *some* of those possibilities. From this point of view, a declaration that understanding in a certain area is beyond our ken is a declaration that there will be no scientific advance in that area. Such declarations may reflect an admirable humility, but that provides no reason why we should accept them.

The second point is that theories of concept formation are themselves scientific theories and are subject to revision in the light of further investigation. Now, this kind of point might be merely skeptical if we had an extremely fruitful and well-established theory of concept formation. In fact, however, there is much we do not understand about cognitive theory, and much we do not understand about how we come to revise concepts or form new ones.[16] We have no theory of concept formation that has the kind of detail, development, and support that would make it reasonable to draw from it any conclusions about the possibility of concepts suitable for progress in any area of inquiry.[17] Thus, it would be contrary to the spirit

---

15 There is a wonderful exploration of this idea in A. Doxiadis's novel of mathematical obsession, *Uncle Petros and Goldbach's Conjecture* (Bloomsbury, 2000).

16 On the depth of our ignorance in cognitive theory, see Fodor (2000).

17 McGinn offers an account of concept formation according to which we form theoretical concepts by analogical extension from concepts of observables. Analogical extension is illustrated by the example of generating the concept of a molecule from perceptions of macroscopic objects by maintaining many of their properties while conceiving their size to be reduced. McGinn argues that this method will not help us gain a concept that will help

of scientific inquiry to close the door on the possibility of progress on the mind–body problem. And it would likewise be contrary to that spirit to find comfort in a materialist commitment that has to be bolstered by the mere possibility that we can make no such progress.

Evidently, not all materialists are pessimists of the kind we have lately been considering. Some of them offer accounts that claim to give a positive understanding that resolves many questions and makes materialism fully intelligible. The next four chapters examine accounts that purport to have these advantages.

with the mind–body problem, "since analogical extensions of the entities we observe in the brain are precisely as hopeless as the original entities were as solutions to the mind–body problem" (McGinn, 1991, p. 13).

This conclusion has at least three faults. First, it is question begging. It may be that all the analogical extensions we have yet thought of fail as solutions to the mind–body problem, but the question is whether that must always remain the case, and merely saying that the project is hopeless is no argument that it is so. Second, this statement again imagines a limited project, where a less limited project is the one that is really under discussion. That is, it limits us to analogical extensions of "entities we observe in the brain". But there is no reason why we should not be able to draw upon analogical extensions of any concepts we may already have in attempting to arrive at a solution to the mind–body problem. Third, and most importantly, McGinn's discussion suggests that a solution to the mind–body problem must come, if at all, through the grasping of a single property. But in typical advances in physical theory, we need to draw on analogical extensions of many concepts at once. Even understanding something as simple as a molecule at the crudest level is not possible with only an analogical extension of the concept of a (single) object; it requires at least minimizing objects *and* adding rubber-band analogues between them.

4

Representationalism

Representationalism is currently a highly favored version of materialism, and in this chapter we will consider its main attractions and its difficulties. A key part of the view can be expressed in the following summary account of how color comes into seeing.

(R1) Color comes into the story of a person's seeing the red apple in exactly two ways, (a) as a represented property, i.e., as a property that the person represents the apple as having (namely, red) and (b) as a property of the (surface of the) apple.

The meaning of this statement evidently depends on one's account of representation and on what one takes to be the relevant property of an apple. Representationalists have a variety of understandings on both points. I shall begin the discussion of representationalism with a generic account designed to bring out essential commitments that are common to those who claim the label. Differences among accounts will then emerge as they become relevant to assessing the merits of representationalism.

A presumed advantage of representationalism is its naturalism, that is, its commitment to recognizing no entities other than those recognized in the natural sciences. Because advances in science sometimes add new entities – e.g., electromagnetic force, black holes, or quarks – we cannot reduce naturalism to recognition of a list. Instead, we must take naturalism to accept only what is presently admitted in natural science plus whatever will come to be admitted by the methods of natural science. Because of this open-endedness, and because even the methods of science are subject to development, there is a certain vagueness to the concept of naturalism – a vagueness that must be regarded as increasing as we look further and further into the future.

It remains true, however, that qualitative events are not now entities that all would recognize as entities discussed by a natural science. Moreover, one aspect of the explanatory gap is that we do not now readily understand how the methods of science could be used to introduce qualitative events into natural science.[1] Thus, if a theory of representation were to depend on admitting qualitative events, as understood by QER, it would not be a naturalistic theory of representation, and should not be taken to be an acceptable candidate for explaining "representation" as used in (R1). The same conclusion would hold for a theory that held representation to be a simple, unanalyzable relation between a mental act and a state of affairs. For neither mental acts nor their (putatively simple) relations to states of affairs are clearly identifiable as items recognized, or likely soon to be recognized, in a natural science.

While representationalists hold that a naturalistic account of representation can be given, the project of actually giving such an account is far from finished, and there are significant disagreements about how to proceed. There are, however, several ideas in the field that look promising.[2] For example, under favorable conditions, perceptual representations should not occur unless what they represent is present to the senses. Further, any event that represents something should have a role to play in causing appropriate behavior; for example, representations of dangers should lead to appropriate behaviors such as avoidance. And, perhaps, "appropriate behaviors" can only be explained (naturalistically and without circularity) by alluding to historical facts about how representing events came to exist in an organism or how evolution produced the capacity for members of its species to have representing events.

These ideas will not be the focus of extended discussion in this book. They are introduced only to provide a sufficiently concrete grip on the idea that representation may be something we can account for in a naturalistic way. With this understanding in hand, we can summarize the foregoing comments by taking the following claim to be built into representationalism as understood in this chapter.

---

1 Current work in the scientific study of consciousness is gradually reducing the sharpness of the distinction I am making here, and the later chapters of this book aim to further this trend. Representationalism, however, claims to have *present* understanding of phenomenal consciousness. It is thus fair to discuss it in terms of distinctions that presently exist and that are accepted by its proponents.

2 Dretske (1988, 1995) and Millikan (1984) are uppermost in my thoughts in this paragraph, but these and similar ideas are widely known and accepted by many. See Sellars (1963) and Chisholm and Sellars (1958) for early discussions in this field.

(R2) Representation (as used in R1) can be accounted for in a way that is compatible with naturalism.

The second clause of (R1) refers to properties of (surfaces of) things. We have already encountered properties of the kind intended here. These are the P-red properties that were defined in Chapter 2, of which examples are having a reflectance profile of a certain kind and having a molecular structure of a certain kind. As in Chapter 2, differences among P-properties will not concern us. Representationalists must eventually say which property is their preferred candidate for the redness of (surfaces of) apples, but the arguments of this chapter will be the same for any of the P-properties they may designate. It is clear that P-properties can be described in naturalistic terms. Thus, we may take it that

(R3) The properties referred to in part (b) of (R1) are P-properties.

Representationalism, as summarized in (R1) through (R3), agrees that P-colors are not the only things we have to mention in giving an answer to the basic question of how color enters into seeing. The addition made by representationalism, however, does not introduce any items, besides those that have P-colors, that require occurrences of *color* in any sense. Instead, what representationalism introduces are *representations of P-colored* things; and representations of P-colored things are held neither to be colored nor to require anything to be colored other than the ordinary things that have P-colors.

This last point is crucial. To bring out its force, let us reflect for a moment on Ponce de León's search for the fountain of youth.[3] Ponce de León knew what he was looking for, that is to say, he represented to himself what he was looking for. The existence of this representation does not require that anything whatsoever actually be a fountain of youth. Since the representation is a reality of some sort, it has some properties; but being a fountain and being a cause of eternal youth are not among them. If we wish to be in accord with current understandings of cognition, we will likely say that de León's representation of the fountain of youth actually has *brain-constituent* properties, e.g., being a set of neural activations or being a certain condition of some synapses; but, again, there is nothing fountainish or rejuvenating about these properties. Analogies with words provide further illustrations of the key point. Thus, the color

---

3 The example is from Harman (1990). Discussion of Harman's text in presenting this example, and several other aspects of the ensuing discussion, can be found in Robinson (1997b).

red is represented when the word "red" is written, but the word need not be printed in red ink to do its representational job. Unicorns can be represented by inscribing "unicorn", but the word has neither hooves nor horn.

These lessons about representation are to be applied in the case of visual representations. If, for example, Eloise should represent to herself a green and brown tree, she will have neural events of various kinds. These neural events will not be green and brown: green and brown will be represented properties, not properties of the representation. If Eloise is actually seeing something green and brown and tree-shaped, there will be a tree (or a tree-shaped piece of papier-mâché, or a painting of a tree, etc.) that actually has a certain characteristic shape and actually has the P-colors green and brown. If Eloise has been ingesting forbidden substances and is only hallucinating the green and brown tree, she may have the same representations as in the first case, and thus the same green and brown will be represented; but, according to the representationalist view, nothing whatsoever in the situation need actually *be* green or brown.

THE P/T PROBLEM

One reaction philosophers have had to representationalism is that phenomenal consciousness need not be representational. The feeling one has during orgasm, for example, has been offered as a candidate for a phenomenal content that is nonrepresentational.[4] Peacocke (1983) has argued that we must recognize differences in features of experience that do not correspond to represented differences. For example, when we see two trees, one closer than the other, they may look the same in size (be represented by the experience as the same size), even though the nearer one occupies more of our visual field and is thus experienced differently.

Responses of this kind present hard cases for representationalism, but they do not succeed in establishing that phenomenal consciousness need not be representational. The reason is that "representation", although clear in certain respects, is not clear *enough* to allow a decisive disentanglement of representation from features of experience. There are weak and harmless senses of "represent" in which all features of experiences are representational. Unless such senses of "representation" were clearly identified and clearly disowned by representationalists, there could be

---

4   See Block (1995a). For discussion see Tye (1995b) and Block (1995b).

little point in trying to refute the claim that all features of experience are representational.

More importantly, there is a problem for representationalism even in cases where it is most plausible to say that phenomenal consciousness is representational. Critiques that bypass these cases miss what is arguably the most fundamental difficulty in representationalism. This difficulty is that representation occurs in thought as well as in perceptual experience. Thus, representationality does not explain what is different about perceptual experience and mere thought. In perceptual experience, however, we encounter phenomenal consciousness. So, appeal to the presence of representation does not explain what is different about cases where phenomenal consciousness is present and cases where it is absent.[5] For the sake of mnemonic ease, I will refer to this problem as the "P/T problem" – the problem of giving an account, strictly compatible with representationalism, that will be adequate to describe the difference between perception and thought.

Two concrete examples will make it easier to appreciate fully the P/T problem. Thus, let us imagine that Eve has been reading about some of the excesses that occurred during the Cultural Revolution in China. She recalls that some of the Red Guards proposed changing the system of traffic lights, because they regarded it as unfortunate that the color that symbolized their politics should be used to mean "stop". Now, in recalling this, Eve may pause to visualize a red traffic light or may look out the window at a red traffic light, but it is clear that she *need not* do any such thing in order to understand what those youths were thinking. Let us suppose

---

5   This fundamental difficulty in representationalism has been clearly stated by one of its early proponents, namely, Lycan (1996). Although it is somewhat peculiar to cite a proponent of a view in criticism of it, Lycan's formulation of the difficulty is so incisive that I cannot forbear to quote it.

Some people [i.e., opponents of representationalism] think of mere *representation* as a fairly cheap and shallow affair. . . . I can write "red" in chalk on the blackboard . . . or represent the property redness in any of a thousand other simple ways. . . . On this view [i.e., that of Lycan's opponents] representation in and of itself is utterly bloodless, hardly the sort of thing of which *qualia* are made; it could not be representation alone and per se that gives an afterimage its qualitative character, its subjective color. (Lycan, 1996, p. 185; emphases in the original)

It is natural to ask why Lycan himself is not dissuaded from representationalism by this insightful critique. Part of the answer may lie in his not recognizing the need for an *intrinsic* difference between perceptual and thought representations – a need that, in the remainder of this section, I argue must be satisfied. Another part of the answer – the more interesting and important part, in my view – will be considered later in the chapter under "Adverbialism and Intentional Inexistence".

that she has not paused for any such visualization or perception. Then it will be clear that she has not had red in her phenomenal consciousness. (We can allow that she has had auditory imagery of the word "red" and so has had phenomenal consciousness of *something*; but there is no reason to suppose that she has had any phenomenal consciousness of the color red.) But, in following with understanding what the Red Guards were proposing and why they proposed it, she did represent the color red. Or, at least, she did so if our current understandings of cognition as involving representing are correct. Therefore, to say that Eve represents the color red does not imply that she has red in her phenomenal consciousness; and thus, her representing the color red does not tell us what it is for red to be in her phenomenal consciousness on those occasions when it is in her phenomenal consciousness.

This argument does not imply that it is false to say that, when red is in Eve's phenomenal consciousness, she is representing the color red. The conclusion is only that representationalism is an *inadequate* answer to the basic question of how color comes into visual experience. What representationalism provides, in addition to P-colors, is representation of colors, and since this can be provided in cases that do not contain phenomenal consciousness of red, it cannot be the answer to the question of what Eve's having red in her phenomenal consciousness consists in.

We have seen that Ponce de León can search for the fountain of youth without there being any such thing and without there being anything fountainish about him. Suppose, however, that, addled by Florida's heat and humidity, Ponce de León were to have hallucinated a fountain, which he believed would have rejuvenating powers. Then, certainly, he would have represented a fountain. But he had *already* represented a fountain when he was just searching and not yet hallucinating. Thus, his representing a fountain cannot constitute an adequate differentiating feature of his hallucinating a flashing of watery spray rather than merely searching for such an object.[6]

Before considering some responses that representationalists may make to the P/T problem, let us forestall a possible misunderstanding of it. Representationalists (like anyone else) can identify differences among the

---

6 While imagery *may* accompany thought, it need not do so (as, indeed, we assumed in the Red Guard example in the text). But a thought without imagery is still a representation. Thus, representation alone and per se likewise fails to provide a way to distinguish between thought with imagery and thought without imagery.

causal conditions of perceptions and thoughts, and thus can give descriptions that divide the two cases without departing from their view. But distinguishing perceptions and thoughts in this purely relational way gives no explanation or description of the intrinsic difference between perceptions and thoughts. It says nothing about the character of *what* is being distinguished by the extrinsic descriptions.[7] The P/T problem for representationalism is that it has no resources for describing the difference in the relata that are (merely) picked out by relational distinctions; in thought there is representation and in perception there is − representation. But there is an obvious difference between what happens in perception and mere thought. So, the inability to describe such a difference within the resources of representationalism is a decisive objection to the view.

Representationalists will counter that they can, after all, describe an intrinsic difference in representations that will explain our sense of a clear difference between perception and hallucination, on the one hand, and thought on the other. The next two sections examine two approaches one may take to making good on such a claim.

DIFFERENCES OF CONTENT

In the following discussion, "representational content" (or just "content") will be used as a convenient term standing for *what is represented*. It will be helpful to have a notation that enables us to indicate content, and we shall use square brackets for this purpose. For example, the content of Ponce de León's hallucination, imagined in the preceding section, may be taken to be [a fountain]. (We should not take the content to be [a fountain of youth] because, while one can *believe* that [those who enter a certain fountain will be rejuvenated], one cannot *hallucinate* such a content.) Again, we have been treating the content of the representation one has when seeing a red apple as [a red apple].

But perhaps the contents in these examples are actually more complex than our discussion has assumed. According to the refinement of representationalism now to be considered, we should say that what Eve represents when she sees a red apple is [her seeing a red apple], and what Ponce de León represents when he hallucinates a fountain is [his seeing a

---

7   In Levine's (2001, p. 98) useful terminology, pointing to the normal dependence of *looking F* on use of the eyes enables us to specify a *role* but does not tell us what it is that *plays* that role.

fountain].[8] The advantage of this view is clear. If Eve is merely thinking of a red apple, she has represented [a red apple] but not [her seeing a red apple]. Thus, on this refined view, we can no longer hold that everything represented in seeing (or hallucinating) is already present in the representing involved in merely thinking, and the P/T problem appears to be solved.

It is, however, easy to reinstate the point of the problem. To do this, let us imagine that Eve thinks that [Adam sees a red apple]. When she has this thought, Eve may also pause to conjure up a visual image of what she supposes the apple looks like to Adam, but she *need not* do this in order to be a thinker of the thought that Adam sees a red apple. We are thus entitled to consider the case where she thinks that Adam sees a red apple but does not pause to conjure up a visual image of how things look to Adam. Further, Eve can think that Adam sees a red apple without herself either seeing or hallucinating anything red. In this case, if widely accepted theories of cognition are correct, she is representing [Adam sees a red apple] but not having an episode of phenomenal consciousness that involves the color red.

If Eve can think the foregoing thought about Adam, she can think the same thing about herself; that is, she can think that [she (herself) sees a red apple]. That is, she can represent to herself that she sees a red apple. But we have just seen that thinking of a subject seeing a red apple does not require Eve to have phenomenal consciousness that involves the color red. So, if we think of Eve representing to herself that she is the subject of the same predicate that we have described her as applying to Adam, we will have no

---

8 In Robinson (1997b) I argued that this is the best way to construe the view in Harman (1990). Although there are some questions that could be raised about this interpretation, the view is clearly suggested in the following remarks.

> [W]hat Eloise sees before her is a tree, whether or not it is a hallucination. That is to say, the content of her visual experience is that she is presented with a tree, not with an idea of a tree. (p. 36)

> It is true that her perceptual experience represents her as visually presented with something brown and green. (p. 37)

> Eloise's visual experience does not just present a tree. It presents a tree as viewed from a certain place. (p. 38)

> Now, perhaps, Eloise's visual experience even presents a tree as seen by her, that is, as an object of her visual experience. (p. 38)

The argument in the text follows the argument against Harman's view given in Robinson (1997b).

reason to ascribe to her any phenomenal consciousness that involves the color red. Thus, the fact that Eve has a representation with the content [she (herself) sees a red apple] does not give us anything that carries us beyond mere thinking; it does not give us something that is distinctive of cases in which phenomenal consciousness also occurs. Therefore, merely pointing to the fact that Eve represents that [she (herself) sees a red apple] is an *inadequate* response to the P/T problem.

It would be very natural to respond to the foregoing argument by saying that Eve really cannot think that she is (now) seeing a red apple without having a visual experience of a red apple, i.e., an episode of phenomenal consciousness involving red. But this point only reinforces the criticism of representationalism. According to the present refinement of representationalism, *what it is* to have phenomenal consciousness involving red is nothing other than to have a representation of [oneself seeing a red X] (where X is an apple or some other ordinary thing). To say that if we had this thought we would *also* be having phenomenal consciousness involving red is to make such phenomenal consciousness out to be an *addition* to having a representation of [oneself seeing a red X]; and it is just such an addition that the present version of representationalism officially eschews.

It may be objected that representing oneself seeing a red apple is not merely representing something like Adam's seeing a red apple, only with oneself instead of Adam as the subject. There is, so to speak, more of a difference in moving from Adam's seeing a red apple to oneself seeing a red apple than there is in moving from Adam's seeing a red apple to Bob's seeing a red apple. This point has some plausibility, but it is irrelevant to the P/T problem. The evident difference between perception and thought has to do with the way phenomenal qualities come into the two kinds of situation, and the difference between representing oneself and someone else is not that kind of difference. The difference between representing oneself and someone else would be the same kind of difference in every case, but the P/T difference has many distinct cases, i.e., one for each distinct phenomenal quality.[9]

---

9 One may also consider

   (a) seeing a red apple;
   (b) thinking of having seen a red apple 5 seconds ago (with eyes now shut); and
   (c) thinking of having seen a red apple 10 seconds ago (again, with eyes shut).

   All of these involve representing seeing a red apple, but the difference between (a) and (b) is not just like the difference between (b) and (c).

I conclude that complicating the content of representations in the way we have considered does not provide an answer to the P/T problem. Nor do I know of any other way of enriching representational content that will avoid the essential point, namely, that representational contents also occur in mere thought. Nothing in this argument shows, or is intended to show, that perceptions are not representational; the point is rather that the representationality of perception *underdescribes* or is inadequate to what occurs in perception.

DIFFERENCES OF REPRESENTATIONAL TYPE

The P/T problem may be addressed by offering something distinctive about *how* contents are represented in perceptions rather than *what* is represented. Alternatively phrased, representationalists may try to distinguish perception from thought by appeal to type of representation rather than content.

There are constraints on what kind of property representationalists can use to distinguish types of representations, and it will be helpful to make these explicit.

(a) Things can be physically red, i.e., they may have the P-properties defined in Chapter 2. But there is nothing that is red in any other sense, according to representationalism.[10]

(b) Everything to which representationalism appeals must have a naturalistic account (or at least a good prospect of such an account).

(c) There must be some set of properties that meet the other constraints that are present in perception but not thought.

(d) The P/T difference must be intrinsically described, not merely extrinsically or relationally indicated.

To see how these constraints can impose a difficult problem, recall that a key idea of contemporary naturalistic accounts of representation is that perceptual representations should, in general, occur when, and only when, the represented item is present to the senses. Perceptual representations, we may say, should *track* the properties they represent.[11] In virtue of constraint

---

10 Strictly, we have defined only P-colors. I am supposing here that readers can extend the method by which we arrived at P-colors to define physical properties that correspond to any of our phenomenal qualities.

11 For use of "tracking" in this context, and a clear and straightforward exposition of tracking and representation, see Tye (1995a). Tracking and related metaphors are widely used in representationalist accounts.

(a), the only properties available for tracking in representationalist accounts are P-properties – reflectance profiles, molecular surface structures, and the like. Perception does indeed track such properties. But nothing appears *as* having these properties. Reflectance profiles and molecular structures are highly complex. When we see an apple and it looks red, we are tracking a reflectance profile, but we are not representing anything to ourselves *as* anything so complex as that. To generalize, P-red is not what an apple is being represented *as* in ordinary perception. But, in ordinary perception, it is not the case that the apple is represented *as* no color at all. It is not true that there is no way it looks; indeed, an apple's looking red seems to be essential to the perceptual character of seeing it.[12] The problem for representationalism is that looking red cannot be adequately described as tracking P-red, but there is no other redness that is recognized anywhere in a representationalist account.[13]

These considerations may suggest that representationalists should abandon the notion that perceptual representation of red is tracking P-red. Since there is no other redness in representationalist accounts, this suggestion amounts to giving up a tracking account altogether. But we do not have a theory of representing that does not involve tracking, yet is clearly naturalistic; so now the problem is that constraint (b) does not look satisfiable. This point is crucial, for in the absence of a naturalistic account of representation, representationalists cannot be sure that their view is distinct from realism about experiences. That is because experiential realism does not exclude the possibility that experiences are representations, if "representation" is not confined to tracking of P-properties. Absent a certifiably naturalistic account of "representation" that is not so confined, "experiences are representational" may amount merely to a *further* claim about items that involve phenomenal qualities in addition to P-properties. But if this is all that representationalism comes to, then it makes a *false* claim when it affirms that the only properties that are needed in its account are the P-properties of ordinary things and whatever neural

---

12 Followers of Dennett (1991) will take exception to this claim. I will be responding to this denial in Chapter 9. For the moment, we should understand that representationalists do not claim to be eliminativists; they are trying to account for, rather than deny, phenomenal experience.

13 Elements of this paragraph are reminiscent of Raffman (1995), who discusses limits of memory, experiential discriminability, and differences of modes of presentation to excellent effect. Raffman exhibits the importance of including modes of presentation in our theory of experience, and she shows how several "demonstrative variants" of materialism fail by failing to provide any differences in actual modes of presentation that correspond to clear and admitted differences in our experiences.

properties are required for tracking of P-properties by those who represent them.[14]

In my view, representationalism is not able to satisfy all the constraints I have listed. Since the point is crucial, however, I shall examine some ideas that may appear to offer representationalism a more positive outcome.

Noninferential Classification

Perceived items can often be classified without inference. I look at my desk and see a blue mouse pad. One may have questions about the classification as a mouse pad but, at any rate, the blue character is not inferred. I just look and see that the thing I am looking at is blue. Now, perhaps we can promote this fact into a satisfactory way of distinguishing between perception and thought. Perhaps perceptual representations are those that provide bases for classifying something as being of a certain kind without

---

14 To illustrate the choice representationalists must make, consider the following passage from one well-known representationalist.

> To have a pain is to feel a pain, and to feel a pain is to experience pain. Thus, if I have a pain, I undergo a token experience of a certain sort. This token experience is the particular pain I have. Now, in optimal conditions, sensory experiences of the pain sort track certain sorts of disturbances in the body, paradigmatically, bodily damage. So pains represent such disturbances. (Tye, 1995a, pp. 112–113)

The represented properties are properties of bodily damage – broken vessels, separated flesh, severed neurons. But these words do not describe how pain feels, i.e., they do not describe how the bodily damage is represented or what it is represented *as*. Experiential realists will agree with the second sentence of this passage. They will read "experience of a certain sort" as "experience of a certain kind, namely, *painful*", where the property of being painful does not have the complexity of the fibrous separations that constitute bodily damage. Now, either (a) we should read Tye as agreeing that there are experiences of the painful kind, where the property painful is not a P-property (e.g., the property of having fibrous separations). In this case, (i) the next to last sentence of the quoted passage is a further comment on a feature of painful experiences (namely, that besides being of the painful kind, they represent). This is a claim to which experiential realists of all kinds can agree. And (ii) experiences of the painful kind will be *additions* to what is officially recognized in representationalism, for they will be actual bearers of properties that are not identical with any P-properties. Alternatively, (b) we should read Tye's "experience of a certain sort" as meaning no more than "experience that represents bodily damage". But in this case, there will be nothing in the view that corresponds to the way bodily damage *feels*. For it does not feel like a P-property (a multitude of fibrous separations, for example), and there is no other property that is correlated with bodily damage that representationalism, on reading (b), admits.

inference, while representations in mere thought can give rise only to classifications that are based on inference.[15]

A problem for this view, however, is that we can sometimes classify noninferentially without having perceptual experience of the relevant property. For example, chicken sexers have no way of describing what tips them off to their judgment; they simply make the judgment that this chick is male or that it is female.[16] Ordinary perceptual cases are not like that. Similarly, if we accept a certain interpretation of blindsight cases, we find that people can make noninferential judgments (e.g., that an X rather than an O is present), even though they cannot see the figures about which they judge. Thus, merely supporting noninferential classification cannot plausibly be offered as an adequate account of what is distinctive about ordinary perception. It does not matter here if one disputes the relevant interpretation of blindsight cases, i.e., an interpretation that accepts at face value the subjects' claims that they cannot see the shapes that they classify with above-chance percentages. For there is nothing more available in the noninferential classification account than is available in that interpretation of blindsight cases. Thus, if one agrees with the conclusion drawn from that interpretation of blindsight cases, one must draw the same conclusion regarding the noninferential classification account. In short, supporting noninferential classification is at best a usual sign or relational identifier of perception; it does not provide the distinctive intrinsic difference that separates perception from thought.[17]

A third kind of case leads to the same conclusion. I suppose that every teacher of philosophy, and many others, can recall cases in which one

15 A view of this kind occurs in Loar (1990). Loar's term for concepts under which classifications can be made noninferentially is "recognitional concepts".

16 Chicken sexers do, of course, perceive the chicks, their yellowness, and their shape, and these perceptions may cause their judgments. Perhaps we even should say, as Brad Thompson has suggested, that their various judgments depend on variations in what they perceive. The point remains, however, that the recognition of the sex is a judgment provided by thought, which does not stand to perception in the way that is characteristic of judgments about perceptual properties, even though it is noninferential. If it should turn out that the ability to sex chicks depends on olfaction, the conclusion remains the same, for again, we will have noninferential classification that is present when what is distinctive of ordinary perception is not.

17 Loar (1990, p. 98) explicitly recognizes the point we have just made. After discussing blindsight cases, he allows that "not just any ability to identify an inner state in the having of it suffices for having a phenomenal concept". One might naturally expect to be provided with a feature that differentiates those noninferentially applicable concepts that are phenomenal concepts from those that are not. This expectation, however, is not fulfilled in Loar's account; what occurs instead is an excuse for not being able to satisfy it.

realizes that a student has made a logical mistake – e.g., confusion of 'if... then...' with 'if and only if' or commission of a fallacy such as an ad hominem. Now, although one can describe these mistakes, and explain why they are mistakes, the recognition that one has just been committed need not be arrived at by inference and, in the case of those with some experience in discussion, generally is not arrived at in this way. One just sees that the mistake has been made, and then one tries to get the student to see it too. But, of course, this noninferential classification is not a visual seeing; it is a "seeing" only in the metaphorical sense of coming to know without inferring. There is nothing visually phenomenal about a logical mistake. One does, of course, hear the words that constitute the mistake, and those sounds have auditory properties. But the property of being logically confused or fallacious is not a sensory quality of any sort. Thus, once again, supporting noninferential classifiability under a certain concept is at best a frequent concomitant of perception, and not an adequate account of what *makes* the difference between perception and thought.

Nonconceptual Content

When we think about things that we are not now perceiving, we use concepts, i.e., we use abilities to represent various properties of absent things. If we have a normal stock of concepts, we have an ability to represent a large number of properties of things, and we can make many distinctions, some of them quite refined. Normally sighted people know the difference between brick red and cardinal red, and would easily classify a single sample of one of these correctly if it were seen just by itself.

There are, however, distinctions that are palpable when two items are presented together but for which we do not have distinct concepts. For example, two tomatoes that are just a few days apart in the course of ripening might have colors that we can easily see to be different when they are side by side even though we do not have any way of representing that difference when they are absent, and even though we could not tell (by its color) which of them was re-presented when shown by itself. We may describe such cases by saying that perceptual content outstrips our conceptual abilities or that in perception we have nonconceptual content.

Representationalists may appeal to these facts to solve the P/T problem.[18] The representations in thought must be conceptual, on this

18 Tye (1995a) gives a clear expression of this view.

proposal, but the representations in perception are nonconceptual. This latter claim is, of course, not the claim that we cannot bring what we perceive under any concepts at all. It is the claim that for any perceptual representation, there could be another that would be pairwise distinguishable but not conceptually distinguishable, i.e., not representable as distinct in the absence of simultaneous presentation to the senses.

Invoking nonconceptual content is appealing because it does provide a distinguishing mark of perception: we can indeed make perceptual discriminations that are finer than any we can make with concepts that we can remember, and that we can apply correctly upon single presentations.[19] However, this way of distinguishing perceptual representations from thought representations is inadequate, because it provides only an extrinsic, or relational, identification. It distinguishes representations by reference to what subjects who have them can or cannot do, but it does not say what the difference is in the representations themselves. It does not say anything about the intrinsic difference between representations in perception and representations in thought; for example, it says nothing about the difference between something looking red and something being thought of as red.

It is important to be clear that it is not being denied that perceptual representation is nonconceptual. Indeed, this claim is compatible with QER, and, I believe, true. We can, for example, have two parts of an afterimage that we plainly know to be of different shades of red, but for which we have no distinguishing concept. (When they have faded, we know that they were both shades of red rather than blue, but not that the left part was red17 while the right part was red18.) Or, at least, remarks of this kind are both natural and consistent when made by a qualitative event realist. Representationalists, however, can say no such thing; for them, nothing is a shade of red except a physical surface that is P-red. So, when representationalists say that perception involves nonconceptual contents, all that they are entitled to mean is that, for example, we can reliably discriminate between pairs of things without being able to reidentify an item when presented by itself. And this is inadequate, because although it makes a distinction between perception and thought in the right place, it says precisely nothing about what the difference between the two consists in.[20]

---

19 Again, see Raffman (1995) for discussion.
20 Dretske (1995) makes a claim that directly conflicts with our conclusion. He imagines "Mary" (a certain ordinary scientist – not the extraordinary Mary of Jackson's [1982] famous knowledge argument) running discrimination tests on dogfish. According to Dretske,

Adverbialism, strictly understood, is the view that qualitative terms in descriptions of experiences really occur only as adverbs. For example, the "red" in "there is a red spot in my visual field" is to be understood as an adverb – an understanding that might be expressed as "I am experiencing redly (or, red-spot-ly)". Plainly, such odd phrases, and the idea that an apparent adjective is to be taken adverbially, need to be explained. The traditional explanation (which I shall understand to be included in my use of "adverbialism") has been that experiencing redly is having an experience of the kind that one has in normal conditions when viewing red things. This way of speaking leaves it open just what it is that one has when one views red things in normal conditions. It leaves it open that different kinds of experiences are different purely physical kinds, e.g., brain state kinds. It avoids committing one to the existence of anything that actually exemplifies qualities that have anything to do with color, except, of course, the P-red properties of ordinary red things. Thus, an adverbialist gets to talk about differences among kinds of experiences while denying that there is a property that is in any way associated with color that presents any problem for an account in purely physical terms.

Adverbialism without further embellishment is, however, nothing more than euphemism. It sorts experiences extrinsically (i.e., by their causal relations), but it does not provide any argument that the experiences thus sorted do not resemble and differ intrinsically. It cannot get along without some phrase that is equivalent to "experience of the kind that...", where the ellipses are filled in by an extrinsic description. Use of such phrases gives us no more way of avoiding intrinsically qualitied experiences than use of "that substance caused to be ejected by stomach upset" enables us to avoid having to deal with disgusting substances in

---

Mary learns "which deformations of the electric field the dogfish is sensitive to and which it is "blind" to. Mary is thereby learning exactly what it is like (for dogfish) to sense electric fields" (Dretske, 1995, p. 87). In another example, knowing what 18°C is is held to be sufficient for knowing how that temperature feels to an organism that systemically discriminates bodies of that temperature from other, slightly warmer or cooler bodies. (See Dretske, 1995, pp. 82–83.)

It would seem to follow from these claims that if Mary knows all about reflectance profiles (or whatever P-red property one prefers), she must be in the same position with respect to human color experience as she is with respect to dogfish electric field experience – i.e., she must know "exactly what it is like" for people to sense color fields. But this conclusion is a reductio of the position, because Mary could be an actual, ordinary, congenitally blind person who knows what many blind people in fact know about the physics of light and the visual system in sighted people.

the sickroom.[21] Upon being told about experiences of the kind that are caused by red things, experiential realists are entitled to ask "And what kind of experiences are those?" Adverbialists can answer only that experiences of red things and experiences of blue things are distinguished by the fact that the former are caused by red things and the latter by blue things. This answer is not *an account* of experiential differences, e.g., the difference between a red afterimage and a blue one; it is a *failure* to provide such an account.

It may be, however, that adverbialism can be improved upon by admitting that extrinsically differentiated experiences do have intrinsic differences but describing those instrinsic differences as differences in what is represented. Such a view provides something additional to the causes of the different experiences; but it puts phenomenal qualities exclusively within the context of what is represented. Now, as we noted early in this chapter, representation that something is F does not require anything at all to actually *be F*. So, a representationalist adverbialist (as we may call the proponent of the view of this section) gets the best of both worlds – an intrinsic difference among experiences without having to recognize that anything actually *is red*, except, of course, for ordinary things that have

---

21 The seductiveness of adverbialism can be seen in a passage in a brief commentary that Stalnaker (1996) makes on a paper of Lycan's. Stalnaker considers Peacocke's example of seeing two trees that are equal in size but lie at different distances from the viewer. The experience represents the trees as equal in size but, one also wants to say, the nearer one occupies more of the visual field than the more distant one. Is there a way of making this latter point that will not commit one to properties of an experience itself, i.e., properties that are not bound within a representational content? Stalnaker expresses some sympathy for saying that "my visual experience is the way it would be if I were seeing an image (a physical image) that contains two tree images, one bigger than the other. This . . . characterization puts the description of one shape being bigger than another into a counterfactual condition, rather than a that-clause" (Stalnaker, 1996, p. 107). Stalnaker goes on to say of this characterization that it "explains how the size comparison can be used to describe the intrinsic character of an experience without hypothesizing any actual entities – components of the experience – that are compared with respect to size" (Stalnaker, 1996, p. 107).

But the fact that the *description* is in a counterfactual is of little consequence. Stalnaker still has the phrase "the way it [my visual experience] would be", which implies that there is some way that the visual experience would be if a counterfactual were true, and that that is the way it *is* now.

Suppose my friend Jones sits on an antique chair, which creaks under his weight. I describe this situation by saying that the chair sounds the way a certain other, ordinary wooden chair would sound if a Sumo wrestler were to sit on it. This characterization puts the description of the sound into a counterfactual condition. But for all that, we have not explained how we can describe the intrinsic character of the sound that Jones's chair makes without hypothesizing any actual entities that make sounds.

the P-red properties defined in Chapter 2. Or, as one leading proponent of the view puts it:

It is, after all, no surprise to be told that mental states have intentional objects that may not exist. So why should we not suppose that after-images and other sense-data are intentional objects that do not exist? If they do not exist, then – *voila* – they do not exist; there are in reality no such things. And that is why we can consistently admit that phenomenal-color properties qualify individuals without granting that there exist individuals that are the bearers of phenomenal-color properties. (Lycan, 1987, p. 88)

Ingenious though this proposal is, I shall now argue that it will not do. The first step is to remind ourselves that nothing in ordinary perception represents anything to us *as* a reflectance profile or a surface molecular structure – in general, nothing represents anything to us *as* P-red. But things in ordinary perception are not represented as nothing at all. There is a difference between looking red and looking blue, and there is a difference between a red afterimage and a blue one, and these differences are not representations of differences of P-colors as differences of P-colors (although they are *caused by* differences of P-colors). But these differences are represented *as* differences of *some* qualities, and these qualities have *something* to do with color. The differences are naturally described only in color terms and ordinary people unhesitatingly talk about afterimages in terms of their colors. Lycan recognizes the need to talk about these qualities with his term "phenomenal-color properties". Thus, we may take it as the conclusion of the first step of our argument that representationalist adverbialism must recognize properties that are in some sense color properties, but that are additional to the P-color properties we have identified.

The second step of our argument is to notice that representation of these additional phenomenal-color properties is highly problematic. The reason is that we do not know what, if anything, *has* these properties. We can, nonetheless, see that we are in a dilemma. (a) If representation is tracking, then if these properties are represented, they are tracked. But they cannot be tracked if nothing ever has them. So, if representation is tracking, then some things do have phenomenal-color properties, and they are mere intentional inexistents only some of the time (e.g., in afterimages). In that case, either (a1) some items other than ordinary things frequently have phenomenal-color properties or else (a2) ordinary things such as apples have not only P-colors, but phenomenal-color properties too. But it is consequences like these that representationalist adverbialism is designed to avoid. The view (a1) is not distinguishable from QER and other forms of experiential realism. The view (a2) implies that there are two trackings – one of P-color properties and one of phenomenal-color properties. But it is not clear how representationalist adverbialism can make room for the tracking of phenomenal-color properties.

In light of these difficulties, it seems likely that representationalist adverbialists will prefer the other horn of the dilemma, namely, (b) There is representation that is not tracking. But two further difficulties now present themselves. (1) Because we have no account of this kind of representation, it cannot be clear that the required kind of representation can be explicated in a naturalistic way. (2) For the same reason, it is not clear that representationalist adverbialism is more than verbally distinct from experiential realism. Perhaps experiences are representational in an appropriate sense. Perhaps an experience's being red just is the way that phenomenal-red is represented. Of course, representationalist adverbialists will not want to say this; but absent any account of representation that is not tracking, they lack any principled ground for avoiding such a view.

I suspect that the problematic character of representation is not appreciated because it is evident to all that we can represent things in thought that do not exist anywhere. Moreover, in familiar cases, it does not seem that we will have to propose anything that conflicts with naturalism in order to account for such representation. Unicorns will serve as an example: there are none anywhere, but we know perfectly well what they are, and we represent them in stories and in pictures. It would indeed be ludicrous to suggest that in order for us to represent unicorns, there must be something, somewhere, that actually is a unicorn.

At the same time, the only ideas we have for a naturalistic account of representation do require some version of tracking, that is, some way of working in the idea that in normal circumstances, a perceptual representation should occur when, and only when, the thing represented is present to the senses. The reconciliation of this fact with the point of the preceding paragraph lies in the fact that many nonexisting things can be constructed from (or defined by reference to) existing and trackable parts. There are horses, foreheads, horns, and spatial relations, and normal people can track them. Once possessed of the corresponding concepts, they can compound them into the concept of a unicorn, evidently without requiring that any instance of the compound concept actually exist.

This kind of account, however, will not work for phenomenal qualities. The problem is that, while some phenomenal qualities are compounds, what they are compounds of is phenomenal qualities. Colors, for example, do not have any obvious parts or elements other than hue, saturation, and brightness. Tastes may be partly salty and partly bitter, but salty and bitter are themselves taste qualities. Chords are complexes; but what they are complexes of is sounds. And so on. We are not going to make any progress on the issues under discussion by proposing that colors need not exist because their concepts can be compounded out of concepts of hues and saturations, for that will just force the question of how hues are represented, and hues are themselves phenomenal qualities.

CONCLUSION

I have not presented a demonstrative proof that no form of representationalism can succeed. Such an argument is not possible, because there is not sufficient agreement on exactly what may count as representation. I have, however, raised severe difficulties for existing forms of the view. We do not now understand how the view can give an adequate account of the obvious difference between perception and thought. We are not in a position to justify rejecting experiential realism on the ground that we have an alternative view that we understand and that provides a better theory of what happens when we perceive.

The difficulties surveyed in this chapter will probably not be sufficient by themselves to undercut the faith in representationalism so long as it is thought that there are positive reasons for thinking that some form of the view *must* work. In the following chapter, I shall turn to such an argument and show that it fails to support its intended conclusion.

5

Transparency

In this chapter I examine the *transparency argument* for representationalism. Its central idea is this.

(T1) When we attempt to focus on (alleged) qualities of our experiences, we find that we cannot do so. What we find instead is only properties of the things that are represented in our experiences. The experiences themselves are transparent; we look right through them, so to speak, to the qualities of the things represented in them.[1]

If we accept this idea at face value, then

(T2) Experiences must be either (a) things we are not directly aware of at all or (b) things we are directly aware of without being aware of any of their qualities.

(T3) Awareness of experiences without awareness of any of their qualities is both peculiar in itself and useless in accounting for phenomenal consciousness. Thus, we ought to reject alternative (b).

(T4) Alternative (a) is acceptable. Experiences can be regarded as brain events that represent things as being colored, flavored, and so on. In having them we are aware of the qualities of things, not of experiences. We are not directly aware of experiences; rather, we infer them as events that represent to us the qualities of things.

Therefore,

(T5) Experiences are transparent representers of qualities of things.

Against this argument, qualitative event realists will say that the properties that ordinary things actually have are P-properties, and nothing is

---

1   See, e.g., Harman (1990) and Tye (1995a) for clear expressions of this widely held argument.

73

represented to us in ordinary experience as having those. For example, when an apple looks red to us, it does not look to have a complex molecular surface structure or a large set of reflectance percentages at various wavelengths. Tracking accounts can give plausible, naturalistic explanations of how such properties can be represented in our brains, but these explanations do not explain what looking red is. The qualities that *are* the ways ordinary things look to us are difficult to fit into a naturalistic account. It is not clear what items can be properly said to have them once experiences are rejected as the appropriate candidates; and if they are held to be always represented, but never actually had by anything, then it is no longer clear that representation can be given a naturalistic account.

Nothing in this brief review implies that QER rejects the phenomenological fact that is encapsulated in (T1) and, indeed, the disagreement between QER and representationalism is emphatically not about any phenomenological fact. Qualitative event realists hold only that the mutually recognized phenomenological fact is misconstrued (misdescribed, mistheorized) by representationalists. The alternative description advanced by QER is that much of our experience – visual experience in particular – is three-dimensional. The idea that we "look through" our experiences to qualities of things is plausible only because our visual experience has depth – the redness of our experiences is redness out there, farther away than some other colors, nearer than still others. When we attempt to focus on the qualities of our experience, we do so with ease; those qualities are the phenomenal qualities – colors, pitches, timbres, odors, flavors, various kinds of pain, itchiness, nausea, and so on – and many of these are located in various places. Experiences are not inferred; they are the qualitied events that collectively constitute our phenomenal consciousness.

We shall soon see some reasons why visual experience is not commonly thought of in the way just described, but let us first dwell for a moment on how natural it is to take experience to be literally three-dimensional. It has often been pointed out that tables look rectangular from many angles, even those from which they present two-dimensional projections that are trapezoids or parallelograms. Likewise, plates viewed from most angles look round, not elliptical. They are not inferred to be round; the roundness is right there in the experience. But if experience were really only two-dimensional, it would be difficult to account for the difference in the experiences of the same plate from different angles in any way other than to refer to different degrees of ellipticality. As it is, we see round plates at different angles of tilt. But difference of angle of tilt *requires* a third dimension. So, to the extent that roundness at different angles of tilt is experienced rather than inferred, three-dimensionality is experienced rather than inferred.

We can find support for the same point in the fact that learning to draw is difficult. Drawing requires the creation of a two-dimensional projection of what we see. If experience were two-dimensional, we ought to be able simply to reproduce our experience on paper. But we cannot easily do this. Just trying to trace our visual experience makes us want to put our hand *into* the paper; it takes effort and practice to overcome our natural reactions and learn to make a two-dimensional projection.

Stereoscopes and IMAX movies give us illusory experiences with exaggerated depth. Despite their atypical character, these experiences are useful in focusing our attention on the point that depth is in the experience itself. It is not an afterthought and it is not an accompanying thought. Again, readers may try looking out a window with one eye closed. It is fair to say that different objects will seem to be at different distances. However, after a scene has been appreciated for a while, one may open the other eye. Something different will then take place, and the difference can be described naturally and without special terminology as an addition of a fuller sense of depth.

We may experience two trees as being of the same size − they *look* like they're the same size − even though one is considerably farther away than the other. If experience were flat, the visual impressions of the trees would have to be of different sizes, and their sameness of size would have to be a conclusion that overrules the difference in impression. But, while, of course, there are brain processes that generate experiences from our retinal inputs, there is no inference about the trees. They come to us in experience *as* laid out in space, i.e., at different places not only as regards left and right, but also as regards as near and far.

Similar points are equally obvious for bodily sensations. Pains, itches, coldness, and so on are located in various parts of the body. They are not inferred to be in those places; being in those places is as much a part of the character of the experience as is the painful quality or the coldness. Our experience of our body is not like a set of qualities with coordinates attached; it is a field of locations with various qualities at various places. Again, auditory experiences occur in a space in which various sounds are at various locations.

Although there are many descriptions in philosophical literature that implicitly recognize the three-dimensional character of visual and bodily experiences, explicit description of such experiences as three-dimensional will be likely to evoke substantial resistance.[2] In Chapter 2, I noted one reason for this resistance, namely, Descartes' identification of three-dimensionality with materiality. In the next section, I shall examine some of the other sources of this resistance.

REASONS AGAINST THREE-DIMENSIONALITY
OF EXPERIENCES

Representational Because *Locational?*

There is sometimes a temptation to conclude that experiences are representations *because* they have a locational aspect.[3] Or it may be that representationality is not clearly distinguished from having three-dimensionality, and so the latter is automatically taken as indicating the former. In either case, the response that is needed is the same. In the previous section, representationality and locational aspect have been clearly distinguished, and it should now be evident how a qualitative event realist can insist on the three-dimensionality of some of our experiences while rejecting the representationalist account of this fact. In light of these explanations, it would be question-begging to simply move from the phenomenal fact of "out-thereness" to a representationalist conclusion.

It must be borne in mind that QER does not deny that experiences represent; it is only the idea that they are representations *rather than* events

---

2 Just to take one example of recognition of three-dimensionality, from a source that is otherwise quite unsympathetic to QER, consider the following from Clark (2000, p. 170). "[T]hese apparent locations are just as much features of the appearances presented by bodily sensations as are the qualities that appear to occupy them. . . . [D]ifferences that are purely spatial tend to sink out of view when one surveys the qualities of sensation. But discrimination among the locations of itches and tingles is just as much a characteristic of the modality as is the qualitative variation."

3 Although it is entwined with a number of other points, this move from location to representation is evident in Tye's (1995a, pp. 30–31) discussion of transparency. Surprisingly, we can also see the temptation at work in a critic of representationalism, namely, Block (1995a, p. 230). In the following passage, "P-consciousness" abbreviates "phenomenal consciousness".

   A feature of P-consciousness that is often missed is that differences in intentional content often make a P-conscious difference. What it is like to hear a sound as coming from the left differs from what it is like to hear a sound as coming from the right. P-consciousness is often representational.

   It is possible that the last sentence of this passage is intended simply to be an additional item on a list of features of P-consciousness. But I read it as a conclusion drawn from the second sentence; and on this reading, Block is concluding representationality from the fact that sounds have locational properties.

with intrinsic qualities in their own right to which it objects. QER can thus turn the tables on representationalism and say that visual experiences are able to represent things in the way that they do *because* they are intrinsically three-dimensional. Experience is a three-dimensional field, and that is why colors appear on the objects, i.e., *where* the objects are taken to be, even though science tells us that the physical surfaces of objects have a molecular complexity that appears nowhere in experience.[4]

In oral presentations, representationalists often accompany explanations of the transparency argument with a revealing gesture. At the point where they say "examine your experiences", they will lift their hands and point at their heads.[5] Then, when they come to the point that all you experience is the qualities of objects, they will extend their arms toward the room. But there is not the faintest suggestion in QER, or in any experiential realism of which I am aware, that phenomenal qualities are experienced as being in the head. It is to be hoped that the gesturing does not really represent what representationalists are actually thinking. To the extent that it may do so, it is woefully misdirected.

Fear of Sense Data

Russell (1912) accepted a key point of Moore's (1903/1922) argument for separating awarenesses from their objects, but he also introduced a revision. Namely, he regarded the objects of (direct) awareness as individuals – individuals that exemplified the qualities, e.g., green and blue, that Moore had regarded as the objects of awareness. These qualitied individuals are Russell's *sense data*. Russell's conception of a sensory awareness, or sensory experience, may be diagrammed as follows.

(1)   aw — A — sd + F(sd)

---

4   Compare Clark (2000): "The 'aboutness' of sensation reduces to its spatial character" (p. 165). "The sensation of having a pain in your foot is about your foot because that is where the pain appears to be. The intentional character of the experience is nothing more or less than its spatial character" (p. 117). Clark is no friend of QER; his agreement in the direction of these reductions thus seems especially significant.

5   Compare Tye's discussion of a case that begins with attention to a blue-painted square.

> Intuitively, you are directly aware of blueness and squareness as out there in the world away from you, as features of an external surface. Now shift your gaze inward and try to become aware of your experience itself, inside you, apart from its objects. (Tye, 1995a, p. 30)

> It is no wonder that Tye does not succeed in this effort. But this "inward" and "inside" correspond to nothing that is proposed in QER.

The first part of this diagram depicts an awareness relation holding between an awareness and a sense datum, and the second depicts the fact that the sense datum exemplifies F. This conception of sense data became widely shared in the early decades of the twentieth century, and I shall refer to the view as "Classical sense datum theory".

Classical visual sense data were regarded as two-dimensional items. Rectangular tables were often supposed to cause trapezoidal or rhomboidal sense data when viewed from locations other than a point above their centers. Because these shapes were both ephemeral, and not shapes of the physical table, sense data could not be regarded as physically identical with any part of a table. Nor were they held to be any other kind of physical thing. They were, however, not regarded as mental on the ground that they were distinct from awarenesses.

Such entities now seem peculiar excesses to most philosophers. They are ontologically suspect and, more importantly, the view that embraces them falsifies our experience. We do not, in evident fact, see the world as a series of flat, colored shapes and then infer three-dimensional objects as the best explanation of the series of sense data. Thus, any view that implies that experience consists of (Classical) sense data is certainly to be rejected. If experiential realism is thought of as proposing that we are directly aware only of sense data, it will seem that there is every reason to reject it.

Representationalists sometimes say they are rejecting sense data. Because the term "sense data" has not always been confined to its Classical meaning, it is not quite evident just what these rejections amount to. It is, however, a reasonable suspicion that representationalism is sometimes thought to be supported by the fact that it avoids (Classical) sense data. The response of QER to such a line of support should be evident: QER equally rejects (Classical) sense data, and therefore that rejection offers no support for representationalism *as distinguished from* QER.

This point generalizes to any description of experience that proposes what might be called "intermediaries". Seeing the Grand Canyon is not like looking at a series of pictures of the Grand Canyon. If representationalists think of experiential realism as proposing intermediaries, they have excellent motivation for rejecting that view. But QER has no truck with intermediaries. It says that when we see the Grand Canyon, we have three-dimensional experiences in which various colors are at various distances. It holds that these experiences are realities that intrinsically differ from other experiences in such properties as color, shape, and distance.

Having such experiences is just what the Grand Canyon looking like it does consists in. This view does not falsify our experience.

As noted, the present limits of the term "sense data" are not clear. It is therefore possible that some will give the term a sense in which it would apply to experiences as these are understood in QER. Because of possible confusion with Classical sense data, however, it seems best to avoid the term altogether, and I shall do so from this point on.

The Measurement Problem

Depth in experience can hardly be taken seriously if one already balks at the idea of literal spread-outness (or homogeneity) of red experiences or pains. I have argued for the latter idea, holding that colors are respects in which experiences themselves differ, that colors can occur only as color expanses, and that one cannot successfully pack colors off into merely represented properties. But if there is a direct objection to literal spread-outness of colored experiences, then there may appear to be a successful *modus tollens* against QER; and then it may seem that representationalism must somehow be able to work, despite the difficulties we have seen.

Such a direct objection can be given by arguing that if experience is literally spatial, then it must make sense to measure it, i.e., it must make sense to attribute some definite quantity to the extent of redness of a red experience. For example, if there are two bright lights of different sizes, then one's afterimage will have two distinctive regions of different sizes. If we go this far, it seems we should be required to say *how large* these regions are. But on the face of it, it seems ludicrous to say that some region in an afterimage is 2 inches across, or 3 feet, or that it has any definite quantity.[6] It thus seems that QER must either reject the demand for such a measure or explain how it is to be provided, despite the initial implausibility of the idea.

To begin the reply to this objection, let us note that we *can* give a measure of sorts, namely, a measure of a visual angle subtended by an afterimage. If we had a measure of depth, we could convert visual angle into actual lateral measure; but, of course, this observation merely throws the measurement problem onto the problem of measuring depth.

The same point can be made in another way. Suppose we want to measure the extent of the part of our visual experience that is caused by

---

6 Thus O'Shaughnessy (1980, p. 180): "While visual sensations are two-dimensionally arrayed, the given distances therein have no linear measure in millimetres or miles."

a bookcase. Suppose we try to do this by laying a yardstick on the floor immediately in front of the bookcase. Evidently, this will not do. The part of the visual experience caused by the yardstick will stand in the same relation to the edges of the part of the visual experience caused by the bookcase whether these items are 8 feet away or 20 feet away. But the extent of the color of the bookcase would be less in the latter case. "One yard" is not an acceptable answer to our measurement question, even if the ends of the yardstick coincide with the sides of the bookcase. Of course, if we could designate a particular distance as a standard, we could lay a yardstick at that distance and at right angles to the line of vision. This would provide us with a way of measuring sizes relative to the yardstick and its parts; and if we can compare everything to the yardstick (at standard distance), we can get a size measure in terms of (proper or improper) fractions of the yardstick for all regions of our visual experience. But, just as in the case of conversion of visual angle, this idea will not work without a measure of depth.

There is, however, a natural and workable way of assigning measure to depth. To do this, lay another yardstick – or, rather, several yardsticks – end to end from one's feet to an object, e.g., the bookcase of the preceding paragraph. The visual experience will include parts that are caused by the yardsticks and by the bookcase. If we allow a little stretch of time in which we look at our feet and then along the yardsticks to the bookcase, we can satisfy ourselves that the bookcase is 8 feet away. The look of the lateral yardstick (i.e., the one across the base of the bookcase) is the look of 1 yard at 8 feet. Suppose a fat book on the bottom shelf lines up with graduations on the yardstick that are 3 inches apart. The part of our experience caused by that book has a definite measure, namely, 3 inches at 8 feet. Suppose the bookcase is next to a doorway, through which we can see another bookcase that is 20 feet away. Let us imagine laying another yardstick across the doorway, also at 8 feet away. That part of our experience that is caused by the second bookcase will align with certain graduations on the second yardstick, and that will give the measure of that portion of our visual experience – for example, as it might be, 18 inches at 8 feet.

Now, x inches at y feet is not a true lateral measure. Since this is the best we can do, we should agree that there is no plain number of inches or feet in which lateral extent of regions of visual experience can be measured. But the reason for this lack of lateral measure is that there is no nonarbitrary distance that we should take as the standard distance for such measures. Given a depth (a number for the y in "y feet"), a definite lateral measure is determined; but there is no feature in experience that offers a reason to prefer one depth (one substitution for y) rather than another.

If this account is correct, the lack of lateral measure of regions of visual experience is due to the arbitrariness of any choice of a standard for depth assignment. But this arbitrariness is not the kind of reason that should lead us to deny genuine spatiality to experience. Choice of inches rather than centimeters is arbitrary, and no length can be assigned without a convention about some such units; but this arbitrariness does not show that the things we measure are not spatial. Similarly, if we appoint a particular depth as a standard, we can get a measure, in feet, inches, and so on, of regions of visual experience. The arbitrariness of choice of depth does not show that there is no genuine spatiality. The disanalogy between the cases I have just mentioned is only that we *have not* made a convention about a depth for measuring experiential regions – presumably because we have no practical use for the spatial measure that such a convention would afford us.[7]

Conceptual Involvement

It is plausible that our judgments of distance are sometimes influenced by our knowledge of what we are seeing.[8] But it seems that sensory experience should not depend on conceptualization. It may thus be concluded that depth cannot really be a feature of experience itself, but only an inference introduced by cognitive activity that is added to experience.[9]

---

7   Afterimages had while one's eyes are open seem to be at the same distance as whatever surface one's eyes are focused on. If that surface had graduations marked on it, we could measure the size of the afterimage at the distance of the surface and calculate its extent at whatever standard distance we might choose. Afterimages had while one's eyes are closed and phosphenes seem to occupy a certain fraction of the visual field. These can be given a measure by reference to the same fraction of occupancy by an object at a chosen standard distance.

8   Anscombe (1963/1981) provides two striking examples. In one of these, she awoke to find a post in her room a few feet away from her bed. This "post" turned out to be a matchbox, standing on end, a few inches from her eye. (The other case was similar but involved a nearby prayer book.) In another sort of case, I was once uncertain whether a sound was a loud whistle from a distant source or a lesser noise some tens of feet away. After moving around a little, I discovered that the source was a very small noise emanating from a thermostat that had been about 6 inches from my ear. Once I knew that, and returned my head to its original position, the noise sounded soft and close.

9   See O'Shaughnessy (1980, pp. 171–174). O'Shaughnessy combines this conceptual consideration with the idea that objects at different distances create the same retinal impression. This latter point, however, ignores both binocularity and information contained in texture.

This argument, however, confuses causation with inference. Acquisition of beliefs may cause our experience to change, but not all changes that depend on acquisition of beliefs are changes in conclusions drawn by inference.[10] Even if one infers that an object is a certain distance away on the basis of coming to believe that it is an object of a certain kind, there is an additional change, namely, a change in where it looks to be. This is a difference in the experience itself and is not merely a matter of a difference of beliefs. This point may be easier to appreciate if we note that a change in apparent location leaves us still with location as part of the experience prior to the change. Illusory depth is as much experiential depth as illusory color is experiential color.

The Sore Finger Argument

If a pain is literally located in one of my fingers and I put my finger in my mouth, then it would seem that it ought to be true that I have a pain in my mouth. But such a conclusion evidently need not be true (i.e., there need be no pain in my teeth, tongue, gums, etc.). It may be concluded from these facts that the "in" of "pain *in* my finger" must be only a metaphorical "in" and not a genuinely spatial attribution.

This conclusion should, however, not be accepted. There is an alternative resolution, namely, that "in" need not be transitive even when strictly and literally spatial. And, in fact, we can produce many examples of this kind in contexts where no one would suggest that we were not speaking in a literally spatial way. So, for example, a dog may have swallowed a rat very recently, and may now be comfortably snoozing inside my house. Does it follow that there is a rat in my house? Of course, there is a sense in which it does; and, in the same sense, we may also say that a pain in my finger is in my mouth if my finger is in my mouth. But in a quite ordinary sense, having a rat in my house means having it somewhere in the woodwork, and it would be distinctly odd to say that I have a rat in my house in the envisaged circumstances. Again, there is a stomach in Jones's body, and Jones may be inside a ship. So, in one sense, there is a stomach in the ship. But it would be a kind of joke to say so.

---

10 Many connectionist devices provide possible models for the structure envisaged here – namely, those in which a hidden layer (B) receives inputs both from an input layer (A) and from a later layer (C) to which (B) also gives inputs.

There is a variation on the transparency theme that itself comes up in many guises. It can be stated as follows.

(V1) Phenomenal qualities are the ways ordinary things seem or appear.
(V2) Things sometimes actually are the way they seem.

Therefore,

(V3) Things sometimes actually have phenomenal qualities.

That is,

(V4) Phenomenal qualities are the very properties that ordinary things actually have (when, as we may put it, nothing untoward is occurring).[11]

QER holds, to the contrary, that things like tomatoes, but not conscious experiences, actually have P-colors (e.g., molecular surface structures), that conscious events are constituted by occurrences of phenomenal qualities, and that, therefore, no tomato literally exemplifies a phenomenal quality. According to QER, some phenomenal qualities are ways tomatoes may look, or appear, but none are ever literally exemplified by tomatoes. This commitment conflicts with the foregoing argument, and it is thus necessary to identify where the latter goes wrong.

The (V) argument is question-begging because, if we are to preserve validity, (V2) has to be read in a way that, by itself, is already equivalent to the conclusion. That is, we have to read (V2) as saying that things sometimes exemplify the very properties that are the ways that they seem. All that is left for the rest of the argument is to introduce "phenomenal qualities" as an abbreviation for "properties that are the ways that ordinary things seem or appear".

Now, if there were no other plausible reading of (V2), one could hardly complain about the argument – for (V2) is evidently *true*. But in fact there is another, obvious and well-known way to read (V2). To wit: things are the way they seem (e.g., red and round) if they actually exemplify physical

---

11 Dretske gives an explicit statement of this argument.

> The first fact is that qualia are supposed to be the way things seem or appear in the sense modality in question. So, for example, if a tomato looks red and round to S, then redness and roundness are the qualia of S's visual experience of the tomato. If this is so, then (second fact) if things ever *are* the way they seem, it follows that qualia, the properties that define what it is like to have that experience, are exactly the properties the object being perceived *has* when the perception is veridical. (Dretske, 1995, pp. 83–84; emphases in the original)

properties that, under normal conditions, cause a normal observer S to have the same kinds of phenomenal qualities that S is now having.[12] Things are not the way they seem if restoring normal conditions would make S have different phenomenal qualities when confronted in the same sense modality with those same things.

This rejection of the (V) argument does not beg the question in a reverse direction by simply assuming that the second reading of (V2) is the only possible one or even the correct one. All that is required is the neutral assumption that the second reading of (V2) is an as-yet-open possibility. This neutral assumption is enough to require a separate argument for the reading of (V2) that leads to the conclusion of the (V) argument; and that fact is enough to entirely remove any force from the (V) argument itself.

THE TRUE RELATION BETWEEN EXPERIENCE AND REPRESENTATION

Representationalism presents itself as a materialist alternative to experiential realism. It claims to show that we do not need to refer to intrinsic qualities of experiences because we can hold phenomenal qualities to be merely represented qualities. Where F is a phenomenal quality, there are no F experiences; there are only, so to speak, *of F* experiences. In the previous chapter, we saw that there are deep difficulties for this view, and in this chapter we have seen that there are problems with what is supposed to be a key positive reason for representationalism, namely, the transparency argument.

Nowhere in this discussion has it been denied that we represent the world to ourselves or that F experiences are, *in addition to being F*, representations of things. Here and there, I have said some things about how experiential realists should think about representation as an additional fact about experiences. It seems useful, however, to collect these ideas in one place.

According to QER, experiences represent things in virtue of the fact that normally, each person has an experience of a certain kind when and

---

12 Normal observers are noncircularly identifiable by reference to their discriminative abilities. This remains the case even if we suppose that inversions or displacements of spectra actually occur: our statement makes no comparison between subjects and thus is implicitly relativized to individual subjects. The phenomenon of perceptual constancy should also be borne in mind here. One consequence of this phenomenon is that things can appear the way they are even in some conditions that are not normal. Just which kinds of variance from normal conditions change or fail to change the way things appear is an empirical question.

only when certain kinds of things are present to the senses. If we want to *say* what kind of thing might be present to the senses, we have to use a public word, e.g., "red" or "sweet". A basic fact is that we can learn to use such words to classify things. We do not have to have either a philosophical account of experience or a science of molecular structures, reflectance profiles, or sugar chemistry in order to learn such words, and without those words, neither philosophical accounts nor science could begin. Once we do have such words, we can use them to classify our experiences, and we can do a scientific investigation of the physical properties of the things we have learned to classify.

Nothing appears *as* having a molecular structure or a reflectance profile. Thus, representation of things is not representation of them as having their physical properties. Nor is it represented in our experience that the physical properties of red or sweet things are the properties of the experiences that are caused by those things. What is true, and what may lead to confusion here, is that our visual experience is three-dimensional, and the location of colors is generally the same as the location of the things that are causing us to have those colors as properties of our experiences.[13] To understand this point more fully, consider a case in which I reach out and touch a red tomato. My visual field will then contain not only redness, but also flesh tone, and these parts of my visual experience will be at the same depth. It is thus natural to think of colors as on the objects; but this naturalness is no support for a philosophical theory that holds that the redness of our experience must be identical with some physical property of tomatoes.

These remarks will remind some philosophers of "projective theories of color". Many of the statements used in describing projective theories of color are statements with which qualitative event realists can agree.[14] But the metaphor of projection is fundamentally misleading. It is infected with the error that was noted earlier, namely, the error of thinking of experience as something to be found by "looking within" – for only if something is in some way inside to begin with can it be projected outward. What QER says, by contrast, is that visual experience is itself

---

13 The exception allowed by "generally" concerns extremely distant objects, e.g., heavenly bodies. Stars and planets do not look to be at different distances, so we should not say that the yellow of Arcturus is located farther away than the white of Jupiter. This observation raises the question of what the maximal distance is in visual experience. It is to be answered by finding the limits of distance discrimination (independently of differential illumination or occlusion), but I do not know what these are.

14 For a good example, see Baldwin (1992).

three-dimensional. Likewise, bodily sensations and sounds are not pro-jected onto body parts or spatial locations; instead, their locationality is an aspect of the experience itself.

These remarks may lead to the question of what the depth of experi-ence represents. The problem behind this question is that space does not seem to be a thing, and thus it is not a thing that can be tracked, i.e., represented in virtue of a causal relation. Now, it is true that while colors, flavors, sounds, and so on have causes that are physical structures, there is no physical property corresponding to distance. There is, for example, no quantity of intervening ether that varies according to how far away a thing is. There is, however, a regular relation, in normal circumstances, between the relative width of objects at the same distance and the sizes of colored regions of our visual experiences. And there is a regular relation between the depth of our experiences and the distance between ourselves and their causes. These regular relations are a sufficient foundation for us to speak of a representational relation between the spatial aspects of our experiences and the spatial character of the physical world.

QER is not only a theory that opposes representationalism. It is a the-ory of phenomenal consciousness. It holds that experiences are episodes of – temporal stretches of – consciousness. It says that consciousness itself is a reality that consists in the occurring of phenomenal qualities, including not only colors, flavors, sounds, pains, and so on, but shape and depth as well. In explaining and defending this theory, we have lately focused on a rival account of the status of phenomenal qualities. But QER also faces a fundamental challenge from a view that is put forward as an alternative account of consciousness itself. It is to this challenge that I will turn in the following chapter.

6

Higher Order Theories

Higher order, or HO, theories of consciousness claim to give a naturalistic explanation of the difference between conscious and unconscious occurrences. These theories present two kinds of challenge to QER. On the one hand, they provide positive accounts of consciousness, and a fortiori of phenomenal consciousness, that are incompatible with QER. On the other hand, HO theories also offer arguments that, if sound, would undercut the key claim that phenomenal qualities can occur only in episodes of consciousness. These two kinds of challenge are closely related and cannot be considered in complete isolation from each other. Roughly speaking, however, I will begin with the first and move on to the second in the section titled "Unconscious Pains and Tastes?".

To introduce HO theories, let us consider cases in which people rely on assumptions without realizing it. They take in some information and they pronounce a conclusion, where the conclusion would not be rationally connected with what they took in unless a further assumption were being made. But they did not utter that assumption, either overtly or subvocally. If advised of the dependence of their conclusion on the assumption, they might deny that they relied on it and even deny its truth; and these denials might be made with every feeling of sincerity. In cases of this kind, it would be natural to say that the assumption was made unconsciously. If one holds a cognitive theory according to which unconscious assumptions must take occurrent form (i.e., must be "tokened") in order to affect behavior, it would also be natural to speak of the (occurrent) assumption as an unconscious thought.

What is the difference between a conscious (occurrent) thought and an unconscious one? HO theories answer, roughly, that a conscious thought is one that is represented, i.e., thought of, by its possessor. An unconscious thought, like all thoughts, represents something, but it is not, in turn, represented.[1] To increase generality, and to begin to introduce some necessary refinements, it will be convenient to have the following summary statement of HO theories.

(HO1) Consciousness obtains in a subject if and only if (a) the subject has a mental state, M, and (b) M is represented by a representation that we may call R_1, and (c) certain conditions on R_1 are met.

In this statement, R_1 is a higher order representation. In normal cases, it is assumed that M causally contributes to the occurrence of R_1. However, since, in general, representation occurs only where misrepresentation is possible, the presence of M is not a necessary condition for the occurrence of R_1. A plausible example of a condition on R_1 is that it not be arrived at by inference. For example, suppose I become convinced that some assumption is operative in my thinking, but only because you seem sincere when you point it out to me and I think you are an excellent logician. Then I have the thought that I am making a certain assumption. But if this is all there is to the case, HO theorists would not count the assumption as being made consciously, since my thought about the assumption is held only inferentially. I cannot say to myself "*Here* is where I assume *p*" or "*This* is my thought that *p*".[2]

HO theories are not aimed directly at our basic question of how phenomenal qualities enter into a perceptual situation; they are theories of what makes a mental state conscious. An answer to the basic question is, however, implicit in many HO theories. I will proceed by giving a first-pass explanation of this answer and explaining why it is inadequate. Then I will introduce a complication that will lead to a more extended discussion.

When Eve sees a red apple, she represents it. If we are particularly interested in her seeing a *red* apple, we shall have to suppose that there is

1 In Robinson (forthcoming), I give a different answer. Very briefly, it is that thoughts we have uttered, either overtly or to ourselves in subvocal speech, are conscious thoughts, and if there are unconscious occurrent thoughts at all, they are occurrents that are unspoken either overtly or subvocally. This view explains consciousness of thoughts in terms of either overt behavior or phenomenal qualities of the imagery (most prominently, auditory imagery) that we have when our mouths are closed. The consciousness of imagery itself is, of course, not explainable in this way: imagery is conscious because it consists of phenomenal qualities, and phenomenal qualities by their very nature can occur only in conscious events.

2 Another condition advanced by some writers is that R_1 itself be represented by a still higher order representation. See Carruthers (1989), and, for discussion of this variant, Robinson (1997a). In this chapter, I will follow the more widely accepted view of Rosenthal (1986, 1990, 1991, 1993), which does not require R_1 to be either represented or itself conscious.

some physical surface property of the apple that her representation tracks.[3] Now, according to HO theories, Eve's *simply* having a representation of the red apple does not involve Eve's having any conscious states.[4] However, if Eve has a representation of her (zero-level) representation, and this representation is of the right sort (i.e., it meets the most defensible proposal for conditions in clause (c) of (HO1)), then she will be having a *conscious* representation of the red apple. We may summarize this answer to the basic question as follows.

(HO2a) (a) Red comes into Eve's seeing a red apple as a surface physical property (a P-red) that is one of a set of such properties that divide objects into classes corresponding to our color classifications. This property is represented by some state of Eve's sensory neurons or of neurons in her sensory projection areas. Let R_0 be this (first order) representation. (b) In some cases — namely, those in which Eve consciously sees a red apple — red comes into Eve's seeing a red apple as a property that she represents again in a (higher order) representation, R_1, of the representation referred to in (a), i.e., R_0.[5] If Eve has R_0 without R_1, she is not conscious of her seeing the red apple. (She may be said to be conscious *of* the red apple, but her seeing of it is not a *conscious* seeing.)

(HO2a), however, is not a promising answer to our basic question. There is no red mentioned in its first clause, except for the physical surface property

3 HO theorists can allow for a wide range of theories about what physical-color precisely is, but they are under heavy pressure to hold that there is *some* good theory of it. The reason is that if there is no suitable set of P-properties, then it will not be possible to have a set of neural properties whose similarities and differences map in a regular way onto color similarities and differences (and analogously for qualities in other sense modalities). But HO theories rely on such regular mapping. (See Rosenthal [1991] and the discussion under "Burdens" later in this chapter.)

4 HO theories hold that Eve may be conscious *of* the red apple without having any conscious states, and even without being (creaturely) conscious. "[T]ransitive consciousness can occur without intransitive state consciousness. One is transitively conscious of something if one is in a mental state whose content pertains to that thing: a thought about the thing, or a sensation of it. That mental state need not be a conscious state. And if, as is likely, mental states are possible during sleep, transitive consciousness will not even presuppose creature consciousness" (Rosenthal, 1990, p. 27). In short, consciousness *of* does not imply (either state or creature) consciousness.

5 In light of the criticism in the following paragraph, how can I think I am justified in using "again" in this sentence? The reason is that the content of R_1 is supposed (by HO theorists) to be something like "I see a red apple". "Red" here can only be taken to indicate the same property that R_0 represents, where we take its content to be "red apple here now". No one supposes that we can have a thought about the neural properties that do the (zero-level) representing merely by having a thought about what we are seeing (*even though* if representation is tracking, those neural properties are represented in a higher level representation).

89

that is not what red is represented *as*. The first clause, that is, evidently does not provide any phenomenal red. But all that (b) adds is a tracking of an event that (i) is not red itself (it is a neural event of some sort) and (ii) does not contain phenomenal red. How it is that tracking such an event should result in a conscious *color* experience is utterly mysterious. Equally mysterious is why a tracking of a tracking should yield consciousness at all. Thus, even if it should turn out that we can construct a set of conditions in part (c) of (HO1) that will apply to all and only cases in which we think Eve consciously sees a red apple, we would still lack an *explanation* of how phenomenal red or phenomenal consciousness of any sort could come into Eve's situation.

One response to these remarks would be to insist that HO theories can be sharply separated from the basic question, in which case their not providing a satisfactory answer is no objection to them.[6] But this response ought to be resisted for two reasons. First, the basic question is aptly named, that is, it is basic to philosophy of mind, and in particular to theories of sensory consciousness. The qualities that enter into phenomenal consciousness have long been felt by many to be a problem. Not every part of a theory of mind needs to solve it, but a theory of consciousness can reasonably be expected to make *some* contribution to the account of phenomenal consciousness. Second, several proponents of HO theories have explicitly held that the difference between conscious pain and unconscious pain coincides with the difference between suffering we have some moral obligation to prevent and a nonsuffering condition that is of little interest to us.[7] If, as I think is the case, (HO1) and (HO2a) provide as little account of phenomenal pain as they do of phenomenal red, their

---

6 Lycan (1996) is explicit: he says that his own view "bears no responsibility for explaining qualia or phenomenal character" (p. 28). But then, we have seen that he thinks that job can be done by appealing to representation. Those who agree are referred to Chapters 4 and 5. This chapter, in effect, addresses those who think that something more than (zero-level) representation is needed in explaining phenomenal consciousness and believe that HO theories can supply this further need.

7 Thus, for example, Rosenthal (1990) argues for unconscious sensory states, e.g., *having* pains; if we not only have the pains but also *feel* them, then they are conscious pains. He recognizes a reluctance to allow for unconscious bodily sensations, and part of the explanation for this fact is that we often speak "interchangeably" (p. 10) of feeling a pain and having a pain. This latter fact is, in turn, partially explained as follows: "Feeling pains and having them seem equivalent only because of our lack of interest in the nonconscious cases" (p. 11). I take it that if we suffered from nonconscious pains, we would be interested in them.

Peter Carruthers (1989) argued that we do not have moral duties concerning what we would call humane treatment of nonhuman animals on the ground that, although such creatures have pains, these pains are not conscious pains.

combination would fail on a matter on which HO theorists have explicitly claimed to provide enlightenment.

A stronger response to the criticism of (HO2a) is to allow for unconscious phenomenal qualities by adding the following claim.

(UPQ) Neural events that track P-properties have phenomenal qualities.[8] (Such events are not conscious in themselves, i.e., not conscious unless represented by a higher order representation.)

This is a theory of phenomenal qualities that is in direct contradiction to QER, which holds that phenomenal qualities are essentially conscious, i.e., cannot occur in a nonconscious event. In thinking about this conflict of views, it is absolutely crucial to understand that the term "phenomenal qualities" in (UPQ) is meant to refer to exactly the same qualities that QER holds to be essentially conscious. The difference between (UPQ) and QER is one of theoretical opposition, and not of senses or uses of the term "phenomenal consciousness". The moment one thinks of this term as having different senses in the two accounts, the issue between them becomes trivialized. For example, if "neural event NEx is phenomenally red" were to be used to *mean* only "neural event NEx is of a type that normally occurs only when its possessor is seeing something that is P-red", then qualitative event realists would have no objection to the claim that would be made by the words "NEx is phenomenally red". (They would, however, still object that such a usage would be likely to introduce confusion.)

Moreover, unless "phenomenal qualities" is meant to refer to exactly the same qualities to which we have been using it to refer all along, adding (UPQ) cannot help to respond to the criticism of (HO2a). To understand how this addition may help respond to that criticism if we do maintain the usual reference of "phenomenal qualities", let us consider the following enriched claim.

(HO2b) Red comes into Eve's seeing a red apple in exactly the ways listed in (HO2a) plus one more. Namely, the representational neural state R_0 is phenomenally red. (But R_0 is not by itself a conscious state, i.e., it is not conscious unless there is an HO representation of it.)

---

8 One form of this view would be to hold that neural event properties (of events of types that track P-properties) are identical with phenomenal qualities. This view would lead us back to the discussion of Chapter 3. But one need not hold this identity in order to affirm (UPQ), and the following discussion will apply to (UPQ) with or without the further commitment to identity.

This view improves upon (HO2a) because we can now no longer complain that there is no red other than physical red mentioned in its first clause. For we now have, besides P-red, the phenomenal redness of the zero-level representation that represents P-red.

Although (HO2b) is an improvement, it is, in my view, not sufficient to make HO theories plausible. It does nothing to explain how adding a representation of an unconscious representation should give rise to consciousness, and it does nothing to explain why the mere fact of standing in a causal relation to P-red things should make a neural event phenomenally red. It does nothing to explain how (UPQ) is possible, e.g., how the very property that distinguishes my red afterimages from my yellow ones should be able to be a property of an unconscious event.

I am, however, not content to leave the matter here. One reason is that QER must deny (UPQ), and therefore arguments in support of (UPQ) must be examined. Another is that many accounts of HO theories do not appear to give (UPQ) the degree of importance that my discussion implies it has. I will begin by reviewing two problems for higher order thought (HOT) theories and show how, in each case, replying to them leads to the introduction of (UPQ).[9] Then I shall begin discussion of arguments that have been advanced in favor of (UPQ).

THE STONE OBJECTION AND SOME REPLIES

It has been noted by several philosophers that if being thought about were enough to make a state conscious, then there would be many states that are (intransitively) conscious states, e.g., the warmth of stones or the greenness of leaves.[10] But no one wants to say that leaves or stones have intransitively conscious states; and if someone did profess a willingness to accept this consequence, we would be sure that the resulting view of "consciousness" would have nothing to do with what the philosophers discussed in this book have been trying to understand.

In considering possible responses to this objection, it is essential to distinguish two ways of understanding what it might be for a transitively

9 HO theories divide into those in which the HO representations are thoughts and those in which the HO representations are modeled on perception. The next two sections focus on HO thought theories (HOT theories); the following chapter will return to a more general consideration of HO theories.
10 Rosenthal (1990, p. 30) mentions Peter Bieri and Fred Dretske as philosophers who have made this objection.

conscious state to *make* its object conscious. To this end, I introduce the following pair of analogies. Being *bothered* and being *brothered* are both relational terms, i.e, in order for either to apply to a person, there must be some other thing to which that person stands in a certain relation. But there is this difference. In order for *s* to be bothered, *s*'s tormentor must produce an intrinsic state in *s*; we might call it a "bothering", meaning a feeling of irritation in *s*. In contrast, a subject, *s*, is brothered just in case *s* has a male sibling. Being brothered consists only in this; it is not further required that *s* have any feeling about having a brother, or that *s* know or suspect the existence of a brother, or that *s* have any intrinsic state at all that is an effect of, or has any other particular relation to, a male sibling.

Making a state intransitively conscious by having a thought of it might be regarded as similar to being bothered. On this model, a HOT would produce consciousness in the (first order) state that it is about by producing some intrinsic property (namely, intransitive consciousness) in the latter state. This interpretation, however, must be avoided. Thinking of intransitive consciousness in this way would make it natural to ask what intrinsic property is caused to occur in first order representations by their being thought of. But if this is a reasonable question, then HOT theory has failed, because it claims to give an answer to the question of what intransitive consciousness is. It cannot be a success if we still have to ask what intransitive consciousness is *after* having received its putative answer. Thus, we must understand HOT theory to offer the "being brothered" model; that is, we must understand it as holding that a state's being intransitively conscious *consists in* the relational fact of its being the object of a certain kind of thought.[11]

One way of responding to the stone objection is to invoke the conditions in clause (c) of (HO1) in order to limit the eligible candidates for conscious states. For example, following Rosenthal (1990), we might hold that any state that will be conscious if it is thought of must be a state that is known immediately, i.e., noninferentially and nonobservationally. Applied to potential phenomenally conscious states, this limitation would restrict eligible states to sensory representations. States of things seen would be observed states, and thus excluded from being potentially

---

11 Rosenthal is quite explicit on both what is to be rejected and what is to be accepted. Regarding what is rejected: "The mistake here is to suppose that a state's being intransitively conscious is an intrinsic property of that state" (1990, p. 31). Regarding what is accepted: "a mental state's being intransitively conscious simply consists in one's being transitively conscious of it" (1990, pp. 30–31).

conscious states. States described in neural terms would be inferentially known states, and thus likewise excluded. The sensory representations, described as such, would be the only states that are closely connected with perception and that remain after these exclusions.

This result seems plausible, but only because thinking of sensory representations, described as such, is thinking of appearances. That is, the only way we have of thinking of sensory representations without inference is to think of them as experiences of things – occasions on which something appears red, round, loud, salty, and so on. That is to say that when we think of sensory states without inference, we are thinking of them in terms of phenomenal qualities – qualities, for example, that differentiate what happens when we look at a ripe tomato from what happens when we look at an unripe one. The higher order thoughts are thoughts that, e.g., something red is appearing to me. This "red" cannot be P-red (since nothing appears as P-red); it can only be the phenomenal quality red.

If sensory representations, thought of without inference, i.e., thought of as appearances of certain kinds, were held to be conscious states just by themselves, then no thought would have to be added to make them conscious, and HOT theory would be false. And thus, we have come upon (UPQ): In virtue of noninferentiality, sensory states must be thought of as involving phenomenal qualities, but for the sake of compatibility with HOT theory, they must be held not to be conscious states when they occur just by themselves.

There is, however, no reason why the unconverted should find any attraction in this account. From an experiential realist point of view, the reason sensory representations are plausible candidates for what is made conscious by being thought of is that they *are* (already, by themselves) conscious states. Applying the immediacy criterion seems to be just an ad hoc way of identifying conscious states, which are then incorrectly treated as mere candidates for being conscious if they are thought of. The more straightforward view of experiential realism will seem all the more compelling because adding a HOT contributes no explanation of how or why consciousness should arise. That aspect of the stone objection remains in full force; there is nothing in the concept of immediacy that explains consciousness. Immediacy picks out a class that has the right extension, but the plausibility of the idea that there is some connection with consciousness comes from the phenomenal character of what is picked out, not from immediacy as such.

Let us turn to another way of replying to the stone objection. Many HO theorists say that what is special about the states that will be conscious if they are thought of is that they are mental states.[12] Perhaps this criterion will prove to be the nonarbitrary feature that, when combined with being thought of, will explain why consciousness occurs.

It is evident that "mental" in this context cannot be understood to mean "conscious". That understanding would render the resulting theory circular, "explaining" consciousness as what happens when conscious states are unmediatedly thought of.

One way to avoid this circularity would be to take "mental" as a commonsense, previously understood way of picking out a certain class of states that does not make any theoretical commitments. Now, I am doubtful that there is any such use of "mental". But if there were, it would not give us an explanatory theory of consciousness. An obvious question to ask of such an account would be this: What is it about mental states that makes intransitive consciousness arise from thinking about *them* but not about nonmental states? Without a well-motivated answer to this question, we would have at best extensional adequacy, but no explanation.

If we are to make good use of the idea that consciousness arises from having thoughts about mental states, we must find a property of mental states that has some promise of contributing something explanatory to our theory of consciousness. As far as I can see, there is only one candidate for such a property, namely, that mental states are *representational* states. According to this proposal, if we are having a state, S1, that represents another state, S0, then S0 is intransitively conscious if S0 itself represents something but not conscious if it doesn't. (And, if S0 represents, but we do not have any S1 that represents S0, then again, S0 is not an intransitively conscious state.)

If this is right, however, we are brought right back to where we were a few paragraphs ago. If we are concerned with perception, the only states that will seem evidently mental are sensory representations, thought of as experiences or appearances of things. To qualitative event realists, these representations will seem to be episodes of consciousness as they

12 See quotations in previous notes from Rosenthal. See also Lycan:

> What is it that is so special about physical states of this sort that consciousness *of* them makes them conscious? That they are themselves mental. Stomachs and freckled patches of skin are not mental. It seems that psychological states are called "conscious states" when we are conscious of them, but nonpsychological things are not. (Lycan, 1996, p. 24)

stand. HOT theorists, however, will have to regard them as exhibiting phenomenal qualities (to preserve the idea that they count as mental) but as not yet conscious in themselves.

It may be tempting here to try to "improve" HOT theory by saying that sensory representations do not have phenomenal qualities (conscious or not) but only represent phenomenal qualities. But there are three problems. First, this is not what HOT theorists actually say. They argue, instead, for unconscious pains and other states in which phenomenal qualities are present but not conscious. Second, making HOT theorists into representationalists would subject them to the criticisms of that view explained in Chapter 4. Finally, sensory representations are supposed to represent properties of physical things by tracking them. But we never have noninferential thoughts that we are representing F things, where F is a P-red property. Thus, if sensory representations do not have (unconscious) phenomenal qualities, then thoughts to the effect that I am now having a sensory representation of red are always false. This result is not a contradiction, but it would be a very strange consequence for a theory of phenomenal consciousness to be committed to.

A DILEMMA FOR HOT THEORY

It is a principle of most versions of HOT theory that the higher order thought about a sensory representation need not itself be a conscious thought.[13] This means that that thought need not itself be thought of in order for it and its object to constitute a case of intransitive consciousness. Let us diagram this absence of a higher (or second order) HOT by using "Null" in a diagram, where the rightmost item is a lowest order representation, and any non-Null item to the left is an HO representation of the adjacent rightward item. "HOT" in (D1) thus depicts a higher order thought, and "SR" depicts a sensory representation that the HOT in the diagram is a thought about. With these conventions, a typical case of phenomenal consciousness, according to HOT theory, would look like this.

(D1)   Null + HOT + SR

Now consider the state of affairs in the following diagram.

(D2)   Null + HOT + Null

---

13   Carruthers, as noted previously, is an exception.

The question we can now formulate is: Is there any difference in consciousness between these cases?[14]

(A) No. In this case, the thought labeled "HOT" is sufficient for consciousness if (D1) is. But in (D2) there is no case of a structure that consists of a state plus a HOT about that state. So, on this supposition, such a structure is not necessary for (intransitive) consciousness to occur, and therefore such a structure cannot be what constitutes consciousness. In short, HOT theory is false.

(B) Yes. In this case, the presence of SR contributes something to consciousness. But SR by itself is not a conscious state, so it does not contribute something to consciousness by, so to speak, just contributing itself. Nor does it contribute something to consciousness by being the intentional object of the HOT, for it is also the intentional object of the HOT in (D2), where, on the present supposition, there is no intransitive consciousness. So long as HOT theory does not provide a further, definite indication of how the presence of SR can contribute to the difference in consciousness that separates (D1) from (D2) (according to the present alternative), it is at best an incomplete theory.

Here are some comments on this dilemma.[15]

(1) One may try to reject the dilemma on the ground that the state of affairs depicted in (D2) is impossible, i.e., there cannot be the supposed kind of HOT without the corresponding SR. However, it is in the nature of thoughts (as of representations generally) to be able to be false. Therefore, if it is held that the thoughts needed in HOT theory *cannot* be false, that would merely raise a question about what is meant by "thought". The point here is not a mere matter of semantics. If "thought" is not being used in its customary sense, then we have no assurance that the qualitative event realist's occurrences of phenomenal qualities are not, after all, being recognized, but merely being (mis)*labeled* "higher order thoughts".

(2) It might be held that HOTs, just in so far as they are thoughts, could be false, but that some additional feature ensures that they never can be false. But this alleged feature has to be explained before this idea can be supposed to defend the theory. To see this, note that an obvious reason

14 It is interesting to note that Rosenthal takes the negative horn of this dilemma. "Still, a case in which one has a HOT along with the mental state it is about might well be subjectively indistinguishable from a case in which the HOT occurs but not the mental state" (1990, p. 48).

15 See Seager (1999, pp. 76–78) for further discussion of the difficulties presented by the possibility of false HOTs.

why two things can never be separated is that "they" are really one thing under two names. So, a natural presumption is that, if a HOT cannot be mistaken, then what is being called a HOT is really a conscious sensory representation. Under that description, again, it might be that QER is the best account of what conscious sensory representations are. Thus, until the alleged "additional feature" is adequately articulated and explained, we have no assurance that HOT theory isn't a view that has the same actual content as QER but is stated in a highly misleading way.

(3) It might be held, finally, that we should adopt the positive horn of the dilemma, and answer the challenge to make HOT theory complete by saying that SR contributes phenomenal qualities. This answer, which I think is the strongest way to develop alternative (B), requires that unconscious states can have phenomenal qualities, i.e., it brings us back to (UPQ).

I have been explaining the relation between HOT theory and the view that there are unconscious occurrences of phenomenal qualities. It is time to turn to the arguments that have been offered in support of the latter notion. In the next section, I respond to some arguments that can be understood and discussed relatively briefly. In the following chapter, I will examine an older and very widely accepted argument for unconscious phenomenal qualities that requires a more complex discussion.

UNCONSCIOUS PAINS AND TASTES?

Pain would seem to be a phenomenal quality, if anything is. Any reason that suggests there can be unconscious pains is thus of considerable interest in an investigation of the claims of QER and its alternatives. Several authors have advanced the view that common sense recognizes unconscious pains. If this view can be sustained, then QER must carry the burden of contradicting common sense. Perhaps such a burden can be borne; after all, no one criticizes physics on the ground that it rules out possibilities allowed by common sense. It would, however, be preferable for QER if it did not have to bear such a burden. Thus, some of the discussion of this section will concern not only the truth about phenomenal qualities, but also the commitments of common sense.

Before proceeding, let us note two preliminaries. (1) QER, like many other views, assumes that there are causes of conscious events, and it allows (indeed, it positively proposes) that these causes show systematic variations that parallel variations both in phenomenal qualities and in the properties of external things or bodily states.[16] It would thus not be to the present point to show only that there are some neural properties that are systematically related to occurrences of phenomenal pain. The opposition between HOT theory and QER is about phenomenal qualities, not about properties that are merely related to phenomenal qualities in some way. (2) The relevant alternatives about commonsense commitments are not limited to the view that common sense embraces unconscious phenomenal qualities and the view that it rules them out. There is a third possibility, namely, that common sense is neutral on such a question. This possibility would seem to be the most likely; it would be extraordinary if common sense really implied a firm position on the somewhat recondite issues that are under consideration in this chapter.

All-Day Headaches

We sometimes make remarks such as "I've had a headache all day". But those who make such remarks do not always mean that they were suffering at every moment. They may mean only that they had recurrent periods of suffering, separated by periods in which they were absorbed in their work and not actually suffering.

One possible interpretation of these facts is what I shall call the "enduring pain view", which is short for the "enduring, but intermittently conscious, pain view". According to this view, the pain is there all the time, but we are not always conscious of it. The times of actual suffering are times when we are conscious of the pain, and the intermittent interruptions are times when the pain is still there but we are not conscious of it.[17]

If this were the only possible interpretation of the facts noted two paragraphs ago, we might fairly take common sense to be implicitly committed to the enduring pain view. There is, however, another way of interpreting those facts. To understand this alternative, we may take a cue from Hobbes (1651), who tells us that the nature of war "consists not in actual

---

16 Systematic variation is intended to be weaker than isomorphism, which seems to be ruled out by, e.g., metamers in color vision.

17 Rosenthal takes this view. "It is arguable that even bodily sensations such as pains can at times go wholly unnoticed, and so can exist without being conscious. When one is intermittently distracted from a headache or pain, it is natural to speak of having had a single, persistent pain or ache during the entire period. It would be odd to say that one had had a sequence of brief, distinct, but qualitatively identical pains or aches. Similarly for itches and other bodily sensations" (1991, p. 17).

fighting; but in the known disposition thereto." Proceeding analogously, we may think of remarks such as "I've had a miserable headache all day" as saying that, throughout the day, the speaker has had a disposition to have an ache in the head – a disposition that would, perhaps, be triggered by excitement, frustration, or sudden movement. Such a disposition is compatible with the speaker's not actually having had an ache at all times, but only various aches at various times. Let us call this view the "discontinuous pain view". To have a positive motivation for this view, observe that, in "all-day headache" cases, there is *something* that is intermittent; and when we identify what it is that occurs sometimes, but not always, during the day, it seems that "aching" or "hurting" are the natural terms to use.

I confess to finding this latter interpretation of the preceding facts the obvious and natural one. Others profess to find the enduring pain view more natural. The conclusion I draw is that common sense is simply not committed one way or the other. It offers no support for QER, but it offers nothing that undercuts QER either.[18]

It may be thought that the discontinuous pain view commits one to affirming something that is unacceptably odd, namely, that during a stretch of time, one has had a series of brief, distinct, and qualitatively similar aches. We may agree that it would be odd to say such a thing; the reason, however, is that it is difficult to imagine circumstances in which such precision would be useful. For the same reason, it would be odd to say "My sump pump produces a series of brief, distinct, and qualitatively similar noises". Nonetheless, that is exactly what it does.

18 It is possible that Rosenthal agrees, for in a footnote (1991, p. 18) he says, "But all I am arguing here is that common sense be open to nonconscious pains; plainly common sense does not insist on the discontinuous-pain interpretation." However, the sentence to which this is a footnote is "Common sense thus undeniably countenances the existence of unconscious pains." This sounds far less neutral to my ear, and remarks about oddity of the discontinuous-pain interpretation and other similar expressions in the paper lead me to believe that Rosenthal holds the view that the enduring (but intermittently conscious) pain view is the more "natural" interpretation, or the interpretation one would take if one's common sense were not corrupted by bad philosophical theory. It is that view (often put forward by others in conversation) that I find both counterintuitive and utterly unsupported by argument.

Later in the same paper, Rosenthal describes the discontinuous pain view as "requiring some reinterpretation of the data" that amounts to "gerrymandering" (p. 33). But the data in this area can be nothing but the *utterances* of nonphilosophers, and neither the enduring pain view nor the discontinuous pain view is to be found in such utterances. The views are thus each as much an interpretation of the data as the other, and neither is gerrymandering unless both are.

We occasionally find statements in contexts remote from philosophy that seem to make explicit commitments to unfelt pains. Lycan quotes an interesting example from Grisham.[19]

(1) "Each step was painful, but the pain was not felt. He moved at a controlled jog down the escalators and out of the building."

To read this passage as supporting commonsense recognition of unfelt pains is to read it as presenting the following scenario.

(2) Each step caused him to have a pain but, fortunately, these pains were unfelt. So, he was able to move at a controlled jog down the escalators and out of the building.

This reading, however, is not the only one possible. An alternative is the following.

(3) Each step was excruciating, and almost completely filled his consciousness with its searing presence. But because he was exceedingly brave, determined, and driven by mortal necessity, he nonetheless, despite the pain, steeled himself to move at a controlled jog down the escalators and out of the building.

This same interpretation can be brought a little more into line with the form of Grisham's actual text.

(4) Each step was painful, but he behaved as if this were not so. He moved at a controlled jog down the escalators and out of the building.

The readings in (3) and (4) offer an interpretation of Grisham's intended scenario that is preferable to that given in (2). The reason is that Grisham is a superior dramatist who makes his living by engaging his readers' attention through the creation of exciting, tension-filled scenes. But the scenario in (2) is flat, unexciting, and, in one word, boring. By contrast, the scenario indicated by (3) and (4) can generate tension by conjuring up in the reader's mind lively images of gritting one's teeth and carrying on in the face of discomfort of which one is all too well aware. Because the latter interpretation fits so much better with Grisham's authorial properties,

---

19 See Lycan (1996, chap. 2, n. 6). The quotation is from p. 443 of Grisham's novel, *The Firm* (1991).

Lycan (personal communication) has collected a long list of Grisham-like examples. My suspicion, naturally, is that they are all open to interpretation either as somewhat hyperbolic speech or as indications of dispositions to have (discontinuous) pains.

(1) is best taken as a literary device for suggesting it. But the scenario of (3) and (4) does not imply that there are unfelt pains. Thus, the appearance of (1) in popular literature should not be taken as offering support for the idea that ordinary people are prepared to countenance unfelt pains.

Another suggestion of apparent commonsense commitment to unfelt pains comes from phrases such as "insensitive to pain", which may be used in connection with a certain congenital condition or applied to patients under analgesia.[20] The most one can garner from such phrases, however, is that their grammatical structure allows a possible reading according to which there is pain that is not sensed. But this fact offers absolutely no support for the view that this grammatically possible reading is the way in which anyone ever actually understands these phrases. An alternative reading of "insensitive to pain" is that subjects are insensitive to tissue-damaging events that would cause most people to suffer painful sensations – i.e., those tissue-damaging events do not cause pains in congenital pain insensitives or in those protected by analgesics.[21] In favor of

20 Dennett provides some examples.

> A textbook announces that nitrous oxide renders one "insensible to pain", a perfectly ordinary turn of phrase which elicits no "deviancy" startle in the acutest ear, but it suggests that nitrous oxide doesn't prevent the occurrence of pain at all, but merely makes one insensible to it when it does occur (as one can be rendered insensitive to the occurrence of flashing lights by a good blindfold). (Dennett, 1978, p. 221)

(Dennett points out that the same textbook also refers to nitrous oxide as an analgesic, i.e., a preventer of pain. The fact that the interpretation given in the main text makes the textbook author consistent is some reason to accept it.) A second source for the unfelt pains view is

> discussions of people who are "congenitally insensitive to pain". Our *prima facie* obligation not to cause pain in others is surely understood not to exclude these unfortunate individuals from the class of subjects. (Dennett, 1978, p. 225)

(Again, the view in the main text explains why we should agree without agreeing to unfelt pains.) It should be said that, while Dennett evidently takes these examples to support commonsense tolerance of unfelt pains, he also believes there are other commonsense remarks that suggest that being felt is essential to pain. See Dennett (1978, p. 225).

21 Lycan has pointed out (in conversation) that congenital pain insensitives may resemble normal subjects not only in tissue damage but also in some, perhaps considerable, portion of subsequent neural processing. In light of this possibility, one might form the hypothesis that the (possible) overlap in neural processes shows that pain insensitives really do have pain, and the remaining differences account (only) for their not feeling it.

Some doubt about this hypothesis may be raised by the facts that it is not only verbal behavior in which pain insensitives differ from normal subjects, and that the large behavioral difference is at least some evidence of substantial difference in neural processing. It should also be borne in mind that neural causes of pains are not pains (but at best "pains"; see the preliminary remarks to this section) – unless one is holding that phenomenal pain itself is

this alternative reading, I note that people do not easily accept that there are unfelt pains when that view is proferred explicitly; considerations of charity thus suggest that we should regard "insensitivity to pain" as insensitivity, strictly speaking, to damage, i.e., insensitivity to the usual causes of pain. It is true, in any case, that the subjects in question are insensitive to the tissue damage. But there does not appear to be any evidence that would suggest that anyone is ever disposed to say that pain insensitives are *also* insensitive to tissue damage (or *also* insensitive to pain); that is, there is no evidence that would suggest that people think of pain insensitivity as anything *additional to* insensitivity to tissue damage. This again suggests that people do not understand talk of insensitivity to pain in a way that would support an attribution of commitment to unfelt pains.

Wine and Music

It is widely believed that our sensory experience gets richer when our store of applicable concepts becomes larger. Learning about tannins is supposed to enable us to find more complexity in the taste of wine, and learning a bit about music theory is supposed to enable us to hear chords differently and with more richness.

One way to interpret such a putative change in experiential content is to suppose that our sensory experience is the same before and after our concept acquisition, and that the learning of concepts enables us to become conscious of (or to notice) what was there all along. If that is what we say, however, then we must suppose that there were phenomenal qualities present in our experience before our concept learning and before our noticing or our becoming conscious of those qualities. Hence, it is sometimes thought, experiential change under concept learning shows us that there are unconscious phenomenal qualities.[22] Or, at the very least, it is thought that we have to admit that there are properties that are fully determinate in our experience even though we are conscious only of a corresponding determinable property.

a property of neural events. However, the main point to notice at the present stage of the argument is that even if one accepts the hypothesis of considerable overlap, that gives no reason to accept the view that commonsense supports the possibility of unconscious pains. For common sense is surely silent about the question of neural overlap.

Lycan's remarks can be used to introduce deeper issues. The latter will be addressed in the next chapter.

22 See Churchland (1979) for a view of this kind. Rosenthal (1991) has a more guarded and carefully developed version.

As one may expect, there is an alternative account that does not support unconscious phenomenal qualities. Before giving it, however, I want to describe an experiment that anyone can easily try, and that severs the dependence of experiential richness on conceptual development. Those not trained in oenology can try this experiment with wine, just as I shall describe it; those who are should try an analogous experiment in some other field. The experiment is to ask your local restaurateur to pour a little of each of two different wines into two different glasses. Have a taste of each. It is nearly certain that you will judge their tastes to be different, and it is likely that you will have a preference for one over the other. But if we ask you to describe the difference, you may well be speechless, or able to give only very general descriptions that would fail to distinguish either of these tastes from those of a large number of other wines.[23] The conclusion to be drawn from this experiment is that you can perfectly well be conscious of qualities of complex tastes without having concepts for the various qualities of which you are conscious.

When we do acquire fine-grained concepts for the qualities in our experience, we undergo a period of *training*. When we learn to recognize tannin, for example, someone tells us that there is more tannin in this sample than in that one, for several pairs of wines that also differ in other respects, while we try to be attentive. Or we are given a highly concentrated sample of tannin to taste. This process changes one's conceptual structure somewhat, but it would be very contentious to assume that this is all that is changed. It is safe to assume that new neural connections are made in the course of the training process, but it would be question-begging to assume that these new connections are confined to changing one's *concepts*. It is perfectly possible that they also change the connectivity of one's sensory apparatus (i.e., the connectivity between neurons in primary sensory areas and the neurons onto which they project, or the connectivity between the latter neurons and the neurons onto which *they* project, etc.). In this case, there would be changes in the character of sensory states themselves, and not merely in the conceptual apparatus by which one is able to connect one's sensory experience with classificatory and other behavioral activities.[24] Now, if this is what happens, there is no

---

23 This point is, evidently, an aspect of what many have in mind when they speak of nonconceptual content. See the discussion in Chapter 4 and, again, that of Raffman (1995).

24 Skarda and Freeman (1987) provide evidence in this direction. Upon exposure to new odors, the activity in the olfactory bulb in rabbits developed attractors only when the new odor was used as a conditioned stimulus.

reason to suppose that there are any phenomenal qualities of which we are not conscious.

There is another possibility for the way in which the training process may affect us, and that is to give us capabilities of attention that we did not previously have. If we have not learned to detect tannin reliably, putting the question to ourselves "How much tannin is in this wine?" may have very little effect upon us. After training, it may cause us to attend to tannin, and that taste may then loom rather larger in our taste consciousness than before. This change, however, is a change in the kind of experience we have. Allowing for it does not lead to the view that there are unconscious phenomenal qualities. Instead, it leads to the view that training can cause us to be capable of new kinds of experiences – hardly a surprising idea.

BURDENS

I have now considered several arguments that have been offered in support of unconscious pains, tastes, and so on, and have found each of them wanting. At this point, however, it may be suggested that the whole strategy of considering such arguments and offering objections to their success is misguided, because it is insufficient to bear a required burden of proof. Behind this suggestion lies the fact that, in general, properties do not have to be conscious to be exemplified. Even if some properties can be identified only through our consciousness of them, that does not show that they are dependent on consciousness. For example, the class of surface molecular properties that constitute physical-red surfaces cannot be identified without reference to the normally conscious classificatory abilities of English speakers. But the surface molecular properties that are members of that class might have existed in nature even if there had never evolved a creature with a human ability for color vision. In light of these facts, it may seem that the prima facie acceptable position is that sensory qualities can be exemplified in unconscious states; that the burden of proof is on the qualitative event realist to show otherwise; and that it is therefore

Evidence of neural plasticity also provides some indirect support for the hypothesis of change of connectivity under training conditions. See the section in Kandel et al. (1995) on "The internal representation of personal space is modifiable by experience", esp. p. 329.

Some readers may be reminded of Dennett's (1988) discussion of the coffee tasters, Chase and Sanborn. I shall return to this topic in the discussion, in Chapter 9, of skeptical dismissals of phenomenal qualities.

insufficient to show only that the foregoing arguments are by themselves no proofs of unconscious sensory qualities.[25]

In response to this point, I agree that the reasoning that disarms the arguments considered in the previous section does not establish the qualitative event realist's claim that phenomenal qualities occur only in conscious events. That task is the job of the whole argument so far and that which is yet to come. I do not claim that there is any *short* argument that will establish such an important conclusion, but such an argument cannot be fairly demanded. It is, in the meantime, appropriate and necessary to show how attempts to close the door on this central claim of QER can be turned aside.

I have, however, not yet faced the most formidable attempt of this kind. That attempt will be taken up immediately in the next chapter. For the present, progress with respect to HOT theory can be described as follows. Possibilities for replying to the stone objection have been examined, and a severe dilemma for HOT theories has been described. Arguments have been given that narrow the possibilities for a successful version of HOT theory. The success of HOT theory has been shown to depend on its ability to sustain the view that phenomenal qualities can occur in unconscious states, and to explain how the addition of such unconscious states to thoughts about them can provide consciousness, when the thoughts alone cannot do so. I take it that the burden is on HOT theory to show how it can do these things. That burden will increase when the most persuasive reason to accept unconscious phenomenal qualities is shown to be a failure.

---

25 Something close to this argument occurs in Rosenthal (1991), and versions of it have been put to me in conversation by several other philosophers. So, it is necessary to comment on it. However, no one has put forward this argument in the context of the whole discussion of this book so far. Thus, it would be unfair to represent anyone as having offered the argument at the present stage of our dialectic.

7

Monitoring

Some higher order theories model their higher order representations on perception rather than thought. For these theories, the relation between higher order and lower order states is naturally described by the equivalent terms "monitoring" and "scanning". Theories of this kind have some distinctive features, but share with HOT theories both a two-layered structure and a corresponding interest in sensory representations that are not conscious just by themselves.

ARMSTRONG'S DRIVERS

Armstrong (1968) mentions a case that is frequently referred to in discussions of consciousness.

This is something that can happen when one is driving very long distances in monotonous conditions. One can 'come to' at some point and realize that one has driven many miles without consciousness of the driving, or, perhaps, anything else. One has kept the car on the road, changed gears, even, or used the brake, but all in a state of 'automatism'. (Armstrong, 1968, p. 93)

I shall refer to the part of such cases before one has "come to" as "autopilot cases" or as "being on autopilot". These terms are intended as handy mnemonic labels and are stipulated to lack any theoretical content.

It would be very contentious to suppose that people on autopilot are not conscious of anything at all. I will, however, not be concerned with thoughts or perceptions that are extraneous to the driving. It will be interesting enough, and difficult enough, to consider just the perceptions of the road. It is clear that in autopilot cases, as Armstrong says, "one must *in some sense* have been perceiving, and acting purposively. Otherwise the car would have ended in a ditch" (Armstrong, 1968, pp. 93–94; emphasis in the original). This plain fact licenses the question of whether the perception that enabled the driver to keep the car out of the ditch was conscious or not. Armstrong has a clear and unambiguous answer: such perceptions are not conscious. Many philosophers have accepted this answer and, indeed, apparently believe that Armstrong's answer is compellingly obvious.

Armstrong's conclusion leads naturally to another question, namely, what is the difference between an unconscious perception and a conscious one? Armstrong's answer is that "consciousness is no more than *awareness* (perception) of inner mental states by the person whose states they are" (Armstrong, 1968, p. 94; emphasis in the original). Armstrong is quite clear that this awareness of inner mental states is perception in the same sense that an unperceived inner state is a perception of outer situations: "In perception the brain scans the environment. In awareness of the perception another process in the brain scans that scanning" (Armstrong, 1968, p. 94).

Leaving aside cases in particle physics that introduce quantum-mechanical considerations, we may say that scanning does not change its object. Ordinary scanning merely reveals to the scanner what is already in the scanned items and makes information about what is in the scanned items available for use by the scanner or, perhaps, its user. Thus, in Armstrong's model, it would seem that color is already present in un-conscious perception – for all that awareness of unconscious perception does is to make available to us information about what is already in it.

Despite the anecdotal character of the evidence, it is very widely accepted that Armstrong's description points to *some* sort of peculiarity that is apt to occur on long-distance drives; that is, in our stipulatively neutral terminology, it is widely accepted that *there are* autopilot cases. Armstrong's account is at least a plausible suggestion about what these cases are and how they differ from nonautopilot cases. If his account is the only, or the best, account of such cases, then the claim of QER that there are some properties that can occur only in consciousness is jeopardized. I shall therefore ask whether alternative accounts are possible and, if so, how well they explain autopilot cases. In this section, I shall introduce and clarify three hypotheses concerning autopilot cases and consider their relationships. The following sections will focus on evaluation of these hypotheses.

Armstrong's view has two parts: (a) perceptions had while on autopilot are unconscious and (b) what makes a perception conscious (when it is) is the scanning of an unconscious perception (i.e., the scanning of a perception that is *in itself* unconscious, i.e., that would have been an unconscious perception if it had happened not to have been scanned). It is possible to hold (a) but deny (b). If one denies (b), one is obliged to explain how an alternative is possible. This can be done by appealing to intensity. Intensity, in turn, could be a matter of the number of neurons involved in the perceptual results of retinal inputs from the road or it could be a matter of the frequency of neural firings. For example, perhaps perception depends on ratios of firings of certain neurons, but the same ratios could obtain at low rates of firing or at higher rates. In this case, it might be proposed that a low-rate instantiation of certain ratios would be an unconscious perception, and the same ratios instantiated at higher rates would be a conscious perception. As these higher rates could be firing rates of the very same neurons that are involved in low-rate cases, there would seem to be no way of applying the idea of scanning to this model. The same holds if we look at the number of neurons involved. The cases with the greater number might include the same neurons that would have been involved if the number had been smaller; and the activity of the "extra" neurons might be caused by retinal inputs and factors affecting thresholds, and not by the activity of the smaller set that would have been firing in the low-number case. On these assumptions, again, there would be no reason to speak of scanning. Thus, on either way of understanding intensity, appeal to it offers a possible account that is genuinely different from Armstrong's, even though it accepts (a).

A different kind of alternative to Armstrong's view rejects (a). Rejecting (a) means holding that, after all, drivers are conscious of the road in autopilot cases. This proposal leads naturally to the question of why it seems that one was not conscious of the road, and the answer that suggests itself is that the perceptions of the road, although conscious, were not stored in memory. Now, there are many cases in which we do not remember what we must have perceived that do not suggest to us that we perceived unconsciously; so there must be some special feature of autopilot cases besides simply not remembering what we perceived. On Armstrong's view, this special feature can be the fact that the perceptions were unconscious to begin with. Rejecting that assumption, however, still leaves available a further feature that could make autopilot cases seem special – namely, that we think we ought to remember seeing the road, because it was recent, and tracking road conditions is important for our safety. These facts make it surprising that we fail to remember seeing the road conditions, whereas we are not surprised that we don't remember seeing our toast at some long-past breakfast.

Before proceeding, let us introduce labels for the competing hypotheses we have to consider.

(H1) (a) Autopilot cases are cases in which there is unconscious perception.

(b) Conscious perception occurs when there is a representation (a scanning or monitoring) of an event that would be an unconscious perception if it occurred just by itself (i.e., if it occurred unscanned).

(H2) (a) Autopilot cases are cases in which there is unconscious perception.

(b) Conscious perception requires processes to occur that are additional to what is required for unconscious perception, but these additional processes are not representations (scannings, monitorings) of what occurs in (the corresponding) unconscious perceptions.

(H3) (a) The perceptions that keep us out of the ditch in autopilot cases are conscious perceptions.

(b) In autopilot cases, asking ourselves whether we remember the passing of roadway scenes returns a (largely) negative result. In nonautopilot cases, the same kind of self-cueing for memory of the recent past returns positive results.[1]

It might be argued that (H3) is not clearly different from (H1) on the ground that (episodic) memories are representations of remembered events, and so a remembered event is a represented event. Having got this far, one might think that (H3) makes the difference between autopilot cases and nonautopilot cases to be a matter of memory, i.e., of representation; and if this is right, then perhaps the difference between (H1) and (H3) is merely a verbal difference, i.e., a difference in whether to call an irretrievable episode "unconscious" or merely "conscious but irretrievable". The impression of mere verbal difference can, perhaps, be increased by imagining memory being moved closer and closer in time to the remembered event, until we are remembering what happened only moments ago.

A large part of the answer to this worry can be given by making the point that, while the time between an event and the memory of it can be small, it cannot be zero. There are empirical questions that can arise here, and they will be addressed later. For now, I want to emphasize that (H1) demands a *contemporaneous* representing for consciousness to occur, and uses the distinction between contemporaneous representing and lack of contemporaneous representing in its explanation of the

---

1 I state (H3) in this circumspect way because (so far as I know) there is little evidence concerning what memories other kinds of cueing might produce. Such evidence as I am aware of will be discussed later.

difference between nonautopilot and autopilot cases. (H3) does not base the nonautopilot/autopilot difference in the presence or absence of contemporaneous representing; rather, it bases the difference in a difference of retrievability (in the self-cueing condition). We should bear in mind that irretrievability might be due to absence of any memory trace ever having been made, or it might be due to certain conditions that prevent the accessing of an existing trace.

This last observation may lead to a further doubt as to whether (H1) and (H3) are more than verbally distinct. If it is possible to remember an event, then a process that is at least partly contemporaneous with that event must create a trace that enables later memory retrieval. But memory traces are representations of the events for which they enable memory retrieval. So perhaps, after all, even (H3) (or, at least, the "never any trace" version of it) will have to divide nonautopilot cases from autopilot cases on the basis of whether or not there is a contemporaneous representation.

To allay this doubt, it is necessary to make a distinction between a passive representation, or trace, and an active representation. The point of this distinction can be introduced by explaining the somewhat oxymoronic, but evident, claim that there are many events I remember now that I am not now remembering. Actually remembering some event requires having an active representation of it. At such a time, there are many events that I could actually remember, and would actually remember if probed in certain ways, but that are not now actually in mind. When I do remember them, there is no miracle necessary; that is, I am able (actively) to remember them because my brain is (all along) arranged in certain ways that, with appropriate triggers, will lead to an active memory. There are representations in my brain of events that I *can* actually remember but am not now actually remembering; for clarity, let us call these "passive representations" or "traces".[2]

Applying this distinction, we can say that (H1) holds that consciousness occurs through contemporaneous active representation of what would otherwise be unconscious representations (of, e.g., conditions in the roadway), while (H3) does not require any such double representation for consciousness to occur. (H1) divides nonautopilot cases from autopilot cases by whether or not (first level) perceptions are accompanied by active representations. (H3) divides nonautopilot cases from autopilot cases

---

2 Those familiar with connectionism will likely think of the difference between representation in the sense of distributions of weights between units (= passive representation) and representation in the sense of a pattern of activity across units (= active representation).

according to whether or not perception (which it takes to be conscious in both cases) is accompanied by a process that leads to passive representations that can be retrieved (turned into active representations) by self-cueing. Since we need the active/passive distinction in any case, in order to give a nonmiraculous accounting of our ability to remember, this difference is a substantive difference, not a verbal one.

In discussing intensity, I have already explained how (H2) is distinct from (H1). The difference between (H2) and (H3) is less clear, because it could be that intensity is causally relevant to the occurrence of a process that eventuates in a self-cueable trace of an event. If there is such causal relevance, then there is a problem about classifying low intensity events, i.e., events that do not issue in self-cueable traces. Namely, it is not clear on what principle they should be classified as (i) conscious (although not retrievable by self-cueing) or (ii) unconscious (and not retrievable by self-cueing). It is, however, conceivable that all events of the same types as those that are able to lay down traces that enable self-cueable memories of perceptual events are of roughly equal intensity; that is, it might turn out empirically that there is no actual series of brain events that begins with clearly rememberable perceptions and proceeds through incremental differences of intensity alone. In that case, (H2) would be ruled out, while (H3) would not be; thus, the hypotheses are substantively different.

It is clear that (H2) is incompatible with HO theories of consciousness, i.e., (H2) does not make the conscious status of perception a matter of that perception's being represented. But how does (H2) stand with respect to QER? QER holds that there is a way that color (for example) enters into perceptions that can occur only by the color's being the phenomenal quality of a conscious event. One could hold a version of (H2) that conflicts with this claim. That is, one could hold that even the unconscious, low-intensity perceptions of (H2) have colors entering into them in every way that any perception ever has colors entering into it. The formulation of (H2), however, leaves open an alternative version, according to which colors enter into high-intensity perceptions in a way that they do not enter into low-intensity perceptions. This version of (H2) would be compatible with QER (and still incompatible with HO representation theories). Since (H2) as stated does not entail either of the two versions just outlined, (H2) is *compatible with* QER, although it *does not entail* that view (or even the key claim that there is a way that color enters into perception that entails consciousness).

So far, I have merely been clarifying the relations among our hypotheses and the relations between them and QER. The next task is to try to decide among them. If my exposition has been successful, it will be apparent that all three hypotheses are coherent; thus, if we can separate them on their merits, that will have to be done by finding empirical evidence that weighs more heavily for or against one than the others. The following two sections examine what can be done along this line.

EMPIRICAL CONSIDERATIONS

The attractiveness of (H1) is based on the impressive phenomenon of apparently having no recoverable memory of mile upon mile of driving, but, as we have seen, this phenomenon is equally explainable on the other hypotheses. (H2) has not often been articulated, and I am unaware of any attempt to support it.[3] (H3) is somewhat more familiar, and Block (1995a, 1995b) seems to commit himself to the idea of conscious perceptions that are unmonitored, unattended, unnoticed, and not retrievable very long after their occurrence. He cites some preliminary results from a Nissan-funded study at MIT.

If you probe "unconscious" drivers, what you find is that they can always recall (accurately) the road, decisions, perception, and so on, for the prior 30–45 seconds, but farther back than that it's all a blank. (Block, 1995b, p, 280)

Block goes on to comment that "This seems a clear case of experience as genuine as any but quickly forgotten, a moving window of memory" (Block, 1995b, p. 280).

Supposing these preliminary results prove to hold up in attempts at replication, let us ask what they would show.[4] One line of attack on their significance is a triggering scenario: the probe might trigger an (active) memory of something that was unconscious at the time it was

---

3 Hill (1991, pp. 118–126) discusses "volume adjustment" and its relation to attention, Armstrong's scanning, and the question of whether introspection changes its object. Hill's context and the questions he addresses are, however, rather different from those in our text. It is, for example, not at all clear that difference of volume is intended by Hill to correspond to the difference between conscious and unconscious perception.

4 The discussion to follow will be a logical one in which we discuss the significance of the preliminary results noted by Block. Since we have little evidence, we should try to accept views that are compatible with what evidence we have. But the views to be considered are merely *compatible* with the preliminary results and do not entail them. In particular, they do not entail that there is a mechanism that creates traces that are preserved and accessible only during a 30–45-second window. Thus, whether or not further studies support the existence of such a mechanism, the main conclusions that will be drawn about the relation of autopilot cases to questions about unconscious perception and monitoring views will stand.

experienced and that was stored in a trace that either fades or becomes irretrievable even by external probe after 30 to 45 seconds.[5] ("External probe" here means any form of cueing other than asking oneself, after coming to, what one remembers.) If this scenario is possible, the study's results would not support the view that autopilot cases involve continual conscious experiences that become irretrievable after 30–45 seconds. But the triggering scenario is visibly noncontradictory, and so the Nissan results offer no positive support for continual conscious perceiving in autopilot cases. I note, however, that the clear possibility of the triggering scenario is no proof of its actuality; so the failure of support for the continual conscious perception supposed by (H3) does not provide any positive support for (H1). Thus, the proper conclusion is that the Nissan results, by themselves, would offer no evidence one way or the other on the choice between (H1) and (H3).

Nor would they offer any evidence on the question of whether consciousness consists in monitoring a perceptual state. For *all* of the following accounts are compatible with those results. (i) Consciousness does not consist in monitoring a perceptual state. Drivers in autopilot cases are continually conscious, but traces of their conscious states either degrade or become inaccessible (even to external probes) after 30–45 seconds. (ii) Consciousness consists in monitoring a perceptual state. Drivers in autopilot cases continually monitor their perceptual states, but traces of the resulting conscious states degrade or become inaccessible even to external probes after 30–45 seconds. (iii) Consciousness consists in monitoring a perceptual state. Drivers in autopilot cases do not continually monitor their perceptions of road conditions; they have only unconscious perceptions, but (as in the triggering scenario) those perceptions cause traces that can be accessed by external probes for 30–45 seconds. The result of external probing during that time is the "developing" of the trace into an active memory that is indistinguishable from an active memory of a conscious perception. (iv) Consciousness does not consist in monitoring a perceptual state. But drivers in autopilot cases are often not consciously perceiving the road conditions, because the activations in secondary visual areas that result from their retinal inputs are (as (H2) hypothesizes) of low intensity. This low-intensity activity causes traces that can be accessed by external probes for 30–45 seconds, with the same result as in case (iii).

---

5 Lycan (1996, p. 178) has offered this scenario in criticism of Block's interpretation of the Nissan evidence.

It might be thought that the first two cases can be ruled out on the ground that traces, or access to traces by external probe, could not have the required 30–45-second brevity if they were effects of conscious events. This view, however, is contradicted by experimental evidence. Muter (1980) presented sets of three consonants (trigrams) for 1 second to subjects who were instructed to report the last three letters they had seen whenever prompted by "LETTERS", and who were told that this would be an infrequent (2%) occurrence if they had seen numbers after the trigrams. Numbers were to initiate the task of counting backward by threes. Letters from the trigrams were reported 95% correctly on trials where the prompt occurred immediately after the trigram; this figure was reduced to less than 35% after just 4 seconds of distractor task (with the number displayed for 1 second).[6] Simons and Levin (1997) found that a substitution of one stranger for another who had asked directions, when a door was carried between naive subjects and the inquiring stranger, was not noticed by subjects about 50% of the time. Wolfe (1999) found that attentional (and thus overwhelmingly plausibly conscious) processing of a display letter (necessary to establish absence of match to a target) conferred no advantage on time to identify a match to the next target (presented 50 milliseconds after the response to the previous target), even though the display remained continuously visible. Rensink et al. (1997) have shown that large parts of plainly and consciously visible scenes can be grossly changed or removed after flicker interruptions without subjects' noticing the change. These results all involve distractors that can act as masks, and thus are not fully comparable to the long distance driving situation, in which one scene is only gradually replaced by another. However, they establish that fully conscious perception can, under some conditions, be forgotten with extraordinary rapidity. We thus cannot rule out that fully conscious perceptions of the roadway while driving are simply forgotten (due either to degradation of trace or loss of accessibility to it), even within a 30–45-second time frame. Indeed, such a possibility is supported by experiments showing that gradual changes in a scene often fail to be noticed when they take place slowly, even when subjects are actively trying to detect them.[7]

I am unaware of any other kind of experimental work that might support a choice among the views that were sketched two paragraphs ago. Before turning to indirect considerations, however, I would like to make

6 Numbers are approximate because they are taken from a presentation in graphic form.
7 See, e.g., Simons et al. (2000).

two points that are based on my own experience. Because these are anecdotal observations, I do not wish to make too much of them. On the other hand, they are observations that readers can test against their own experience. This puts them in the same probative position as the observations that have been taken to support the monitoring view of consciousness. To appreciate this point, note that the impressive phenomenon of realizing that we can remember little about all those miles of driving is nothing other than an observation we each make for our own case and find that others agree in making about themselves. If readers find that their impression of their own experience agrees with what I am about to say, they will have as much reason to accept those impressions as they do to accept the existence of autopilot cases.

The first observation requires a bit of driving. The next time you have to drive on an uncongested stretch of interstate highway for a half hour or so, think of the problems we are discussing here and set yourself to notice your perceiving of the road conditions. Attend to the fact that you are perceiving the road; if you prefer the monitoring view, tell yourself that you must not only keep your car on the road, but also monitor the perceptions you have while doing so. At the end of the drive, ask yourself how much of it you remember.

I have tried this informal experiment, with the following results. (i) It is difficult to stay on task. One's mind wanders; one recalls what has been said about autopilot cases and gets to thinking about the merits or demerits of various views. One speculates on the significance of imagined outcomes. (ii) Nonetheless, it is completely compelling, both during and after the drive, that there were *many* occasions on which one was attentively, consciously seeing the roadway and the traffic. (iii) At the end of the drive, one has no more sense of "connection" with most of the experiences during the drive than one does in long drives where one has not been thinking of any philosophical problems whatsoever. One has the same sense of surprise about how one could have been through all that, and yet have so little sense of having been through it, that one does in standard autopilot cases. (iv) In a few cases, there will have been something interesting in the scene or something that triggered a significant memory. Those events will be remembered.

These informal observations are consistent with the previously cited experimental results that support rapid forgetting of consciously perceived material, and they concern a condition that is very similar to the standard autopilot cases. They offer some support for the proposition that conscious perceptions in autopilot case conditions can be quickly forgotten. Suppose we accept this conclusion: what follows? It does *not*, of course, follow that consciousness is not monitoring. Maybe consciousness is monitoring and, under certain conditions, we can forget monitored perceptions just as fast as unmonitored ones. What *does* follow, however, is this: *autopilot cases provide no reason in favor of a monitoring view of consciousness.* If it is clear that conscious perception can be forgotten quickly, then the fact that we are soon unable to remember perceptions while driving is simply no reason one way or the other for thinking that they are conscious or unconscious.

The second experiential observation I want to make is that the frequently used phrase "come to" is misleading. If traffic becomes congested, one may become more attentive to the roadway, and it is on such occasions that one may have the somewhat disconcerting thought that one has been on autopilot for a while. This is not at all like being suddenly awakened. There is no sense of discontinuity between one's previous condition and one's present perception of, say, the unusually slow car just ahead. The only things that are sudden in the situation are (a) the realization that the car ahead presents a problem that requires immediate reaction and (b) the coming on of the sense of disconnection with all those past miles.

Monitoring could, perhaps, come in degrees, and if so, a monitoring view of consciousness could grant that what I have just said accurately describes our experience. But, if that accuracy is granted, then, once again, autopilot cases provide no reason in favor of a monitoring view of consciousness.

These reflections lead me to despair of giving any direct argument that will separate our hypotheses. But there are other phenomena that bear on the question of unconscious perception, and the best hypothesis would be one that fits best with all the relevant cases. We should thus turn to some of these other cases to see whether they can lead us to more definite conclusions.

QUADRANGLE BELLS AND OTHER PUZZLING CASES

The first of these related cases is the quadrangle bell phenomenon. It can happen that while absorbed in reading or calculating, one fails to notice the striking of the hour until three or four bells have sounded. Upon realizing that the hour is striking, one can have an impression of how many bells have already gone by or, more accurately, one can have an impression that the bell one has first noticed is, say, number five. One can test the accuracy of this impression by counting the rest of the series and checking the result against one's watch. Impressions so checked usually turn out to be correct. This means that some part of one's brain was either counting the bells or forming traces that allow counting, even though one was completely absorbed in one's work and, as we would say, was not aware of them. If one counted the bells accurately or formed accurate traces of them, one must in some sense have heard them, and this fact leads to the question of whether this hearing was conscious or not.

A difference between this case and the autopilot case is that the early bells are quite recent – well within the putative 30–45-second window. It thus seems that if they were consciously heard, we ought to remember them as such – whereas, in fact, we have only an impression of the number of the first-noticed bell, without any (episodic) recollection of the first four. This reflection, therefore, seems to support the unconscious perception view, (H1). Before affirming that view, however, we should notice another difference between the cases. In driving, one may be lost in one's own thoughts, or conversing with a passenger, or listening to music or audiotaped stories. These activities, however, do not require the same depth of concentration that is required by the activities that form the background of the bell cases. In the latter cases, one must be thoroughly absorbed in one's task; and, of course, one is free to be thus thoroughly absorbed, because one is not at any level doing anything analogous to tracking the road conditions. Thus, it is possible that one had conscious perceptions of the first few bells, but that one's absorption caused a strong suppression of memory-forming mechanisms for the auditory contents of those perceptions, leaving only traces that permitted simultaneous or immediately subsequent counting. Because of this offsetting difference, we cannot draw any conclusions from the bell case that will enable us to separate (H1) and (H3).

Nor can we rule out (H2). On this hypothesis, when we are absorbed, some sensory area never reaches an intensity that is required for conscious hearing. Low-intensity processes can, however, have effects, and one of these might be sufficient to allow a counting mechanism to operate reliably and to deliver its state to consciousness when we finally notice the striking of the hour. One would not be committed by this account to supposing that conscious hearing is a monitoring of the same low-intensity process that occurs during unconscious hearing, for conscious hearing could, instead, be a more intense version of the same kind of process that occurs when the bells are only counted but not consciously perceived.

Faced with this inconclusive result, we may be moved to turn elsewhere and, in particular, we might suppose that we will find some help in experimental psychological studies. Shiffrin (1997, p. 51) remarks on the fact that there are "numerous" demonstrations that stimuli about which subjects can report neither their type nor even their occurrence can produce measurable effects.[8] Such cases have the advantage of providing clear examples of unconscious perception. Unfortunately, however, they do not provide anything with which to *separate* our hypotheses. That is because all of the hypotheses are compatible with there being detectable effects of unconscious perceptions. This point seems obvious for (H1) and (H2). Regarding (H3), it may be helpful to remark that it is not the claim that there cannot be any cases of inputs that have effects without being conscious. A background issue of our discussion is whether there can be phenomenal qualities without consciousness. (H3) allows phenomenal qualities to occur during autopilot cases and merely insists that consciousness is found there too. As to whether there can also be cases where there is neither phenomenal quality nor consciousness, it is silent; and thus it allows for that possibility in cases of masked brief exposure with measurable priming.

It would be difficult to maintain (H3) in the face of such priming cases if there were no principled reason for distinguishing between these cases and autopilot cases. But evidently there is such a reason. Priming experiments of the kind described can be done when subjects know that there may or may not be a stimulus in the presentation, have no other task when the stimulus is given, and can be presumed to be following an instruction to attend to the location where the stimulus is presented. Still, they cannot detect the stimulus or respond explicitly to its character. Drivers in autopilot cases *could* easily report on what they see, and have plenty of time for visual processing to proceed without interference. The stimulus conditions in the masked priming and autopilot cases could thus hardly be more divergent.

The point just made might be conceded, and yet it might be argued that the occurrence of measurable effects of unconscious perception in masked brief exposure cases is enough to show that phenomenal qualities occur in unconscious events, and is thus enough to undercut QER. Such an argument, however, must assume that the measurable effects require the presence of phenomenal qualities; and there is no reason to make this

8 Some of the cases that might be cited here are controversial. For example, Dark (1988) and Dark and Benson (1991) have shown that semantic priming is conditional on reportability and recognizability of primes. However, even if such priming results are discounted, there remain other cases of detectable effects, even under the stringent conditions Shiffrin states.

assumption. To make this last claim clear, let us remind ourselves that phenomenal colors do not enter the eye; what enters the eye are photons of various energy levels.[9] Similarly, the (partial) blindness resulting from occipital lobe scotomas shows that phenomenal color is not simply a result of occurrences in the retina alone. Again, spinal blocks show that nociceptor activity is not a sufficient condition of pain. The point of these reminders is to argue that phenomenal qualities depend on some process that is stretched out over several neural regions and thus over some time, however brief. Once this point is borne in mind, the possibility is clearly open that there can be measurable effects of very early events in the process – that is, measurable effects of events that come earlier in the processing than any sufficient condition for phenomenal qualities. It is thus clearly open to qualitative event realists to hold that the results of masked, brief exposure experiments are due to events that are normally parts of sequences that lead to phenomenal qualitied conscious events but that, because of the special conditions, are not followed in these cases by any phenomenal qualities at all.

It may now be wondered why we cannot simply apply the argument of the preceding paragraph to the allegedly unconscious perceptions in autopilot cases. The answer is that, in autopilot cases, the exposures are not at all brief, and the gradual change of scene as one proceeds down the roadway does not plausibly act in the same way as masks in the experiments to which Shiffrin alludes. It would thus not be plausible to deny that phenomenal qualities occur in autopilot cases; and it is thus necessary for qualitative event realists to argue that there is no reason to suppose that consciousness is lacking in these cases.

The foregoing discussion may lead some to want to bring in the idea of "attention". There are many difficult issues that pertain to this concept, and I shall assume nothing about it except that (i) attention requires brain processes that occur subsequently to sensory input and (ii) attentional processes have limited capacity. This specification of the concept of attention clearly allows for the possibility of having perceptual receptions that do not undergo limited-capacity processing. These will be cases of perception without attention, and a natural suggestion is that what Armstrong's drivers lack is attention to their perceptions. However, if we invoke lack of attention, we must be very careful about how we describe what is unattended. (a) We might say that drivers in autopilot

9 Locke (1690) was already clear on this point – although, of course, his ocular entrants were not photons.

cases are not attending to *the road conditions*. We might still say that they see the road conditions, and even that they consciously see them. If they had attended to them, they would have been more likely to remember them, but as it was, they saw the road but did not attend to it, so they were able to use the steering wheel and the brake appropriately but have no recollection of what they saw. This description will seem natural for those who favor (H3). (b) We might begin the same way, i.e., we might say that drivers in autopilot cases are not attending to the road conditions. But we might continue by saying that although they saw the roadway, they did not consciously see it. They would have consciously seen it if they had attended to it; but, on the present alternative, their attending to *the roadway* would just have *consisted* in the fact that some effects of their retinal inputs were more intense. That extra intensity would have made recollection more likely; but as it is, they had enough processing to operate their vehicles properly, but only just enough. This would be a description that would come naturally to those who prefer (H2). (c) We might say that drivers on autopilot are not attending to *their perception* of the road conditions. They see the road conditions (although not consciously), but since they did not attend to their seeing, they do not remember seeing the road conditions. This description would seem natural to devotees of (H1).[10]

Before saying more about how to think of attentional mechanisms, let us notice that we are not entitled *simply* to identify consciousness with attention. One reason is already clear: descriptions (a) and (b) make distinctions using "attention" in a way that does not violate any clearly established constraints on that concept, yet neither of these descriptions makes attention a matter of HO representing, and neither makes attention the source of consciousness. (In the case of (b) the two do go together, but that is because both consist in the higher intensity of processing of the input from the roadway.) A second reason for not conflating attention and consciousness is that there seem to be cases in which we are clearly conscious of a (relatively inclusive) scene but attend to only part of it.[11]

---

10   Lycan describes his theory in just such terms. "An internal monitor is an attention mechanism, which presumably can be directed upon representational subsystems and stages of same" (1996, p. 32). "I hold that awareness is a product of attention mechanisms that are perceptionlike in some ways (though not in all)" (1996, p. 30). "Consciousness is the functioning of internal *attention mechanisms* directed at lower-order psychological states and events" (1996, p. 14; emphasis in the original).
11   Lycan (1996, pp. 16–17) himself holds that we can voluntarily shift our attention to various parts of the visual field.

Further, we need not lack visual consciousness if we are attending to an auditory task with our eyes open.[12]

The result of the discussion of attention thus far is, once again, disappointing: the supposition that autopilot cases involve lack of attention can be understood as compatible with all of the hypotheses that we are entertaining about these cases. However, there is another possibility concerning attention that we should now consider, namely, that there are at least two "levels" of attention. This idea is suggested by the rapid forgetting experiments cited earlier. In Wolfe's experiment, for example, display characters are attended sufficiently to be known to be nonidentical to a target but are then immediately forgotten. In the experiment of Simons and Levin, the first stranger is engaged in conversation with a subject, yet is often not realized by the subject to have been replaced. A natural suggestion here would be that a first level of attention is sufficient for conscious perception, but a further level of attention, or a further amount of processing, is required if rapid forgetting is to be avoided. If one makes such a distinction, then one could plausibly suppose that autopilot cases include a first level of attention, and thus conscious perception, but not the second level of attentional processing that would be required to enable subsequent conscious memories. It would, of course, not follow that either level of processing is a scanning or monitoring of an earlier perceptual state.

Controversies in the experimental psychology of attention make it difficult to use this term in a way that is both precise and likely to be generally accepted. However, it is not necessary to use this term in discussing the results of the rapid forgetting experiments, and it seems that these experiments do support the view that conscious perceptions can be quickly forgotten.[13] To review, they do so by offering presentations that are clearly supraliminal (so that they clearly *can* be consciously perceived) and that, in some cases, must have been processed sufficiently to influence a reported decision, yet become inaccessible in a very short (less than

---

12 As Shiffrin (1997, p. 52) points out.
13 Kihlstrom (1999) is cited by Wolfe (1999) as disagreeing. However, (a) most of Kihlstrom's discussion is concerned with *cognitive* representations, not perception. And (b), in his section on implicit *perception*, Kihlstrom considers masked brief presentations, blindsight, implicit memory for presentations to patients under general anesthesia, hypnotic analgesia, and functionally blind "hysterical" patients. Each of these cases presents special obstacles to perception that are not present in Wolfe's experiment or the other rapid forgetting work I have cited. I have already noted that (H3), which is a hypothesis about autopilot cases, is fully compatible with measurable effects of unconscious perception in masked priming experiments.

122

1 second) time frame. This conclusion strongly suggests, although it does not conclusively prove, that (H3) ought to be accepted as our best account of autopilot cases. If this is allowed, then we have removed the threat to QER that arose from the monitoring theory, namely, the possibility of unconscious phenomenal qualities. There is, however, a possible source of future evidence that has not yet been considered, and to this I shall now turn.

FUTURE EMPIRICAL SUPPORT FOR MONITORS?

Monitoring theories require a certain structure; there must be internal mechanisms that monitor internal states that are closely dependent on sensory inputs.[14] Since existing empirical support for any of our hypotheses is thin, we are obligated to try to follow out the possibility of future evidence in support of the required structure. Monitoring theorists generally do not describe the internal mechanisms of monitoring in much detail. It will, nonetheless, prove valuable to try to see what a scanning, or monitoring, theory would have to look like from a neural point of view.

Let us assume that S_0 is a neural state or event that is a perception of an external object of some kind, K.[15] This assumption will require that (i) in normal circumstances, S_0 occurs only when its possessor, s, is confronted in normal conditions with K objects. s is allowed to have hallucinations or illusions when drugged, subjected to poor lighting, and so forth; but *normally*, the relationship in (i) holds. Likewise, there may be unusual obstacles that prevent s from perceiving normally; but (ii) normally, S_0 will occur whenever a K object is in an appropriate relation to s's senses. Implicit in (i) and (ii) is that K objects in appropriate relation to s's senses initiate a causal chain that, in normal conditions, leads to S_0. (iii) S_0 is a state that can contribute to s's behavior in a way that enables that behavior to be appropriate to K objects.[16]

---

14 See, e.g., Lycan: "the inner sense theory as I have formulated it makes at least one brutally empirical commitment: to the actual existence of internal attention mechanisms in our brains" (1996, p. 16).

15 In adopting this way of stating the case, I am not assenting to an identity theory. If we suppose an ordinary case of perception (as contrasted with implicit perception as might occur, e.g., in a masked brief presentation), then QER implies that there will be consciousness that is *caused by* some aspect of brain events. But to put matters this way would distort monitoring theory. In this section, I am looking at things from the general point of view of monitoring theory in order to raise questions from within the perspective of that theory.

16 Explaining what exactly this appropriateness consists in is a very large task. I leave it open how much of s's history has to be invoked in order to unpack (iii); see Millikan (1984) or

I shall return shortly to a question about how states near the input end of our cognitive processes contribute to behavior. For now, I continue to sketch monitoring from a neural point of view. It is reasonable to say that the brain area, or "module", in which S_0 occurs (along with other states that bear similar relations to other kinds of things) is a scanner *of the environment*. A monitoring theory adds a scanner *of* S_0. This addition requires a new brain area or module that has a state S_1 that stands to S_0 in much the way that the latter stands to K objects. Thus, (i') normally, S_1 occurs only when s is having a state S_0 in a certain brain area (other than the one in which S_1 occurs). Following (H1), we want to allow for unconscious perception in autopilot cases. It is not clear that these are abnormal cases, so we cannot have an exact analogue of (ii). But perhaps there is some reasonably well-behaved condition set, C, such that (ii') normally, S_1 will occur whenever s has S_0 while C is satisfied. (The point of introducing the set C is that it can fail to be satisfied without conditions being abnormal; and thus, autopilot cases can be handled, in accordance with (H1), as cases of normal conditions that fail to satisfy C. A candidate for C might be a condition in which the monitoring region is "turned on" or "turned toward" the region in which S_0 occurs.) Implicit in (i') and (ii') is that, when C is satisfied and conditions are otherwise normal, S_0 states initiate a causal chain that leads to S_1. (iii') S_1 is a state that can contribute to s's behavior in a way that enables behavior to be appropriate to occurrences of S_0. (Roughly, (iii') says that the scanning state leads to behavior that is appropriate to perception of K objects.)

Satisfying (i') through (iii') makes S_1 a monitor of S_0. Evidently, it is an empirical matter whether there are neural states that satisfy the requirements for being monitoring states, subject to the caveat that it could turn out that attempts to specify C in a noncircular way would encounter insurmountable difficulties. What must now be clarified, however, is the relation between the monitoring of S_0 and S_0's contributing to behavior.

A state can contribute to behavior if it permits a computation that is useful and that, in turn, actually affects behavior. Let us unpack this statement by reference to an example taken from Gallistel (1990). Let us suppose there is some portion of an animal's brain, $R1$, states of which track amounts of food that have been observed to have been distributed.

Dretske (1988, 1995) for discussion of this issue and Robinson (1988) for a quite different approach. If (iii) *cannot* be satisfactorily clarified, then the project of naturalizing the mind is in deep trouble. Here, I merely assume that (iii) can be satisfactorily explained in order to exhibit key questions that still come up regarding a monitoring theory of consciousness.

Call one of these state types "S_f". (We are to imagine that food arrives over a period of time and that some of it is eaten or moves out of sight quickly. Thus, S_f is not a sensory input, but a representation that already rests on accumulation of information from several sensory inputs.) It may be that a successful strategy for this animal depends not on absolute amounts of food observed, but on the *rate* at which it becomes available. If the animal can perform according to that strategy (and ducks, for example, can do so), it must have another region, $R2$, states of which (e.g., S_t) track elapsed time. Moreover, it must be able to derive a state that tracks rate. Here is one way in which that could happen. The brain regions in which S_f and S_t occur are neurally connected to a third brain region, $R3$, in which states occur that depend on both S_f and S_t; and, because of the topology of the connectivity and the synaptic weights, a state in $R3$, say, S_r, tracks a rate at which the observed food becomes available. If S_r enters into similar connections with states in further brain areas, and these latter states enter into further such connections, behavior may result that is sensitive to rate.[17] In this case, we should count S_r as having contributed to behavior; and since S_f was necessary to produce S_r, we should likewise say that it has contributed to behavior. We can reiterate the reasoning and say that each of the several sensory inputs that contributed to bringing about S_f also contributed to behavior.

The point to be drawn from this discussion is that in the case described, S_f contributes to behavior without being monitored. In particular, S_r does not monitor S_f. This is easily seen from the fact that S_r violates condition (i'). It does so because it tracks rate; thus, it will occur, and occur normally, in cases when food is being distributed at the same rate, but in absolute amounts *not* represented by S_f. Likewise, S_f does not monitor the sensory inputs that contribute to it, since it may be brought about, and be brought about in a normal way, by many different sets of possible observations of variably sized clumps of food, from a variety of angles and distances

---

17 I am not assuming that there is anything necessary about any of these states affecting behavior. There can always be interactions with effects of other inputs or preexisting states that cause inhibitory neurons to fire and prevent a potentially useful representation from actually having any effect on behavior. Of course, evolutionary considerations imply that there would not likely be many potentially useful representations for which there were not sets of conditions that could be reasonably counted as normal, and under which they would usually have actual effects on behavior, in cases where there were no representations that meet the same conditions but tend to lead to incompatible behavior. (For example, sighting prey when hungry should usually lead to pursuit, but not if one has recently seen a danger to which pursuit might increase one's proximity.)

of view.[18] The generalization to be drawn from these examples is that monitoring is not necessary for our perceptions to make a behavioral contribution.

Evolutionary considerations suggest a stronger result, namely, that it is unlikely that we will find monitors, because these amount to uselessly redundant representations. Redundancy can, of course, be useful in systems whose components are prone to failure; but the useful kind of redundancy is parallel redundancy. Parallel redundancy is what we would have if we had more than one *first-level* state that represented the same thing; if one such state failed, another might still permit processing leading to a useful response. But the redundancy of monitors is serial redundancy. Whatever processing depends on the monitor depends on *two* states, i.e., the first order state and the monitoring state, and this arrangement merely increases the chances for failure.[19]

It may, however, be urged that monitors are likely to be found because they are required for introspection, and the ability of organisms to represent their own internal states can be useful. We should not deny the second premise of this argument, but the first would seem to be false. In brief, the reason is that introspection requires concepts, and concepts are not monitors. To make this brief statement cogent, however, I must clarify some assumptions about concepts that are implicit in it.

I take possession of a concept to be a certain kind of ability to be in a state that represents a thing or a kind of thing. A use of a concept is the actualization of such an ability, i.e., actually being in a state that represents. But there is a key constraint on the abilities that are possessions of concepts, namely, they can be normally actualized when the represented item is not perceptually present. Concept possession confers the ability to represent things when they are absent. So, for example, if Eve can *want* a red apple when she is not seeing one, she must have the concepts "red" and "apple", and she must be able to use these concepts when she is not perceiving a red apple. (Eve can want *what is being offered* without having the concepts "red" or "apple", where what is being offered happens to be a red apple,

---

18 A special case to which this reasoning applies is the suggestion that monitors might prove useful by abstracting particular features. For example, there might be states that represent (just) the intensity of pains. If there are such states, however, they are not monitors of pains, since they would fail to covary with any of the differences among pains except intensity. Their claim to be analogous to *perceptions* would be undercut, as would the view that being thus represented would be that in virtue of which a pain is a conscious pain.

19 For those old enough to remember, the old-style serial strings of Christmas tree lights provide a compelling illustration of the point being made here.

but in that case "red" and "apple" do not enter into the description of the content of her desire, but only into the description of the object of it.) Of course, *one* (normal) use of (a certain class of) concepts is to classify things that are perceptually present; but, on the understanding of "concept" presupposed here, this cannot be the only case in which a concept possessor can make normal use of a concept.

Subjects who have the thought "I am seeing a K" are introspecting, and are using the concepts "seeing" and "K". Such thoughts will provide whatever survival advantages might be thought to accrue from having concurrent representations of our internal states.[20] But because concepts must be able to have normal uses in the absence of perceptual presentations of what they are concepts of, the states that are uses of concepts are not monitoring states; that is, uses of concepts violate condition (i'). Thus, once again, the supposed advantage of introducing monitoring states is obtainable without them, and it is hard to see why there should be redundant monitoring states at all.

It may be suggested that the thought "I am seeing a K" is itself the monitoring state since, in normal conditions, this thought would occur only if the subject were seeing a K. One might add that, provided the condition set C is satisfied, this thought would occur whenever its possessor was seeing a K. This suggestion, however, misses the point that a tokening of the thought "I am seeing a K" involves the tokening of the concept, K, i.e., an event of the same kind that can occur in the absence of K objects. Thus, even if I think I am seeing K objects on exactly those occasions on which I am, that thought is not a state of a system that qualifies as a monitoring system, and that state is not a monitoring state. It may also be noted that a conflation of monitoring and introspection would reduce monitoring theory to the HOT view. Such a reduction would both violate the point of analogizing monitoring to *perception* and expose the view to the criticisms of HOT theories that were advanced in the previous chapter.

I have been giving reasons, though not conclusive ones, for doubting that there are monitoring states. I am, however, not reneging on my agreement that it is an empirical matter whether such states will be found.

---

20 Memory traces will also be useful, of course, as will use of them to cause images at a later time. I take it as evident that memory traces are not monitor states. (a) Monitor states would have to be active representations (see the earlier discussion of active/passive memory). (b) If having memory traces were counted as having monitoring states, then the difference between monitoring theory and (H3) would collapse, contrary to the evident intent of monitoring theorists.

If neural investigation fails to find them, then of course, a monitoring theory of consciousness must be false. But even if neural investigation does find them, that would not count as empirical support for a monitoring theory of consciousness. (a) Some theories of consciousness – we may call them "teleological theories" – require that conscious states *do* something that unconscious states do not do, but we have seen reasons to doubt that monitoring is needed for anything. We cannot, of course, rule out that neural investigation that found monitoring states might also find some useful function for which they are essential; but such a finding would be a large addition to merely finding monitoring states. (b) Even if we do not demand that consciousness has a function, we would still have no explanation of why the occurrence of a second state that very nearly duplicates the occurrence of an earlier perceptual state should have anything to do with consciousness. An empirical finding of monitoring states would not count as empirical support for the claim that monitoring states *explain* consciousness.

CONCLUSIONS ABOUT HIGHER ORDER THEORIES

One main conclusion of this chapter is that, contrary to popular belief among philosophers, we do not have good reason to believe that we have unconscious perceptions in autopilot cases. To the extent that acceptance of phenomenal qualities in unconscious states depends on such a belief, that acceptance is unwarranted. There is also reason for significant doubt about monitoring theories. Thus, again, to the extent that acceptance of phenomenal qualities in unconscious states depends on such theories, that acceptance is unwarranted.

In Chapter 6, I proposed a dilemma for HOT theories and argued that they could not escape from it unless they could explain why adding sensory representations to thoughts about sensory representations should result in consciousness. It is by no means clear that we would have such an explanation even if unconscious sensory states did have phenomenal qualities, but the suggestion that they might seemed to offer *some* help. In the meantime, however, several approaches to unconscious phenomenal qualities have been examined, and have been found not to warrant acceptance of such occurrences.

It will be pointed out that I have not demonstratively refuted the unconscious phenomenal quality theory, and nor have I demonstrated that there is not some other way in which HOT theories can escape from the proposed dilemma. These truths, however, cannot carry us very far.

Without an *actual* account of how unconscious sensory states may contribute to consciousness, when thoughts that have such states as intentional objects are insufficient for consciousness, HOT theories are seriously *incomplete*. It is not clear what their actual content amounts to. Faith in their future would thus be an empty faith that some unspecified way of completing the theory will be found. In view of this fact, HOT theories cannot be taken as support for materialism with respect to phenomenal consciousness.

8

Functionalism

I define a *functional property* as any property P such that

(F) *x* has P if and only if

    (1) there is at least one other individual (perhaps of specified kind(s)) with which
    (2) *x* stands in certain relation(s), and
    (3) the set of relations to individuals of the right kind(s) in which *x* stands meets some condition, **C**.[1]

C is allowed to be vacuous; in that case, P is just a relational property. For example, being a (full) sibling counts as a functional property because for a thing to be a sibling, there must be at least one other individual who is coparented by two further individuals. The point of speaking of functional properties is, however, best seen by considering less degenerate cases. For example, a thing, *x*, can be a *pump* only if there is a fluid and two places such that *x*'s activity causes the fluid to flow from one place to the other; and anything that causes such a flow is a pump.[2]

---

1   In symbolese, $Px \Leftrightarrow \exists y \ldots [x \neq y \ \& \ldots \& \ Gy \ldots \& \ \exists R \ldots (Rxy \ \& \ldots \& \ \mathbf{C}(R \ldots))]$.

2   I am suppressing the point that a pump could still rightly be called a pump if it were removed from its position in a system and laid on a shelf by itself. (In the case of a heart, the analogous claim is not so clear, having, perhaps, been denied by Aristotle.) One could recognize this point by defining "*x* has functional property P in system S" instead of "functional property" (where, however, generality would require allowing that S may be vacuous). Or one could make (F) modal, saying that Px iff there *can* be the required other items of various kinds in various relations, where a commentary on this modality would be required. I recognize that careful formulation of these ideas would be a nontrivial task, but I forgo it because such care would not change any of the arguments to come and would only obscure the focal points of the discussion.

A variety of functionalisms can be generated by making **C** nonvacuous in various ways. For example, we may require that the set of relations in (F) be such as to make *x* perform a *biological* function, where biological function is specified according to one or another theory of biological function. We get a different kind of variation in functional properties by selecting one specification of **C** and filling in the kinds and relations in (1) and (2) in different ways. We also get different functionalisms by giving different readings to the "if and only if" in (F). For example, it might be read as logical coentailment, or as indicating only causal necessity and sufficiency.

A "functionalist theory of mind", as understood here, is any theory according to which all mental properties are functional properties. This usage is wider than the standard one, because, as we shall see, it includes behaviorism, which is often regarded as a theory that has been superseded by functionalism. I adopt the present usage because I believe that there is an essential continuity between behaviorism and the views usually included under "functionalism", and that there is no uniquely preferable way of introducing a borderline into this continuity. Those who are not persuaded by the following analysis, however, can still make some use of (F) in defining their preferred notion of "functionalism", namely, by introducing constraints on the kinds, relations, or condition **C** on the right side of (F).

Because of the many possibilities for specifying functional properties, there can be many versions of functionalism; and because of this potential variety, there are limitations on what one can say about functionalism in general. There is, however, one key aspect that is common to differing functionalist views. In the remainder of this section, I identify this aspect and explain the structure of the discussion to follow.

The common aspect of functionalism follows from the fact that a functional property, P, is defined in terms of relations. Because of this fact, there is always the possibility that things of more than one intrinsic kind can stand in those relations and thus have the property P. To have a non-controversial illustration of this point, let us refer again to a pump. The functional specification of a pump is silent on many things, e.g., what materials it is made of, what size it is, what design (e.g., piston, rotary, diaphragm) it has, and how it came into existence. We could, of course, add specifications that would yield other predicates that would not be so open in all these ways; for example, by specifying that the flow must have low pressure variation, we might rule out the possibility of realization by piston designs. But the common idea of functionalism is that a function can be *realized* in various ways, i.e., that more than one kind of thing might stand in all the relations required to specify a functional property (even if, in fact, only one kind of thing does so).

A crude move toward naturalizing the mind might consist in specifying a relatively simple function and claiming that anything that satisfies (realizes, performs) that function has a certain mental property. Consider, for example, a proposal to the effect that x perceives Fs if it reliably acts appropriately to the presence of Fs. Such a proposal will surely be met with the objection that supermarket door openers reliably act appropriately to the presence of customers advancing toward the door, but, as far as we have any reason to think, they lack perceptual experience and they lack mentality.

One might improve the plausibility of the claim that a certain object is a perceiver by enriching the functional specification in various ways. Without pretending to give an exhaustive survey, let us consider some possible steps in this direction. (i) One might enrich the number of different reactions a device might have to various circumstances. For example, a second-generation door opener might respond not only to presence, but also to speed of approach, and might adjust the timing of the door-opening appropriately. (ii) One might enrich the number of levels of response. "Enrichment of levels" here means the addition of abilities that depend on other (lower level) abilities. For example, we might add to our door opener the ability to give a report ("Customer approaching!"), or to record the number of openings, or to record the number of openings and use the record to draw conclusions about the number of customers per day, the weekday that usually has the most customers, recommendations for inventory adjustment, and so on. (iii) One might increase the details of responses to be taken into account; for example, one might specify a small range of reaction times within which any of the identified responses must fall. (iv) One might enrich the specification of the mechanism required to come between the input and the output as specified in either (i), (ii), or (iii). One might do this at a relatively gross level in which, say, the number and connectivity of computational units are specified, but not the structure internal to those units. (v) One might enrich the specification of the input-output connecting mechanism at a finer level, for example, by imposing very narrow time intervals within which operations have to be completed. (vi) One might enrich specification of internal processing by requiring that it be done by a mechanism that will work only in the presence of certain chemicals, or that is interrupted in characteristic and differential ways by the administration of certain other chemicals.[3]

If we specify functions solely with materials indicated in (i) and (ii), we have species of behaviorism. If we add (iii) alone, we still have a form of behaviorism. However, studies of reaction times are often thought of as indirect ways of getting evidence about the structure and relations of brain mechanisms. If such mechanisms are found to be successively decomposable into smaller and smaller mechanisms, and if such decomposition is thought of as part of the way in which a function is to be specified, we have "homuncular functionalism". With (v) and (vi), we move past the relations of homunculi, or the jobs they perform, to facts that constrain the possible mechanisms by which they perform their jobs. This type of view may be called "microfunctionalism". The divisions among these views are evidently not sharp, and a bit of reflection on (i) through (vi) will make it obvious that they encompass a multitude of shades and degrees.

Despite the fact that behaviorism, homuncular functionalism, and microfunctionalism shade into one another, there are genuine tendencies and pressures to go toward one or another, and it will be useful to organize the following discussion by reference to these views. The focus will be on questions that arise for functionalism in regard to phenomenal consciousness. We shall see that as functionalist views are developed in a way that makes them most plausible, their divergence from the QER of this book (rhetoric aside) reduces to zero.

BEHAVIORISM

Many of the views considered in this book are of relatively recent vintage, and were formulated against the background of a widely accepted failure of behaviorism to give an adequate account of phenomenal consciousness. Briefly, if all one can talk about is pain behavior – e.g., groaning, favoring injured parts of the body, taking aspirin, complaining, and uttering "I am in pain" – one seems to be limited to talking about the concomitants of pain while leaving out the essential, awful thing *of* which they are concomitants. It is difficult to imagine how one might add anything to expose the inadequacy of behaviorism that cannot already be found in the mountain of literature on this subject.[4] In the nature of

---

3 This list is inspired by many sources, the most important of which is Dennett's "Why You Can't Make a Computer That Feels Pain" in Dennett (1978).
4 See, for an influential example, Putnam (1965) on super-Spartans.

the case, one can only ask readers to test accounts of phenomenal consciousness against their own experience. We have by now seen numerous ways of approaching a focus on the relevant aspect of one's experience, and if these efforts have not already succeeded in enabling readers to recognize the relevant aspect of their experience, there is little hope of success now.

Reflection on Turing's (1950) famous test, however, may provide one source of lingering resistance to dismissing behaviorism. If the possibility of machine mentality is not ruled out a priori, then something must count as a criterion for discovering its presence; and Turing's test has seemed to many to be a strong candidate for the right criterion.[5] Because this test is behavioristic, it may come to seem that we are driven either to accept behaviorism or else be deprived of any reasonable way of being nonaprioristic about machine mentality.

The solution to this dilemma is to accept Turing's test as appropriate for the purpose that he advertised in the title of his paper, which was "Computing Machinery and Intelligence". In Robinson (1992a), I defended Turing's test as a test of *intelligence*. This defense does not require that we regard Turing's test as worth anything as a test of *phenomenal consciousness*. Turing's test for intelligence does not depend on assuming anything one way or the other about phenomenal consciousness. We can thus avoid the threatened dilemma by accepting a behavioristic test of intelligence, which we can well imagine that a machine might pass, while denying a behavioristic test of phenomenal consciousness.

HOMUNCULAR FUNCTIONALISM

Homuncular functionalism invokes specification at level (iv) in the introductory list of directions in which functionalism may be developed. This level, let us recall, describes units of our processing mechanism in terms of inputs, outputs, and operations without specifying the fine structure of how these mechanisms work. Unlike behavior, these processing mechanisms are not directly observable; they are inside the brain and spinal cord and must be painstakingly inferred. An appropriate device for setting out homuncular functionalist views is the flow chart. Connections among boxes of such a chart specify the relations among mechanisms, and the fact that the boxes are merely labeled, without their innards being specified, corresponds to the absence of specification of fine structure.

---

5 Dennett (1985), for example, has defended it.

In discussing homuncular functionalism, it is important to note that no one has a priori knowledge of the flow chart structure for any state of phenomenal consciousness.[6] We have only a few general ideas to guide us. For visual experience, there should be some boxes that receive inputs from the eyes; for pains, there should be some boxes that receive inputs from nociceptors. Outputs from these boxes should reach other boxes, whose outputs reach other boxes . . . whose outputs reach the muscles required for linguistic or nonlinguistic behavior appropriate to what we have seen or felt. How many layers of boxes should come in between input and output? What, exactly, should their jobs be, and how should they be connected? Our ordinary concepts of seeing or suffering contain at best a few clues for answering these questions. Most of the answers will have to come from careful and systematic research. Lesion studies may provide reasons to multiply boxes, so that some functions can be carried out when the wherewithal for others has been destroyed. Double dissociations in normal subjects of performances on finely measured tasks may provide reasons to postulate a plurality of mechanisms at work in the use of perceptual inputs. Anatomical considerations or scanning techniques may suggest division of modular mechanisms, and electrode insertions (in non-human primates) may yield clues as to what various parts of the brain are doing.

Let us imagine that our arsenal of empirical methods has enabled us to arrive at a flow chart, **FC**, of Mary Smith's processing of nociceptor input. There are three competing views that might be taken to apply to this flow chart.

(V1) One of the boxes can properly be labeled "pain generator". What we have discovered is that Mary's pain generator receives inputs from certain boxes and gives outputs to others (possibly including some of the boxes from which it also receives input).

(V2) There is no box that can be properly labeled "pain generator". Instead, Mary's having a pain is Mary's having a certain set of boxes being in certain states of activation (i.e., Mary has a pain when activity is actually flowing in the way indicated in **FC**).

(V3) There is a box that can properly be labeled "pain generator", but this label is appropriate *only* at times when activity is actually flowing in the way indicated in the flow chart.

6 In Robinson (1992a) I considered a flow chart used in Dennett (1978) at some length. Here, I am attempting a more general discussion and will only summarize some of the conclusions reached in that previous work.

(V1) is a coherent attitude toward a flow chart, but it is not compatible with homuncular functionalism. According to (V1), pain is generated by one box, and the flow chart merely describes (a) the input conditions under which it will do its generating and (b) how the output is used by the rest of the system. (V1) raises the question of how the pain generator generates pain. Perhaps we can answer this question by looking inside the pain generator; but then the remainder of the flow chart becomes irrelevant to the answer, which contradicts the point of homuncular functionalism. If we do look inside the pain generator, we will have moved away from homuncular functionalism and toward microfunctionalism (which will be discussed later).

(V2) is the true homuncular functionalist view. Once this view is clearly distinguished from the others, however, the basis of the claim that having pain is having the indicated activations in **FC** becomes problematic, and the empirical character of the claim is not evident. We may, indeed, discover that when Mary has a pain, activity is flowing through her system in the way that **FC** describes; but we would not thereby know that any of the boxes in **FC** are *essential* to her having a pain. For example, suppose Mary has a pain gate – a device in which box B feeds inhibitory signals to box A, from which box B also receives excitatory input. Is this part of Mary's flow chart something that *has* to be there in order for her to feel pain? The description of the device as a pain gate suggests a negative answer, for it would seem that one could have pain even if one did not have a device that controlled its intensity in a certain way. (Compare a light with a rheostatic control. One could still have light even if one only had an on–off switch.) Again, suppose Mary has a box whose activation corresponds to believing she has a pain. Is that essential to her having a pain? To suppose so is to be committed to the implausible supposition that a being with less cognitive equipment than Mary could not have pains. To suppose that *all* of Mary's boxes are essential is to be committed to the even less plausible supposition that a being with equally complex, but different, cognitive equipment could not have pains.

These considerations create pressure in the direction of whittling away at **FC** until we have found the irreducible core activity that produces pain – that is, they press us toward microfunctionalism. One might, however, try to resist this pressure by allowing that pain sufferers might have a wide variety of flow charts. The natural question for this view is, what holds the set of flow charts together, i.e., what is the criterion for a flow chart to qualify as a member of the set of flow charts whose possessors suffer pain when activation is flowing as indicated in the chart? There does not seem to be any plausible way to answer this question other than by appealing to behavior. That is, one would first have to identify the pain sufferers behaviorally and then hold that their flow charts all qualify as pain-supporting charts. This view, however, is tantamount to behaviorism plus a nearly vacuous addition, for it says no more than that for an object to have a pain is for it to behave in certain ways under certain conditions and to have some mechanism or other by which it produces those behaviors under those conditions. This view seems to be no more plausible than behaviorism as previously stated. (Behaviorists thought that internal mechanisms of behavior production were to be excluded from conceptual analysis and from study by experimental psychologists, but presumably, none doubted that such internal mechanisms existed.) Once this point is clear, the pressure toward microfunctionalism threatens to become irresistible.

Before moving on to the latter view, let us pause to consider (V3). There is an easily available model that we can use to make some sense of this view, namely, words. For example, we can tell whether there are marks that spell the word "cliff" in a certain place just by looking in that place. There is, however, an obvious sense in which such marks would not properly be called a "word" unless they were related in a complex way to the habits of the users of some language. Now, analogously, one might hold that activity in some brain part produces pains, but these effects are not properly called "pains" unless they are caught up in a system of relations that causes them to occur only under certain conditions and to lead normally to certain kinds of behavioral responses.

The attraction of this view seems strongest at those moments when we are primarily concerned with epistemology. If we want to know something about the causes of pains, we will naturally start with people we think are having pains, and our paradigm cases will be people whom we can see to be injured, and who are complaining about their pain and seeking relief from it. Following the usual ways of searching for causes, we will look for something that is common to our paradigm subjects and absent from those we think are not having pains. If it were not usual for people with pains to be injured, and to complain and seek relief, we would not have the concept of pain, and the project of looking for the causes of pain would not be coherently describable.

These facts, however, are compatible with there being a disanalogy between words and pains. To wit: there would be nothing "wordish" whatsoever about the marks in "cliff" if there were not a surrounding set of relations to linguistic habits; but there is no contradiction in holding that the painfulness of pain could exist in the absence of the system of relations that are necessary in order for us to know it and to investigate its causes. In view of this disanalogy, it is not clear that (V3) is coherent; deprived of the analogy with words, it seems to be an unstable mixture that must collapse into either (V1) or (V2). We have just reviewed the consequences of the latter alternative (i.e., homuncular functionalism); let us therefore move forward to the other alternative, i.e., microfunctionalism.

MICROFUNCTIONALISM

The relation between brain events and pains can be approached by refining our knowledge of normal human reactions to injurious or potentially injurious stimuli. Pointlike results are not to be expected in such an enterprise, for people do not have one single reaction time to stimuli of a given kind, nor do they all react to drugs, or particular dosages of drugs, in the same way. But we can make some progress in the study of pains by requiring that subjects to whom we are willing to attribute pains have reaction times to normally painful stimuli that fall within the same range as the range for most people. Again, we might limit our studies of pains to subjects who exhibit drug reactions within a certain range of variability.

The same ideas can be applied to the composition of internal structures involved in cases of pains. That is, we might begin with apparently paradigmatic pain sufferers and look for internal structures, and activations within those structures, that are common to the occasions on which they experience pains. Here again, there would be a range, not a single repeated structure; but it would seem plausible to think that nonparadigmatic subjects who exhibited structures and activations within this range are pain sufferers, despite peculiarities in their behavior.

How far should we go in the indicated direction? There would seem to be no principled way of stopping short of the answer: "as far as we can". We do not have any a priori reason to think that some particular level of detail must be enough, or that some structures and not others are relevant. If we are to avoid arbitrariness, we would just have to try to find the commonalities, or normal ranges of near commonalities, that characterize the structures and activation states of the brains of subjects we are willing to count as normal pain feelers. Similar considerations would apply to the structures and activations that are to be associated with other kinds of phenomenal consciousness.

The absence of a principled limitation on the level of detail to which we may have to descend in looking for the structures and activations essential to pain (or other types of phenomenal consciousness) leads to a curious result. The microfunctionalist will describe the investigation I have outlined as the search for the (internal) functions whose satisfaction is sufficient for being a pain sufferer; but the very same search will be described within QER as the search for the causes of phenomenally conscious events. In light of this equivalence, however, it is no longer clear why the view that a thing has pains if it has certain kinds of neural events should be counted as a species of functionalism at all. Of course, an ideological motivation for claiming functionalism remains, since functionalism is typically associated with materialism. One may wish to preserve the idea that a material thing can be the actual realizer of a function that is specified in "topic neutral" terms, i.e., terms that do not logically commit one to the nature of the realizer. But one is no longer entitled to that kind of comfort if the "functions" are specified in terms of, say, time frames for the processes to take place or wiring diagrams for neural interactions. Again, traditional functionalisms in philosophy of mind often suggest that the relevant functions can be specified at a nontechnical or folk-psychological level; but the microfunctionalism we are now considering foregoes this putative advantage. In light of these traditional associations of "functionalism", it would invite confusion to classify a view as a functionalism if what it says boils down to this: a subject has pains if and only if it has certain activation types, where those types are to be specified at a level of minuteness illustrated by tens of milliseconds ranges of reaction times and particular patterns of neural activations.

The point that satisfaction of very minutely specified functions is the same as occurrence of causes of phenomenal consciousness cuts both ways; that is, we may say that a search for causes of qualitative events has a functionalistic aspect. This is easy to see if we observe that likely candidates for such causes can be regarded as multiply realizable. Consider one such candidate, namely, neural activation states. Two neurons can be similarly activated when they are not exactly the same shape, or when their nutritional condition is not exactly the same, or when the number of neurons synapsing onto them or the distribution of locations of synapses is not the same. So, a neural activation state is realizable in many ways.[7] If we suppose that the causes of phenomenally conscious events are, instead, processes in microtubules, we will still be able to realize those processes in microtubules that are not exactly the same in length or precise chemical

---

7   The same point will apply to the stronger candidate for causes of qualitative events that will be explained in Chapter 12.

composition. Unless we (implausibly) get down to elementary particles, we are going to have multiple realizability of event types that are sufficient to cause qualitative events according to QER; and if multiple realizability is taken as a hallmark of functionalism, QER will thus count as a version of functionalism.

To summarize: when microfunctionalism is pressed far enough, it becomes indistinguishable from the view that brain events of some type cause qualitative events. Once we give up on homuncular functionalism, there is no nonarbitrary way of stopping microfunctionalism's slide into this equivalence. Since equivalence is symmetrical, one could say that QER is a version of functionalism. However, the term "functionalism" has generally been used for views that hold that the characteristic function of pain, and so on, can be described without getting down to the level of brain events. For this reason, it would likely be misleading to describe the qualitative event realism developed in this book as a version of functionalism, and I shall not do so.

IDENTITY AND SUPERVENIENCE

There is one further idea that may be found attractive, and that may be regarded as a way of maintaining a principled difference between the causal view of QER and a meaningfully functionalistic microfunctionalism. This idea is that theoretical simplicity is a virtue, that theoretical simplicity is served by having as few entities as possible, and that we should therefore *identify* what QER calls "causes of conscious events" as simply *being* those (putatively caused) events. This identification need not be a type-identity theory. Qualitative event realists can allow that brain event causes of indistinguishable phenomenally conscious events may be distinguishable by their neural properties, and microfunctionalists can likewise allow that several events that are distinguishable by their neural properties are nonetheless not phenomenally distinguishable. The brain events in such cases will fall within a restricted range of degrees of similarity with each other, but the fact that they are distinguishable as brain event types is enough to prevent type identity and imply a token–identity view.

A review of Chapter 3 will explain why the identity view just described cannot be refuted. But there are good reasons not to adopt it. We have two kinds of properties – phenomenal qualities, e.g., pain or red, on the one hand, and brain event properties, e.g., as it may be, neural firing rates and ratios of these, on the other. We do not understand why

140

these go together, and this means that the assertion that they are identical is an empty claim that neither provides nor reflects any increase in our understanding.[8] This kind of assertion is utterly dissimilar to the identity claims we find in science, e.g., water is H_2O or lightning is electrical discharge. In these cases, the identification comes with a genuine explanation of the observable properties of one term (water, lightning) by reference to its construction out of the items referred to on the other side of the identity. Thus, holding that phenomenally conscious events are identical with brain events would naturally suggest that, scientifically speaking, all is well, and consciousness has been brought within the explanatory orbit of science. That this suggested view is false is a good reason for avoiding the formulation that leads to it. Nor should we be impressed by the putative simplicity. When we have explanations, we have genuine simplification; for example, once we have the explanation of how H_2O molecules permit passage of light (by not resonating to visible frequencies), surround salt molecules, slide past each other at room temperature, and so on, there is no advantage to saying that there are *both* piles of H_2O molecules *and* bodies of water. But with empty identities – identity claims without associated explanations – we have no real theoretical simplification. An empty identity (and the empty materialism that includes it) offers no better theory than its counterpart that refuses the identity; and the latter is preferable, because it is less likely to mislead about the actual state of our explanatory ignorance.

Some philosophers will agree in these discomforts with identity, but will also wish to avoid the view that brain events cause qualitative events. They may prefer to say that qualitative events *strongly supervene* on brain events, where

(SS) A *strongly supervenes* on B just in case, necessarily, for each x and each property F in A, if x has F, then there is a property G in B such that x has G, and *necessarily* if any y has G, it has F. (Kim, 1993, p. 65; emphases in the original)

Carefully handled (as it is in Kim's work), "strong supervenience" is a useful concept. Nonetheless, I shall not use it here for the following reason. As Kim points out (p. 66), each of the occurrences of "necessarily" in

---

8 Identity theorists will object that identities are never explainable. (How can B be identical with A? What is there to say, except that B *is* A?) The following text is one way of responding to this objection. For an excellent alternative treatment, see Levine's (2001) section on "Gappy Identities".

(SS) can be interpreted in more than one way. Thus, there is potential for confusion in using "supervenience", which, in our context, would have to be repeatedly, and tediously, forestalled. Without this care, it would be easy to come to think of supervenience in a way that, in effect, asserted empty necessity, i.e., the necessity of a connection, where we do not understand how the connection can be necessary, i.e., why it should hold in all possible worlds. Just as assertions of empty identity can mislead, so assertions of empty necessity can enable us to lose sight of our ignorance of any logical connection between phenomenal qualities and properties of brain events. This kind of error is especially likely if empty necessity is wrapped in a formulation as complex as (SS).

In Part II of this book, I will return to the question of what kind of necessity might connect phenomenal qualities and properties of brain events. I will consider approaches that offer, or at least appear to offer, some improvement on our present understanding of this relation. To carry out this inquiry in the clearest way, however, we must begin with simple formulations of matters of which we are relatively firmly convinced, and then carefully add only whatever we can find good reason to add. At the present stage of the argument, we can say only that we are justified in thinking that prickings, burnings, crushings, and so on, cause pains, that proximity to hog confinement lagoons causes olfactory experiences, that looking at ripe tomatoes causes red experiences, and so on. Well-known facts about anesthesia and brain lesions give us good reasons to think that these causal connections are mediated by brain events. We are thus on firm ground if we say that phenomenal consciousness is caused by events in the brain; and this is what qualitative event realists should say until they are either forced away from it by objections or able to improve upon it by constructive arguments.

9

Skepticism and the Causes of Qualitative Events

Many forms of materialism can be regarded as accepting a substantial portion of what qualitative event realists say about phenomenal consciousness. In rejecting QER, they attempt to give an alternative account of something that is recognized on both sides. One version of materialism, however, rejects QER in a much more radical way: it regards the qualitative events of QER as illusions. What is to be accounted for is not those events, for there are none, but only the language of seeming (looking, appearing, etc.), and the tendency of philosophers to postulate seemings (appearances, phenomenal occurrences, qualia, etc.) as presuppositions of such language. This skeptical version of materialism is closely related to the view I called "Minimalism" in Chapter 1, and its answer to the question of how color comes into experience can be given as follows.

(S) When Eve sees a red apple in daylight, the apple's P-red surface reflects light with some set of wavelength intensities. This light impinges on Eve's retina, where it causes changes that initiate a number of processes in the brain. Some of these brain processes may lead to behavior appropriate to red things, including reports that something red is seen. Under other conditions, some of these processes may interact with other processes and result only in "proto-judgments", which may (or may not) lead to statements to the effect that something seems to be red but isn't. Under still other conditions, some of these processes may be substantially inhibited by other processes and thus not lead to much of anything. Under abnormal conditions, e.g., in afterimaging and perceptual illusions, some of the processes that are normally initiated by seeing red things can be brought about by other causes. There is no other way or sense in which red enters into Eve's perceptions of red apples, or into afterimaging after looking at bright green things, or into hallucinatory or illusory visual episodes.[1]

To clarify the notion of proto-judgments, consider a view that is similar to (S) but tries to get along without them, namely, the view that all judgments about what seems are *tentative* judgments about what *is*.[2] We can find many cases that illustrate how "seems" and similar expressions can function in this way. For example, we may say that the stock market seems to be turning bearish, that it appears that the mayor has been embezzling, or that it looks as though Derby Dame is about to win the race. These statements do not call attention to qualities in phenomenal consciousness. No one would seek to account for the sensory character of the seeming of bearishness, the appearance of mayoral corruption, or the look of incipient victory. We would have said the same thing had we said "I think the market is turning bearish (or the mayor is corrupt, or Derby Dame will win)".

These latter comments, however, fail to apply in other cases, and we should thus not accept this simple view as a general account of seeming and its ilk. The trouble is that it is uncontroversially correct to assert some "seems" statements when it is perfectly clear to all (including the utterer) that matters are not the way they seem. To use one of Sellars's famous examples, we can correctly say that a tie looks blue when we are fully apprised of the vagaries of fluorescent lighting and are completely convinced that the tie is green. In such a case, the simple account would require that we are tentatively asserting that the tie is blue at the same time that we know full well that the tie is green. But there is no reason to suppose that we must be in such a confused state of mind when we know both that the tie looks blue and that it is green.

If we can avail ourselves of proto-judgments, however, we can say that in these latter sorts of cases, we judge that a tie is green and also report that we have a proto-judgment to the effect that it is blue. We do not judge that the tie is blue, tentatively or otherwise; rather, besides judging that the tie is green, we know that we might have judged it to be blue, because we know that there is something in us that is part of what sometimes occurs when we make judgments that things are blue.

Naturally, qualitative event realists will agree: what we know to be occurring is a blue qualitative event. But this is not what skeptics have

---

1   I take Dennett (1991) to be the leading exponent of the view just described.
2   Ryle (1949) advances a view of this kind.

in mind. Proponents of (S) mean to deny that there are such qualitative events. What we are reporting in the tie case (besides the actual greenness of the tie) is, according to them, solely that we have a proto-judgment, the content of which might be expressed by "the tie is blue". There is no additional seeming, appearing, or looking blue over and above our having that judgmental content.[3]

SKEPTICISM VERSUS QER: HOW MAY WE PROCEED?

The reply that QER will make to this last point is one that was already made in reference to representationalism – namely, there is an obvious difference between perception and thought for which the stated position provides no adequate account. Describing the tie case as involving a proto-judgment that the tie is blue underdescribes what is there in somewhat the same way as "reading a score while moving one's fingers" underdescribes playing a piano or "a day in winter" underdescribes Christmas.

Many materialists would accept this reply and claim that they can account for the difference in a way that is compatible with materialism. But the skeptical response will be that there is no difference between perception and thought of the kind that qualitative event realists and many of their materialist opponents accept. Antiskeptics *think* there is such a difference, but in fact, there is no difference of the kind they imagine. Qualitative event realists may theorize that we have an ability to report on qualities that are somehow in our experiences, but that theory is simply mistaken and there are no phenomenal qualities to be accounted for.

Now, in principle, we are at an impasse. The purpose of this book is to find the best account of something – something that I take to have been successfully introduced in Chapter 1. But skeptics say that there is just

---

3 Does anyone really want to make such a strong denial? Yes. Speaking to his dialogic partner, Otto, about a certain illusion (of a pink region when there is only a grid of red lines on white paper), Dennett says:

> You seem to think there's a difference between thinking (judging, deciding, being of the heartfelt opinion that) something seems pink to you and something *really seeming* pink to you. But there is no difference. There is no such phenomenon as really seeming – over and above the phenomenon of judging in one way or another that something is the case. (1991, p. 364; emphasis in the original)

Or again, referring to putative properties that would be properly called "raw feels", "sensa", "phenomenal qualities", "qualia", etc., Dennett says:

> In the previous chapter I seemed to be denying that there are *any* such properties, and for once what seems so *is* so. I *am* denying that there are any such properties. But ... I agree wholeheartedly that there seem to be qualia. (1991, p. 372; emphases in the original)

nothing to be accounted for here, except the fact that many make a certain mistake and thus have a tendency to produce false theories. In short, skepticism begins by begging the question against the most fundamental assertion of QER, but equally, QER cannot get off the ground without first begging the question against skepticism. We must wonder whether discussion must simply stop or, if not, how it is possible to proceed.

One thing that qualitative event realists can do without begging the question is to make their view and its motivations clearer and more explicit. I have been doing this all along, and I will continue in that task. A second approach is to rebut reasons that may be offered against QER. This path is open because criticisms of QER need not be question-begging, i.e., they may be based on premises less fundamental than the simple denial of qualitative events. I shall consider some arguments of this kind later in this chapter and in Chapter 10. Before doing that, however, it will be helpful to say a little more about the present difficulty and the terms for its resolution.

Our impasse is particularly deep because it concerns what, at least on one side (i.e., on the side of QER), is supposed to be evident. The phenomenal qualities of which QER offers an account are, according to that view, not inferred properties of inferred entities; they are the qualities of our conscious experience itself. But if this is so, it might be wondered whether skepticism is even possible. Or it might be asked whether the very *possibility* of skepticism shows that there is no consciousness of the kind that QER (or any version of experiential realism) proposes.

In responding to these puzzling questions, we should first explicitly recognize that there will be no *proof* that phenomenal consciousness exists by employment of the third-person methods of science. Those methods will give us knowledge of neural events and correlations of neural event types with physical properties of stimulations. If we assume knowledge of phenomenal consciousness, we can use such results to further establish causal relations between neural events and qualitative events. But the existence of the latter cannot be introduced by third-person methods.

While QER holds that there is no establishing of the existence of phenomenal consciousness by third-person means, QER *can* lay claim to what may be called a "subjective test". That is, it is consistent from the point of view of QER to say that we each have conscious experience and, therefore, we each have something against which we can test various theories – including skeptical denials of phenomenal consciousness. Such a stance has been assumed in my remarks about the difference between perception and thought and about colors in afterimages. Moreover, to the extent that people agree in their judgments, the outcomes of subjective tests have a kind of objectivity. Namely, if claims about our experience are consistent and sufficiently clear, and if almost everyone agrees about the results of subjective testing of them, then it is rational to regard those claims as true. Of course, accepting the legitimacy of subjective testing does not mean that people get to say anything they like about experience. Broad agreement is essential. Nor does it imply that intersubjective agreement alone is enough to warrant acceptance of a claim about phenomenal consciousness. That is because clarity and consistency can, in principle, always be challenged.

Another way to put the point just made is that if, after thorough examination, almost everyone agrees that there is phenomenal consciousness, then affirmation of its existence is a reasonable position to adopt. A skeptic will not agree, for intersubjective agreement on the results of subjective test is still not establishment by scientific third-person methods, and if that criterion is demanded, experiential realism will fail. Experiential realists will not be daunted by this observation; they will say that it is illegitimate to demand third-person proof of phenomenal consciousness. Here, I think, we are at a genuine impasse. Readers must decide for themselves whether they find that there is something that experiential realists are talking about and for which it is therefore reasonable to offer some kind of account.

There is, however, one further dialectical problem for QER, and that is to explain how skepticism is so much as possible. Denials of, e.g., a salient difference between perception and thought are certainly puzzling and present some embarrassment for a qualitative realist for which no fully satisfactory resolution is available. Two points, however, show that there is less difficulty here than may appear at first sight. First, we cannot be expected to take *denials* of phenomenal consciousness (under any description) at face value. There is a genuine asymmetry of positions here, for the widespread agreement that there is something to discuss about phenomenal consciousness has to be discounted by skeptics. They cannot consistently follow such a discounting by offering their own subjective sense of absence of such phenomena as something that should carry any weight on the question of whether we should try to account for phenomenal consciousness.

Second, experiential realists should be embarrassed only if there *could not be* a plausible account of skeptical denials of phenomenal consciousness. But there is an obvious possibility, namely, that skeptics are imposed upon by their own ideology. For example, if one begins by demanding third-person evidence for assertions, then one may think that one ought to exclude any statements that lack such evidence, and one may then accept reasons that seem to justify such exclusion. I do not believe that it is possible to prove that such a scenario is actually what produces skepticism about phenomenal consciousness in any particular case. But it would be rash to deny that some such dynamic *could* be operative[4]; and so long as that possibility is on the table, experiential realists should not find skepticism to be a theoretical obstacle.

EXCESSIVE DETERMINATENESS?

Let us turn, then, to objections that rely on premises other than denial of qualitative events. The arguments I shall discuss in this section rest, in part, on the premise that realities are determinate. Experiential realists, in my view, should accept this premise; thus, they should agree that experiences have determinate qualities, e.g., particular shades of red, particular intensities of flavors, particular pitches, and so on. And they should accept that experiences have determinate times of onsets and determinate durations.

The skeptical arguments to come are based on a verificationism that is weaker than the question-begging assumption that whatever is can be established for all competent thinkers by third-person methods.[5] This weaker version might be called "no determinateness without in principle establishability" or, more clearly,

(NDWE) No theory should be held if it implies determinateness of properties that goes beyond what can, in principle, be established.

Perhaps no illustration of this principle is entirely uncontroversial, but we can get a preliminary understanding of its point by imagining that a certain conception of particles implies that they must have an absolutely definite position and momentum at all times. If certain interpretations of quantum mechanics are accepted, it is in principle impossible to come to know such a pair of properties in full determinateness. Application of (NDWE) would then lead us to reject the conception of particles that implies such determinateness in their properties.

How might (NDWE) be applied to qualitative events? The first argument I will consider begins by noting that by the time any record is

---

4 I am put in mind here of a debate in the late 1960s in which some philosophers were led to claim that they were acquainted with bare particulars.

5 Dennett (1988, 1991) has developed arguments of the kind reviewed here. For a more detailed discussion of some of them, see Robinson (1994).

made of a putative experience – even just expressing a judgment as to what it is – some memory (perhaps extremely short-term memory) must be relied upon. But, then, the question can arise as to how reliable the memory is, or how much of our impression that we have had an F experience is due to reliable memory of an F experience and how much is due to faulty memory of an experience that was not F. Now, for the sake of the argument, skeptics might concede that if we take events that are, say, several seconds apart, it will make sense to distinguish between the quality of the earlier event and the quality represented in the later memory event. But it may seem that we cannot maintain such a separation, even in principle, if we consider a stretch of brain processing that lies within the 100 to 300–millisecond range.

In its present form, this objection appears to be based on a self-contradictory conception. It is first supposed that memory can be distinguished from experience, and then it is supposed that, in very brief time frames, the distinction cannot be made. The obvious reply is that, if we have grounds for distinguishing a memory mechanism, then, in principle, we can distinguish between what is represented in memory and what actually happened in experience. If we have no such grounds, then we just have the experience, and there is no question about accuracy of memory to be asked.

This reply will not satisfy skeptics, however, for they can give a reformulation of the objection that cuts more deeply. The real problem, they may say, is that we cannot tell how much of brain activity to assign to causation of experiences and how much to assign to memory thereof. After all, they may point out, the brain occupies a region of space, not a point, and brain processes occur in stretches of time, not instants. So, it may seem, we always *could* divide brain processes into causes of experiences and memories thereof. Since there would always be many ways of choosing to draw the line between one and the other, there is no way of making a principled distinction here. But that means that there is in principle no way of finding out how much of what occurred in the brain was a cause of experience and how much was a memory thereof. By (NDWE), we should conclude that the idea of fully determinate qualities of experience is a myth and reject forms of realism that imply that experiences have determinate qualities.

To reply to this argument, we must have a little more background about how to conceive the causes of episodes of phenomenal consciousness. The remarks in the next few paragraphs are additions to what has already been said, and are to be understood as further specifications of QER. Some of the motivations for these additions should be immediately clear, but I will be returning to causal matters in later chapters and developing some of the ideas introduced here.

To begin, QER assuredly recognizes that brain events are spatially and temporally spread out. For example, it seems likely that the relevant features of brain-event causes of phenomenal consciousness include timing of neural events – perhaps ratios of firing of several neurons, or rates of change of such ratios, or other quantities that depend on such ratios. But ratios of neural firings are undefined until several firings have occurred, and require a region in which the several neurons are located. Thus, from the point of view of QER, it is evident upon the slightest reflection that brain-event causes of experience are not pointlike, but instead occupy spatial regions and temporal durations.

This observation has an important consequence, namely, that interference effects should be expected at small temporal intervals. To illustrate what this means, consider the phi phenomenon. If two lights blink a few seconds apart, people will experience a blink on the left (for example) and a blink on the right. If we arrange for the blinks to come closer together (as on a movie marquee), a new kind of experience will be caused to occur, namely, an experience of motion. Now, if experiences are imagined to arise from pointlike causes, it will be difficult to account for this phenomenon. If, however, the causes of experiences are thought of as spatially and temporally spread out, we should expect that the course of activation due to the first blink will be altered by the effects of the second blink if the two stimluli are sufficiently close together in time. In that case, we should expect the nature of the experience to differ from the mere succession that results when the interval between blinks is longer.

We should also bear in mind that a state of activation of a set of neurons is not determined solely by which neurons have recently shown an increase in their firing rate. An activation state of such a set includes both firing rates that have not changed and those that have become less. A useful analogy here is that of vectors: a vector of length k that happens to have m entries of value zero is not the same thing as a vector of length $k - m$, with no entries at those places where the original was zero. Analogously, a brain event that is relevant to causation of qualitative events should not be thought of as consisting solely of neurons with raised activations, but as an event occurring in a larger set of neurons that have a broad range of activation levels. It is an empirical matter what sets of neurons we will find it necessary to take into account to achieve a good theory of the causes of qualitative events, but the vector analogy suggests that relevant sets might be quite large – as large, perhaps, as the set of all neurons whose firing rates are ever relevant to the phenomenal qualities in any sensory modality.

If a qualitative event is recognized as something that can occur and instantiate a phenomenal quality, then we can understand the sentence frame: phenomenal quality F was instantiated at instant t. But the view that experiences may be instantaneous is not a consequence of this truth. The time course of causes of experiences is an empirical matter, but there is nothing in QER that suggests that the relevant brain events do not last for nonzero intervals. Perhaps an analogy will help to clarify the point here: we can define instantaneous velocity without committing ourselves to the idea that a thing can be in motion for an instant (i.e., a duration of zero length).[6]

It may seem that the commitment of QER to causes of qualitative events that span spatial regions and temporal durations only adds fuel to the skeptic's fire; for, it may seem, the more spatiotemporally extended the events are that are supposed to cause qualitative events, the more latitude we have for arbitrarily dividing them into causes of experiences, on the one hand, and memory mechanisms, on the other. And, in fact, qualitative event realists should agree with skeptics that, *in the absence of other constraints*, there is a field that could be divided in conflicting ways. But they should not agree that there are no other constraints. There are several obvious candidates. (i) The sensory modalities contain events that are relevantly similar to each other and distinctively different from those in other modalities. It is not a necessary truth that the causes of sounds should all have some kind of similarity that unites them, and differentiates them from the causes of taste and color experiences, but it would be astounding if it were not so. (ii) A similar point holds with respect to small variations within sensory modalities. It is not logically impossible that the brain-event causes of reddish orange experiences should be no more similar to the causes of red experiences than they are to the causes

6 This point permits a direct response to Dennett's attempt to get some mileage against his opponents by hanging on them the idea that there could be millionth-of-a-second real seemings. "Suppose something happened in my presence, but left its trace on me for only 'a millionth of a second,' as in the Ariel Dorfman epigram. Whatever could it mean to say that I was, however briefly and ineffectually, conscious of it?" (1991, p. 132). The idea of such a brief consciousness is indeed puzzling; but the puzzle is entirely a construction of Dennett's own to which qualitative event realists are in no way committed. Further indications that Dennett believes that experiential realists must be committed to the possibility of (temporally) pointlike qualitative events are reinforced by his use of metaphors such as "line" (1991, p. 107) and "point" (1991, p. 125) in discussions of experience and memory.

of blue experiences; but again, it would be amazing if that were the case. (iii) Some brain lesions lead to inability to have certain kinds of experiences. It is a natural inference that some part of the causes of experiences lies in those regions where damage produces such inabilities. (iv) There should be systematic relations among the causes of experiences that differ only by arrangement. For example, the causes of an afterimage containing a green square above a red circle should have systematic structural relations to the causes of an afterimage containing a red square above a green circle, a green circle above a red square, and so on.

It would be unscientific to ignore these constraints in an attempt to discover the causes of our experiences. The skeptical worries that we have seen previously amount to the hypothesis that utilizing such constraints will not be enough to establish a credible theory of causes of experience. But this is a skeptical conclusion about the possible progress of science for which no support has been offered, and it would be contrary to usual practice in the sciences to take this kind of skepticism seriously. Objections to QER and rescues of materialism that rest on this kind of skepticism should be firmly rejected.

These points provide the background for a response to a related argument that involves evaluation of our experiences. Overdosing on a favorite food can sometimes make us averse to eating it. Coincidental illness can do the same thing. The notion of an "acquired taste" suggests a change in the opposite direction, i.e., from disliking a taste to liking it. Now, in any such case, we can ask whether the old foods produce the same old tastes, which are now evaluated differently, or whether our evaluations have remained constant while the old foods have come to produce new tastes in us. There is genuine commonsensical bite to this question. We may have definite opinions that a change of one kind or the other has occurred, but it does not seem that we are in any position to defend them.

Matters are worse if we allow the possibility that change of taste production and change of evaluation may both occur at the same time.[7] That is because allowing this possibility presents the problem of discovering how much of our new reaction to a food is due to each kind of process. Perhaps there is no principled way of apportioning responsibility to either process without making unjustified assumptions about how much is to be attributed to the other. Or, we could equally say, perhaps there is no way of assigning some change in the brain to one process or the other

---

7 See the discussion of Chase and Sanborn in Dennett (1988).

unless we already assume we know how changes in these processes work. Experiential realism, however, implies that we definitely have one taste or another on each occasion, and so it is determinate that a later taste is the same, or is not the same, as an earlier one. Further, if the tastes are different, the degree of difference is determinate. In this way, one might argue that applying (NDWE) should lead to rejection of experiential realism.

If we apply our previous discussion to this case, however, we can see that we do not know that we cannot ever have a science of the causes of taste experiences. We are not confined to simply reflecting on our likes and dislikes and our memories of changes. A scientific investigation of the causes of our experiences would narrow down the causes of taste qualities by looking for causes that varied only slightly when tastes were judged to be only slightly different in normal circumstances over short times. It would look for a type of variation that is correlated with intensity across a variety of tastes; for such a variation would be likely to be a variation in the causes of tastes. At the same time, it would legitimately assume that aversion to foods was related to aversions to smells or bodily sensations, and would use that assumption in building a model of an aversion system. As before, it is not logically guaranteed that such efforts would lead to a credible science; there is surely a possible world in which the causes of our sensory qualities have an order that does not neatly map onto the order in our sensory quality space. But to deny the possibility of a science of the causes of tastes would be a colossal presumption. If we must choose between that form of skepticism and experiential realism, it seems quite clear that we should prefer to keep the latter.

INTERNALISM

Part of the realism of QER is that qualitative events have causes, and I have evidently been taking these causes to be brain events. The previous section has added a little detail to this assumption, and later discussions will add more. As these discussions develop, it will become more and more evident that QER is committed to internalism for phenomenal consciousness. This feature of the view will be found objectionable by some proponents of externalism. It is thus necessary to face directly an argument that seeks to establish externalism for phenomenal qualities, and that is our task in this section.[8]

---

8 In this section, I follow Dretske's (1995, pp. 127–141) argument.

Let us begin by considering me and my physical duplicate on Twin Earth. I stipulate that despite physical duplication of me, there are aspects of the surrounding environment in which Earth and Twin Earth differ.[9] I further stipulate that these differences are subliminal. If I were drugged and transported to Twin Earth, I would be none the wiser when I awoke. So long as I am not informed of the switch, and so long as revealing microanalyses are not performed, my verbal and nonverbal responses to given situations would be just like those of my twin.

I shall assume externalism for thoughts. The question is whether externalism can be extended to phenomenal qualities of experiences. I shall further assume that the difference between Earth and Twin Earth is sufficient that none of my twin's concepts are the same as any of my own. When we look at the same Twin Earth object, we say exactly the same things, but, where I think that something is **F**, my twin thinks that that thing is *F*, where the difference between boldface and italic script indicates that the concepts are different, even though the words for them are the same (we both utter "F") and even though Twin Earthers will find my statements acceptable, or not, just as they would isophonic productions from my twin.

Here is the argument.

(1) Either (a) we can know what experiences we are having or (b) we cannot.
(2) To know what experiences we are having involves bringing them under concepts.
(3) I share no concepts with my twin. So,
(4) There is no experiential kind such that I can know I am having an experience of that kind and my twin can also know that he is having one of that kind.[10] So,
(5) If we assume (a), we can never have reason to suppose that my twin's experience is ever of the same kind as any experience that I ever have.
(6) My twin has the same causally relevant brain structure that I have. So,

---

9 Slightly less implausibly, my twin can differ from me in having, say, XYZ where I have water. This supposition does not change the argument, provided that both my twin and I are oblivious to the water/XYZ distinction, i.e., we live in premodern times when no one has a way of detecting the difference between XYZ and water.

10 *Nota bene*: This is *not* the proposition that there is no experiential kind such that I can know that both my twin and I are having an experience of that kind. The present argument is not about the problem of other minds. Likewise, (5) does not raise an inverted spectrum problem. If our spectra are mutually inverted, then our sets of experiential kinds certainly overlap and may (as far as pure inversion hypotheses go) be identical. We just have different members of those sets on similar occasions. The sense of the present argument, however, is that the lack of overlap of concepts leads to mutually exclusive sets of experiential kinds.

(7) It cannot be that sharing causally relevant brain structure gives us a good reason to suppose that my twin's experience is of the same kind as mine. So,

(8) We cannot have a good reason to suppose that causally relevant brain structure is sufficient to determine what kind of experience we are having.

On the other hand,

(9) If we cannot know what kind of experiences we are having (or if there is supposed to be some aspect of experience such that we cannot know we are having *that* kind of aspect), then we cannot have a good reason to suppose that my twin is having the same kind of experience as I am.

Thus, once again,

(10) We cannot have a good reason to suppose that causally relevant brain structure is sufficient to determine what kind of experience we are having.

Cautious though the conclusion of this argument is, I believe we have no reason to accept it. The reason is that (4) does not follow from (2) and (3). To see that this is the case, consider the concepts **F or property I cannot distinguish from F** (**F*** for short) and *F or property I cannot distinguish from F* (*F** for short).[11] Now, if I can know I have an **F** experience, I can know I have an **F*** experience; and likewise, my twin can know he has both an *F* and an *F** experience. But, as far as (2) and (3) tell us, it may be necessary that whatever is **F*** is *F**. So (as far as (2) and (3) tell us), both I and my twin may know that we have an experience of a certain kind, where the kind is the same for both of us. The concepts **F** and *F* are different, but it may be that the kind that **F*** picks out is the same kind in all possible worlds, and is the same kind as the kind that *F** picks out in all possible worlds.

As a possibly helpful analogy, consider that the concepts "shape of the American coin with Washington's head on it" and "shape of the American quarter-dollar" are different concepts, but they pick out the same shape property. Moreover, if one knows that shape through possessing one of these concepts, one knows the same shape that another knows through possessing the other. In thinking about this analogy, however, it should be borne in mind that there are worlds in which the property picked out by one of these concepts is different from the property picked out by

---

11 Even though **F*** is extensionally equivalent to **F** (and *F** to *F*), the *concepts* **F** and **F*** are different, just as "equilateral triangle" and "equiangular triangle" are different concepts, and both are different from the concept "equilateral or equiangular triangle".

the other. But, as far as (2) and (3) tell us, the same may not hold of $\mathbf{F}^*$ and F^*.

It may seem that I am begging the question by assuming that $\mathbf{F}^*$ and F^* pick out the same property for me and my twin, but I am not making this assumption. Clearly, externalists cannot make the opposite assumption (i.e., that there must be a difference in the kind of experience) without begging the question in favor of their argument. My response against externalists does not assert the opposite of their view; instead, it shows that *as far as anything in the argument shows*, there is no reason to accept their view. It does this by showing that there being a common experiential kind shared by my twin and me is coherent upon, i.e, compatible with, the assumptions that externalism offers in the preceding argument (in particular, with (2) and (3)).

It may further be objected that my response to the externalist argument shows something only about some possibly "enriched" versions of me and my twin, that is, about beings who are like us but who have *actually formed* the concepts $\mathbf{F}^*$ and F^*. It might then be thought that the externalist argument can stand if applied only to the original me and twin-me. In response, however, it should be noted that what is $\mathbf{F}$ is necessarily $\mathbf{F}^*$, and what is F is necessarily F^*. If I make the conceptual leap to enrichment (i.e., by forming for the first time the concept $\mathbf{F}^*$), I will not be able to distinguish the phenomenal character of my $\mathbf{F}$ experiences from that of my $\mathbf{F}^*$ experiences. Similarly for my twin and his F and F^* experiences. So, even prior to enrichment, my twin and I have experiences that neither of us will be able to distinguish from our corresponding experiences after our conceptual enrichment. Thus, the reasoning I have given concerning $\mathbf{F}^*$ and F^* experiences should lead to the same conclusion for the experiences of me and my twin when we possessed only the concepts $\mathbf{F}$ and F.

CONCLUSIONS

I conclude that the foregoing argument should not be considered a good reason to give up the view that qualitative events are realities that have causes in the brain events of the people who have them. From earlier sections, I conclude that we have not been given a good skeptical reason to suppose that a science of the causes of qualitative events is impossible. Naturally, I am not denying that there are many difficulties, both conceptual and experimental, that lie in the path of this kind of research; I am only resisting the idea that we have reason to abandon a science of consciousness because we have been shown that, in principle, it cannot achieve its aims.

There is, however, one remaining objection to QER as so far developed. I have deferred it because, although it may arise from a skeptical outlook, it may also arise from within a broadly realist perspective. This objection is that QER leads to epiphenomenalism. It is time to address this implication.

10

Epiphenomenalism

The science of our sensory and neuromuscular systems provides overwhelming evidence that all our behavior is a product of our muscles. This is evident for movements, but even holding oneself still requires muscular involvement, as becomes obvious if one holds one's hand out and tries to keep it steady. Muscles, in turn, contract as a result of chemical changes induced by activation of motor neurons. Motor neurons are activated by depolarization induced by neurotransmitters that cross synaptic clefts from other neurons. These presynaptic neurons are, in turn, activated by depolarization induced by neurotransmitters that cross synaptic clefts from still other neurons.[1] And so on. Perhaps the activity of glial cells is involved at some point, and perhaps the activity of neurons is mediated by conditions in their microtubules. However that may be, these structures are all straightforwardly physical things, and their activities are governed by physical laws. There is ample evidence that neurons do not generate action potentials out of nowhere; on the contrary, decades of ingenious and exacting research show that neural membranes are complex gating structures that control the relation between ions inside and outside the cell and lead to activations under certain specific conditions. The picture that these facts support is one in which all our actions are effects of extremely complex, but completely physical, interactions of the cells in our brains and the neurons that lead into and away from our brains.[2]

---

1 There are also gap junctions that join neurons in a way that is not mediated by neurotransmitters. I suppress this detail, because even if there are large units that effectively act as one enormous neuron, that will make no difference to any of the arguments of this chapter.
2 If we count reflex movements as "actions", we must allow simpler transactions that involve only the spinal cord.

These remarks may be summarized in the following two statements.

(1) Our behavior – nonlinguistic and linguistic – is completely accounted for by the activity of our neuromuscular (and perhaps glial or microtubular) systems.
(2) Our neuromuscular (and perhaps glial or microtubular) systems are entirely material and subject to laws of nature.

In previous chapters, various attempts to fit phenomenal consciousness into a materialist framework have been considered and found to be inadequate. QER has been advanced as the most defensible version of a view that does not suffer from this kind of inadequacy. I have agreed that the position that phenomenal qualities are nonetheless material cannot be refuted; but the tenable versions of this position provide no explanation of *how* phenomenal qualities could be material, i.e., they are empty materialisms. I have argued that empty materialisms are likely to be misleading regarding our explanatory ignorance, and should thus be avoided in favor of riskier hypotheses that keep the "explanatory gap" firmly before our minds. Respecting these principles leads me to the view that

(3) Phenomenal qualities, and the events in which they are instantiated, are not material.

It follows from (1), (2), and (3) that

(4) Phenomenal qualities, and the events in which they are instantiated, are not needed for any causal role that is required to completely account for all of our behavior.

If we set aside the implausible idea of systematic overdetermination, we can move from (4) to the simpler claim that phenomenal qualities, and the events in which they are instantiated, have no effects in our behavior. Further, there is no reason to suspect phenomenal qualities, or the events in which they are instantiated, of having any effects *other* than those that might (directly or indirectly) lead to behavior. Thus, we arrive at the epiphenomenalist conclusion that

(5) Phenomenal qualities, and the events in which they are instantiated, are inefficacious.

Since QER's account of phenomenal consciousness is that it consists in events in which phenomenal qualities are instantiated, QER's commitments can also be expressed by saying that

(6) Phenomenal consciousness is inefficacious.

Epiphenomenalism is widely regarded as an anathema, and the fear of being led to epiphenomenalism is a primary motivation for avoiding qualitative event realism. Or, to put the point more positively, it is held that the assumption that qualitative events are material is the best explanation of their (at least apparent) efficacy in our behavior. This consideration may be thought sufficient to overcome the drawback of emptiness of materialism for which I have argued in earlier chapters. In the following sections, I shall briefly review, and respond to, the most important arguments against epiphenomenalism.[3] These responses are, in my view, sufficient to undermine the force of the appeal to materiality of qualitative events on the ground that this is required for explanation of our behavior.

ANTIEPIPHENOMENALIST INTUITIONS

A common intuition is that we just know that our thoughts and our experiences cause our behavior; this connection lies, so to speak, right on the surface of our experience. Anyone who is willing to bite the bullet of denying *this* intuition may be thought to be intellectually deficient or caught in the grip of a powerful but mistaken ideology.

Despite the wide appeal of this antiepiphenomenalist intuition, there is good reason to doubt its force. To understand why, let us first say a little more about the epiphenomenalistic view that is open to qualitative event realists and would seem to be the view that they ought to hold. QER holds qualitative events to be realities that have causes. These causes are naturally taken to be neural events; for example, we know that pains are produced by impingements that cause neural events and that they are prevented if we block the activation of certain neurons. In general, neural events cause neural events, and there is no reason against supposing that the neural events that cause qualitative events also initiate a series of neural events that lead to behavior. These relations may be usefully represented in the familiar diagram of Figure 1. Here, PQ(e) stands for an event that is an occurrence of a phenomenal quality, the Ni stand for neural events, and B stands for some resulting behavior. Arrows indicate causal relations. Now suppose that there is no cause of PQ(e) other than N1 and no other cause of N2 other than N1. Then there will never be a case of PQ(e) that

---

3 For further detail see Robinson (1982, 1999a). The present discussion covers fewer arguments than does Robinson (1999a). My principle of selection has been to discuss matters on which I believe I can offer some advance, especially on the important matter of knowledge of phenomenal qualities.

$$PQ(e)$$
$$\uparrow$$
$$\ldots \to N1 \to N2 \to N3 \to \ldots \to B$$

Figure 1.

$$\ldots N1 \to PQ(e) \to N2 \to N3 \to \ldots \to B$$

Figure 2.

is not followed by N2, and there will never be a case of N2 that is not preceded by PQ(e). The counterfactual, "If PQ(e) had not occurred, then N2 would not have occurred", will be true. But for all that, PQ(e) and N2 will not be related as cause and effect, but rather as common effects of the cause, N1.

To accept the intuition that N2 must be caused by PQ(e) would be to hold that the structure of Figure 1 can be ruled out solely by the deliverances of intuition. But it is notorious that we are subject to causal illusions, i.e., that we are inclined to attribute causal connection in cases of common effects. Philosophers regularly teach their students to be on their guard against such mistakes, and since Hume's day, it has not been thought that we have any special insight into causal connectivity. To accept the antiepiphenomenalist intuition at face value would thus be to think in a way that is directly contrary to the teachings of nearly all contemporary philosophers.

There is worse to come. To appreciate the further difficulty, let us use an alternative diagram, as in Figure 2. We do not have any common-sense knowledge of the neural events that plausibly cause our phenomenal consciousness or that lead, after much further processing, to our behavior. What we ordinarily know about are our surroundings, our stimuli, our phenomenal consciousness, and our behavioral reactions to our stimuli. Thus, we have no commonsense knowledge of any of the Ni in either Figure 1 or Figure 2 or their relations; and this is to say that we have no commonsense knowledge of the items that make the *difference* between the two figures. Thus, to suppose that we have commonsense knowledge that the structure in Figure 2 holds, rather than the structure in Figure 1, is to embrace a deliverance of experience whose credentials are shrouded in mystery.

There is another way to look at this point. Consider N3 and imagine looking backward from it. Its cause is the neural event N2. Nothing in either figure allows N2 to preserve a mark of the way in which it was

161

caused. Thus, there is nothing in N3 that indicates that it came about through the structure in Figure 2 rather than the structure in Figure 1. This same reasoning will hold for every event later in the series, including the eventual behavioral event, B. Thus, there is nothing in our behavior that could correspond to a difference between the structures in the two figures.

This conclusion might be avoided by holding that causation by PQ(e) is preserved by some mark in every later event in the series. This is to say that PQ(e) could not simply contribute its effect upon one neural event and then retire from the causal scene; it would have to have an effect on each item in the series. This idea, however, runs counter to the entire empirical framework of accounting for our behavior through a serial process of neuromuscular events.

It might be thought that this last point can be avoided by making a distinction between behavior and mere movement. Perhaps, that is, there can be a neuromuscular account that gives the causes of movement of the lips and tongue that produce the sounds "Ai amm inn pein", but there cannot be a *saying* of "I am in pain" unless there is a pain or, at least, unless something like the following is true: I would not normally be producing the sounds "Ai amm inn pein" in these circumstances unless I were having a pain. (We can add, if we like, that this normality had to have come about by a certain kind of process.) But this distinction, and the way of making it, can be accepted without PQ(e) doing any more *causal* work than it does in Figure 1 (which is none at all) or in Figure 2 (where the causal work is limited to producing N2). So, the appropriateness of the demand for a movement/behavior distinction will not support rejection of the conclusion of the preceding paragraph.

I turn now to an empirical study that should increase our willingness to entertain grave doubt about the antiepiphenomenalist intuition. This work concerns the experience of will rather than sensory qualities, but the general point that we are not in a good position to distinguish causation from common effects will be supported. Wegner and Wheatley (1999) mounted a 12-centimeter square board atop a computer mouse. A participant and a confederate placed their finger tips on the board and moved it in slow circles, stopping from time to time. Both could see a computer screen with about 50 small objects depicted and a cursor that was moved by the mouse. Participants and confederates received input through earphones. Participants were instructed to stop the motion of the board a few seconds after they began to hear music. Confederates were mostly passive, but on key trials (forced-stop trials, occurring 4 times in a series of 23 trials in some cases and 32 in others) they were given the name of an object on which they were to force a stop. Participants heard words that sometimes corresponded to objects depicted on the screen and sometimes not, but were not instructed to stop on named objects even when they were on the screen. In non-forced-stop trials, confederates heard nothing and allowed participants to stop where they would.

It is important to the argument of Wegner and Wheatley (1999) that participants were not stopping at an object just because they had heard the word for it before stopping – for, if that is what was happening, then it would not be possible to separate the contribution of confederates from the contribution of participants in the key forced-stop trials. To test for this possibility, the authors examined records, for *non-forced-stop* trials, of the distance between the point of stopping and any object that was ever used as the target of a forced stop. There were eight of these targets; let us illustrate the procedure for one such target, a picture of a swan. There are two cases. (a) The first was nonforced trials in which participants heard "swan". The distance between the point where the participant stopped and the swan picture was recorded and compared to the following figure. (b) The second was nonforced trials in which participants heard a word for an object that was not represented by any of the pictures on the screen. Distances of the stopping point from the swan picture were recorded, and the mean was calculated and compared with the figure in (a). Now, in (b), participants could not have been influenced in their point of stopping by the word they heard; and so, if they were being influenced in their point of stopping by hearing a word that did name an object on the screen, the number arrived at in (a) should have been significantly smaller than the number arrived at in (b). The result, however, was that there was no significant difference between these two numbers – 7.60 (SD = 1.85) for the mean for the eight targets used in case (a) and 7.83 (SD = 0.82) for all the trials in (b). The conclusion drawn from these results is that hearing a word that did correspond to a picture did not significantly influence participants toward stopping on the corresponding picture in non-forced-stop trials; and a natural inference is that there was no such significant contribution from participants in the forced-stop trials.

In forced-stop trials, a word for a displayed object was heard in one of four conditions: 30 seconds prior, 5 seconds prior, 1 second prior, or 1 second posterior to the stop. After each stop, participants rated the extent to which they were involved in the stopping, on a scale from "I allowed the stop to happen" to "I intended to make the stop". Confederates pretended to do the same. Marks on this scale were converted to percentages of intention to make the stop.

Participants rated their percentage of intention in forced-stop trials at a mean of 43.68% (SD = 31.19, SE ± 4.923) for 30-second prior conditions; 61.07% (SD = 28.40, SE ± 5.185) for 5-second prior conditions; 62.33% (SD = 23.72, SE ± 4.565) for 1-second prior conditions; and 47.12% (SD = 32.21, SE ± 5.524) for 1-second posterior conditions. Mean percentage of intention for non-forced-stop trials was 56.09% (SD = 11.76). Differences between the 30-second prior condition and the others, and between the 1-second posterior condition and the others, were significant; none of the other differences were significant.

The conclusion that the authors draw from these results is this: "Apparently, the experience of will can be created by the manipulation of thought and action in accord with the principle of priority, and this experience can occur even when the person's thought cannot have created the action" (p. 489). (The principle of priority is that the experience of will requires thought to precede the action at a proper interval.) This result should not be dismissed on the ground that it shows merely that judgments of efficacy of will are fallible (which is compatible with their being reliable in most circumstances). For the sense of Wegner and Wheatley's (1999) conclusion is that what leads to our impression of efficacy of will is the close temporal relation between thought and action: actual causation has nothing to do with producing the impression, even though, in normal cases, actual causation may be well correlated with the operative temporal relation.

The conclusion that I will carry forward from this discussion of Wegner and Wheatley (1999) is much weaker than that of the authors. I shall suppose only that the conclusion they draw is *possibly* correct, and that they have approached the matter in a way that could be supported in further work and will lead to their conclusion if so supported. This supposition alone is enough to support the firm rejection of the idea that intuitions about the efficacy of our will have any probative value. But if these intuitions are not to be trusted, why should we trust the antiepiphenomenalist intuition? After all, it too concerns the causes of our actions, and it too concerns a case where common effect may be confused with causation. The answer to our question seems clear: there is no reason to assign any weight to the antiepiphenomenalist intuition, and doing so runs positively counter to well-understood and commonly taught principles of critical thinking.

A deep argument against epiphenomenalism is based on the premise that knowledge depends on causation of belief by the fact that is known.[4] Since phenomenal consciousness is inefficacious, according to epiphenomenalism, it cannot cause our belief that we have it. Less abstractly, Eve's having a red qualitative event cannot be the cause of her saying that she has one, or of her saying that she has a red sensation, or is phenomenally conscious of red, or that she sees something red. If we assume that her believing that she is phenomenally conscious of red would be a cause of her saying any of these things, we must also say that her having a red qualitative event cannot be a cause of her believing anything about her phenomenal consciousness or the qualities that she is perceiving. Putting these reflections together, it follows that Eve – and, by parity of reasoning, any of us – does not know that she has a red qualitative event.

It is not open to epiphenomenalists simply to bite this bullet. For their claim is that there are phenomenally conscious events that are inefficacious. If they then say that they do not know that they are phenomenally conscious, they are caught in the self-stultifying position of advancing a claim while affirming that they do not know it. Being in this position does not prove that their claim is false, but it does make it absurd to *make* the claim.

The stance of QER is that we should both eschew empty materialism and accept a scientific account of behavior. In the previous section, we saw how these commitments lead to epiphenomenalism. Thus, if epiphenomenalism is self-stultifying, so is QER.

These unwelcome consequences all rest on the premise that knowledge requires causation by the thing known. This premise can, however, be denied without absurdity, and in what follows, I shall explain how this negative task is to be accomplished. I shall also devote substantial effort to the positive task of explaining what our knowledge of phenomenally conscious events consists in.

The first point to be made is a slight extension of the preceding discussion of Figures 1 and 2. Figure 2 gives PQ(e) a causal role, and would not commonly be thought to raise an epiphenomenalistic problem.[5] However,

---

4   Strictly, the causation of belief would be by the coming into relation (e.g., observation, deduction) of the fact that is known. I suppress this detail in the interest of clear presentation.

5   Figure 2 does, of course, raise a problem about how PQ(e) could be the same event as the neural event that it has to be in order to cause N2. Under the pressure of this question, some might resort to distinguishing "aspects" of a single event. In this case, an epiphenomenalistic

given the assumptions surrounding the discussion of Figures 1 and 2, we are entitled to say, in reference to both figures, that N3 would not have occurred if PQ(e) had not occurred. But the fact that N3 would not have occurred if PQ(e) had not occurred seems to be the crucial fact that is relevant to enabling N3 to transmit knowledge of PQ(e). To appreciate this point, imagine that the behavior, B, is an utterance of "I am having a red experience". No one thinks it is required that this behavior be *directly* caused by a red experience if it is to be an expression of knowledge. (Indeed, if we required direct causation of utterances by events, in order for those events to be known, knowledge of past events would immediately be ruled out.) We accept claims to knowledge if we think the chain of events leading up to the utterance of the claim is of a kind that would not occur if the claim were not true. But this condition is met just as much by the structure in Figure 1 (with its attendant assumptions) as it is by the structure in Figure 2. Thus, Figure 1 has as much claim to provide a structure that allows for knowledge of PQ(e) as does Figure 2.

It can, of course, be objected that Figure 2 provides a property of N3 that N3 lacks in Figure 1, namely, the property: being caused by an event that is directly caused by PQ(e) or, as we may also put it, the property

(IC) Being indirectly caused by PQ(e).

The nearest thing we can say about N3 in the structure in Figure 1 is that it has the property

(ICC) Being indirectly caused by a cause of PQ(e).

But it is not at all clear why (IC) should be thought to bestow any more ability for N3 to transmit knowledge than does (ICC). What is important is that N3 should be a reliable indicator of the occurrence of PQ(e), and this is ensured equally by both properties.

The conclusion of the discussion so far is this. According to a qualitative event realism that embraces epiphenomenalism, we can know that we have phenomenal qualities, and we can know that we are having particular qualitative events that are occurrences of such qualities. These things

worry is likely to return, namely, the possibility that the causation of N2 might be due entirely to the neural aspect and not at all to the phenomenal aspect. This worry, however, does not arise simply from Figure 2, which is compatible with refusing to distinguish aspects and is compatible even with an interactionist dualism that counts PQ(e) as nonmaterial and yet allows it to cause N2. Of course, I have no sympathy for any of these views. The point developed in the text is that Figure 2 actually supplies no advantage for knowledge, as compared with the structure in Figure 1.

are possible because knowledge of phenomenal qualities does not require qualitative events to be the causes of utterances, other behavior, beliefs, or anything else. What is required for knowledge is that we would not normally sincerely assert, or believe, that we had a certain kind of qualitative event unless we actually did so; but this requirement is met by (ICC), which is included in epiphenomenalism (as diagrammed in Figure 1 with its attendant assumptions). So, epiphenomenalists and qualitative event realists who embrace epiphenomenalism are not engaged in the self-stultifying advancement of a claim, the knowledge of which is incompatible with their theory.

CONTINGENCY AND KNOWLEDGE

The foregoing discussion will be defended as actually containing the answer to the deepest sort of objection to epiphenomenalism. By itself, however, it is unlikely to allay everyone's doubts about the view. One likely source of dissatisfaction comes from the thought that the connection between N1 and PQ(e) is only contingently related to the connection between N1 and N2. So, one may say, it could happen that our verbal and nonverbal behavior is in every respect identical to what it actually is, even if there were no PQ(e) at all! And if that could happen, then we *don't* really know that we have phenomenal consciousness, according to the epiphenomenalistic QER that has been advanced in this chapter.[6]

As a first step in replying to this thought, let us note that the contingency of causal connections applies just as much to Figure 2, which would not commonly be thought to raise epiphenomenalistic worries. To explain: what causes what is contingent; therefore, it is possible that N2 could be caused by something other than what actually causes it; and that other cause might be one that is neither identical with PQ(e) nor a cause of it. So, it could happen that all our verbal and nonverbal behavior is in every respect identical to what it actually is, even if there were no PQ(e). So, we might think, even without assuming inefficacy of PQ(e), we don't really know that we have phenomenal consciousness, even if matters are as depicted in Figure 2.

6 For simplicity, I discuss the issue raised here in terms of the worst-case scenario, i.e., the hypothesis that our behavior is the same while we have no phenomenal consciousness at all. But the arguments all apply (though with more complex wording) to inversion scenarios, in which phenomenal consciousness is present but has different neural causes.

This reasoning about Figure 2 is offered only to suggest that something has gone wrong, and that it is the same mistake in the case of the structures in both figures. The mistake arises from trading on an ambiguity that is implicit in the claims about what "could happen". One thing we might mean is

(CH1) There is a possible world in which all the causal laws are the same as those in the actual world, and in which N3 (and all its sequelae) occur even though PQ(e) does not.

This interpretation does, indeed, defeat a knowledge claim. This fact can be easily illustrated by courtroom cases. Defense lawyers do not appeal to possible worlds in which the causal relations differ from those in the actual world (at least they don't if they make a living at their work). Instead, they argue, in effect, that the causal structure of *our* world allows for the prosecution's evidence to have come about, to be exactly what it is, without the defendant's having committed the crime. Now, the contingency of causal relations evidently does not commit epiphenomenalists to (CH1); and thus, they avoid at least one way of being committed to a claim about what "could happen" that would defeat their knowledge claim. Similarly, the contingency of causal relations does not commit those who prefer the structure in Figure 2 to (CH1) or to rejection of knowledge of phenomenal consciousness.

In contrast, epiphenomenalists *are* committed by the contingency of causal relations to the claim that

(CH2) There is a possible world in which the causal laws differ from those of the actual world, and in which N3 (and all its sequelae) occur even though PQ(e) does not.[7]

But a defense lawyer who appealed to facts analogous to (CH2) would be properly rebuked by a prosecutor or a judge who pointed out that we are in *this* world, not some other, and that the existence of possible worlds in which we do not know the defendant committed the crime is no obstacle to our knowing that the defendant is, in fact, guilty. And the analogous reply for epiphenomenalists (or for those who prefer the structure in Figure 2) is equally strong. That is, the possibility of a world

7 I have put (CH2) in a form that parallels (CH1) as closely as possible. But otherwise stated, (CH2) is the possibility that the neural and other physical laws of our world – the connections indicated by the horizontal arrows in Figure 1 – remain what they are, while the connection between neural and phenomenal events – the vertical arrow in Figure 1 – is different from what holds in our world.

in which laws are different and we do not know that our qualitative events occur does not show that in *this* world we do not know that they occur.

Some will now raise a further objection. One way to do so is to ask the question: How do you know which world you are in? Another is to say that we have no ground for supposing that we are in a world such as that depicted in Figure 1. The answer to this objection has two parts. One is that we *have* qualitative events, and we know about them if we believe and speak truly about them and if our believing and speaking truly about them is the result of a reliable process (one that would not have produced the believing and speaking absent the cause of the phenomenal consciousness). These conditions are ensured by QER, so we are entitled to claim that we know we have qualitative events if we do have them and if QER is a defensible theory. The remainder of the answer is that QER *is* a defensible theory. This last statement is, of course, not one for which one can give a *short* argument: the only argument available is the long one that consists of (many parts of) this book so far and material that is yet to come.

This answer is correct, but it will not satisfy everyone. Those whom it does not satisfy will say that it is question-begging for me (and, by parity, any qualitative event realist) to premise that we have qualitative events. For, to state such a premise in the present context is, in effect, to say that I know what I say to be true – but that is just what the objector of the preceding paragraph is doubting.

This response is extremely tempting, but it is mistaken. The objection in the last paragraph but one was that there was no ground for supposing that we are in a world such as that depicted in Figure 1. *This* objection was answered in that same paragraph. The dissatisfaction identified in the immediately preceding paragraph is a different one. This dissatisfaction calls into question the claim that we have qualitative events. Now, this calling into question is either a *denial* or an *assertion of absence of proof.* If it is a denial, it is egregiously question-begging, and we are entitled to ignore it. But how should we reply to those who say, in effect, that epiphenomenalism is unsatisfying because to hold it you must think that you have phenomenal consciousness, but that is something you cannot prove?

To whom can I not prove that I have experiences? (a) It may be said that I cannot prove it to another person. To this, epiphenomenalists should say: that is certainly correct, but that is no reason to reject epiphenomenalism. It is obvious that the contingency of causal relations leaves open the possibility described in (CH2). It follows that my behavior could occur without any phenomenal consciousness; *all* of my behavior could so occur. So, no matter what behavior I exhibit, there can be no entailment between it and the claim that I have phenomenal consciousness; you are not contradicting yourself if you say that I exhibit behavior B but have no phenomenal consciousness, for any behavior B that I may exhibit (where "behavior B" may include all of my behavior over any length of time up to and including my total behavioral output since birth).

But the fact that I can't prove to *you* that I have phenomenal consciousness is no argument against epiphenomenalism. One can, of course, state it as a principle that what can be known must be provable to another; but that is a form of verificationism that it is not absurd to reject. One does not thereby declare oneself against objectivity; one only allows that objectivity may sometimes obtain not in proof to another, but in the common ability for each one to prove something to himself or herself.

This form of objectivity may be rejected on the ground that it would leave us in a position of skepticism regarding other minds: if I cannot prove to you that I have phenomenal consciousness, you cannot prove the analogous proposition about yourself to me. It is, however, mere dogma to hold (as many have) that I know others' minds solely through others' behavior. As I argued in Robinson (1997a), we have strong and readily available reasons to believe that others are constituted very much like ourselves.[8] If events in our brains cause episodes of phenomenal consciousness, similar events in others' brains should be presumed to do likewise. To advance the old saw that such reasoning would be an induction from a single case would be to abandon principles of biology. Biological science does not

---

8   Hill (1991, chap. 9) gives an account of knowledge of other minds with which the account of Robinson (1997a) overlaps in significant respects, including the reply to the "only one case" objection discussed in our immediately following text. However, Hill's statement of his version of the argument from analogy still relies on the idea that qualitative events are efficacious in behavior, and that we reason backward from their role in our own behavior to a similar role in the behavior of those who are like us. Evidently, this line of reasoning is not open to an epiphenomenalist. The account of Robinson (1997a) allows that behavioral *dissimilarity* would be evidence for internal dissimilarity, and thus that absence of gross behavioral dissimilarity indirectly supports our internal likeness to one another. But it puts the direct argument for knowledge of other minds squarely in the other direction, i.e., on the argument from likeness of biological structure, to high probability of similar neural events, and thence to similarity of the effects (namely, occurrences of phenomenal qualities) of (certain kinds among) those neural events.

regard each member of a species as a distinct natural kind. If we follow the classifications familiar to biology, we will regard our actual inductive base as comprising many kinds of brain events (each with multiple instances) that cause many kinds of episodes of phenomenal consciousness, and we will form generalizations to other occurrences of the same natural kinds, i.e., to similar brain events in other people and animals.

But now (b) it may be said that I cannot prove that I have phenomenal consciousness even to myself. This would, indeed, be a serious objection to epiphenomenalism, if true, and so epiphenomenalists must respond to it with care. But let us note the following straightaway. If I could prove to you that I can prove to myself that I have episodes of phenomenal consciousness, I would have proved the latter to you, which we have just seen cannot be done. So it cannot fairly be demanded that epiphenomenalists prove to others that they can prove to themselves that they have episodes of phenomenal consciousness.

Once this point is clear, however, it becomes difficult to see where there is supposed to be a problem – and hence, it is not easy to know what should be said. Perhaps it will be helpful simply to describe some elements of a state of mind that may occur. Suppose, then, that I am looking at my blue mouse pad and thinking about the issues of this chapter. I have a perceptual experience, and, without rehearsing every detail of the argument, I remember the conclusions I have reached and, in particular, that I think that an adequate account of what is going on requires recognition of an intrinsic blue character of my experience. I say these things to myself and, perhaps, I say to myself that I am saying these things to myself. I have an impression that the blue character of my experience is the very quality that my phrase "blue experience" indicates. I also note that I hold that the blue quality of my experience is not the cause of my silently soliloquizing to the effect that I have a blue experience. Does this fact make me worry that my soliloquizing may be mistaken? No. Should it make me have such a worry? How might such a worry get started? Perhaps I say to myself, "You say to yourself that you have a blue experience, but it's just your neurons that make you say that; the blue experience isn't causing anything." I am not moved to doubt by this, partly because I think that the cause of the blue experience is causing events that cause me to say to myself that I have a blue experience; and partly because I reflect that even if the blue experience were a cause, there would be no reason to expect me to be aware of the causal mechanism, and so my state of mind would, as far as I have any reason to believe, be just what it is now – i.e., one in which the experience and the silent soliloquy in which I tell myself about my experience occur together. "But wait," I hear my skeptical side saying, "the fact that you are having a blue experience cannot, according to what you say your view is, have anything to do with producing the feeling that it is right for you to be saying to yourself that you have a blue experience. You might be giving yourself this same silent soliloquy speech, and be having the same feeling that it is appropriate, even if you had no blue experiences at all!" But here I think I can rebuke my skeptical side with two comments. First, it is not a consequence of any view I hold that I might be giving myself this same silent soliloquy speech, and feeling that it is appropriate, even if I had no blue experiences. If I had no blue experiences, I would not have the causes of blue experiences, and then there is no reason to think that I would have the causes of my saying to myself that I have them. Second, it is weird to suppose that I can be having a silent soliloquy, but not the blue experiences that my silent soliloquy is about. (If I couldn't have a silent soliloquy because I don't have *any* phenomenal consciousness, then, of course, I don't have blue experiences; but there is no plausibility at all to the idea that I am having genuine phenomenal auditory imagery but no visual experiences.)

I make no pretensions to being a novelist, but I do think that the foregoing internal dialogue does expose the kind of deep doubt that one may have in coming to grips with epiphenomenalism. Reflection upon this dialogue seems to me to teach the following lesson. If at any point I try to think of the content of the dialogue as proving to *you* that I have experiences, I am done for and am advancing a question-begging claim. And so, if I imaginatively put myself in the position of a third party and try to use my internal dialogue to convince that third party, I am likewise certain to fail. But I am not a third party, and so long as I do not make the mistake of pretending that I am, I simply cannot get a robust doubt going.

Let us put the point in the well-worn language of Zombies. By a (capitalized) "Zombie" I mean a philosopher's zombie, i.e., a being that exhibits *completely and exactly* human behavior but has no phenomenal consciousness. (The contrast is with Hollywood zombies, who stare fixedly and move woodenly.) Suppose someone asks, "Since you're an epiphenomenalist, how do you know you're not a Zombie?" The answer is, if I am a Zombie, I'm a Zombie; I have no phenomenal consciousness, my overt words about my experiences (necessarily overt, because if I'm a Zombie I haven't got any others) are all false, and, of course, I don't know I'm not a Zombie. But if I am not a Zombie, then I do have experiences, and my silent soliloquy about them is true, and caused in a way that makes its

172

truth nonaccidental, and I know I have experiences. And, by the way, I *do* have experiences.[9]

This last sentence is likely to set off a new round of doubts, but we can cut them short. If I think, for a moment, that "And, by the way, I *do* have experiences" should convince *you* that I'm not a Zombie, then I have glaringly begged the question. But if I add it for myself, I have merely told myself the obvious, and there is no mistake or logical impropriety.

From the discussion of this section I conclude that there is no difficulty in epiphenomenalism *provided* that we avoid two mistakes: (i) confusion between (CH1) and (CH2) and (ii) confusion between what I am entitled to say to myself (and, by parity, what all are entitled to say to themselves about themselves) and what can be a proof to others. These mistakes are easy to make, and the second one is especially easy, because one can imaginatively put oneself in the position of another. The ease of these mistakes is sufficient to account for the resistance philosophers have had to epiphenomenalism. But if we do not make these mistakes, then we cannot generate any definite and palpable doubt about epiphenomenalism.

---

9   Perhaps it will be objected that even the minimal use of Zombies that I have made allows too much credibility to the concept. Cottrell (1999) has argued that if we can conceive of zombies, then we can conceive of our being very much as we are, except that we are zombified with respect to one sense modality, say, vision. We give the same detailed reports on the colors, distances, lighting conditions, etc. that we always do, and although we claim not to have any visual experience, our ability to give correct reports is dependent in the standard ways on the position and condition of our eyes. This part of the argument seems to me to be correct. Cottrell then goes on to argue that what we have just described is not possible. "I just don't seem able to form a conception of *this* sort of information's being acquired, via a few moments' gaze out the window, *without* there being 'something it is like' to acquire it, without there being an impression of subjective phenomenology" (1999, p. 8; emphases in the original). The presumed conclusion, that zombies are not really conceivable, then arrives by modus tollens.

But if there being something it is like to acquire information is supposed to be a distinct fact from the acquisition of information, as Cottrell's way of putting his case suggests, then we can coherently describe the obtaining of the one fact in the absence of the other; and this is all that is required for conceivability. It is not also required that we can *imagine*, i.e., form a lively inner portrayal of, this situation. There are all sorts of dissociations that we have excellent medical reasons to accept that are exceedingly difficult to imagine, e.g., hemineglect or prosopagnosia. (In the latter case, we know that a familiar face can be processed in respect of its familiar characteristics without the subject's being aware of who is present or aware that the processing that leads to an emotional reaction is occurring.)

Cottrell's paper also trades on the idea that we would have no good reason to believe a person who gives fully detailed and eye-dependent reports of visual matters but denies having visual experiences. But we saw in our discussion of Dennett (1991) that neurological evidence might carry us where behavioral evidence cannot carry us; and we shall see this point developed in more detail in a later chapter.

Wilfrid Sellars (1956) introduced a deeply important dilemma that must be faced by any experiential realism, and recent resurgence of interest in Sellars's work, most notably in McDowell (1994), has put this dilemma once again before the attention of philosophers.[10] The burden of the present section is to state the problem and explain the best way for QER to respond to it. To introduce the problem, let us consider the following three claims.

(1) Knowledge requires possession of concepts.[11]
(2) Possession of concepts requires a process of acquisition.
(3) Justification is a relation that holds between premises and conclusions.

It follows from (3) that what is believed with justification is what is believed as a conclusion from something else. But inference to a conclusion requires that the basis of the inference already be something that *can* stand in a logical relation to the conclusion; and this requires that the basis be something properly expressible in a sentence, i.e., something that already has a structure that involves conceptualization. In short:

(4) Justifiers must be conceptualized.

Nothing in this book has suggested any departure from a long tradition according to which the having of qualitative events is something that does *not* depend on a process of concept acquisition. For example, I have said nothing to suggest that infants, animals, or normal adults who happen not to possess the concept *F* should thereby be debarred in any way from having *F* qualitative events. Indeed, the ruminations about causation of qualitative events in the previous chapter lead naturally to a view in which those causes are taken not to depend on concept possession. The foregoing argument, however, provides a reason to focus our attention more carefully on these questions, for it forces us to make the following choice.

(5) *Either* (i) Qualitative events are already conceptualized, i.e., are the kinds of things that could not occur in a being that lacked an applicable concept;
    or (ii) Qualitative events cannot be justifiers of any of our beliefs.

---

10 Sellars actually introduces an inconsistent triad, thus suggesting a trilemma, and he uses the terminology of sensing sense contents. I believe my slight repackaging preserves the force of Sellars's problem, and makes it easier to be clear both about my way out and the extent to which I agree with Sellars's background assumptions.

11 Here and in what follows, I am referring to knowledge *that*, not knowledge *how*.

(i) gives up the traditional independence of experience from concept acquisition; (ii) gives up the equally traditional idea that we can be justified in believing certain things "on the basis of" what is given to us in sensory experience.[12]

To the qualitative event realism developed so far, I shall now add the acceptance of (ii) and the rejection of (i). Taking this stance means that I must explain both how qualitative events stand to belief and justification in general, and why rejecting (ii) can ever have seemed attractive. I begin with the latter of these tasks. If it should happen that one does have the concept F, and one has an F qualitative event, then normally one can say to oneself "I have an F qualitative event" (or, at least, "I have an F experience"). This bit of silent soliloquy is in sentential form, and is thus the right sort of thing to enter into relations of justification. Focus on these frequently available cases, and the ease with which we can normally tell ourselves what we are experiencing, could well lead to a confusion that it is qualitative events rather than judgments about them that are appealed to as justifications.

Giving this explanation should lead us to ask about the relation between a qualitative event and the judgment that one has that qualitative event, and this question returns us to the first task of explaining the relation between qualitative event possession and judgment. Happily, the discussion of Wittgenstein in Chapter 2 permits a brief and mostly recapitulatory statement at this point. Acquiring a concept that we can apply to a phenomenal quality normally depends on a complex causal history that includes sensory events and interaction with the world, most usually including interaction with members of a linguistic community. The result of such interactions is to put in place a brain structure that ensures that, under normal conditions, we do not judge that we have an F experience unless we do have such an experience. Thus, when we judge that we are having an F experience, we are normally in a position in which that judgment is an instance of knowledge. In the infrequent cases in which we actually seek to support a further belief by basing it on our judgments about what kind of experience we are having, we are thus in a position that meets both the logical requirement of supporting a conclusion with

---

12 "Given" is, of course, Sellars's term, and the issue at hand is part of his attack on the "Myth of the Given". I have discussed the given at some length in Robinson (1988). In the present discussion, I focus on the argument just outlined, on the issues necessary to understand knowledge of our phenomenal qualities, and on the role of this knowledge in our knowledge in general.

a premise and the epistemological requirement of relying on a premise that expresses something we know.

It will be objected that this explanation is very complex and theoretical. By no stretch of the imagination is the background required for this explanation given to us or even available at all to anyone who has not engaged in a considerable amount of philosophizing. It may therefore be alleged that the account just given fails to match our experience that, as we might say in an unguarded moment, our experiential judgments are simply justified in the face of our experience.

This objection does make a correct phenomenological point. Certain moments in my philosophical reflections about the issues at hand can indeed be described in the following way: I look at a ripe tomato, tell myself I am having a red experience, tell myself that I have just told myself "I'm having a red experience", *and* tell myself that the term "red" seems appropriate to what I am having. This last statement does not come to me as a conclusion of an argument; I just *find* that "red" is the word for this experience. I can say to myself "Maybe 'red' just seems to be the right word, but actually the color I'm experiencing is something else entirely". When I say this to myself, I get an eerie feeling, but nothing by way of argument comes to mind.

I can easily understand how someone might express this eerie feeling by speaking of being justified in the face of experience. Other similar formulations come to mind, e.g., that experience gives the evidence for the judgment, that the quality of the experience is the reason I make the judgment, that the quality of the experience is the cause of my judgment. These formulations probably do no harm if we are not discussing the issues at stake in this chapter. But there is no reason to accept these formulations as literally true and much reason to think that they are false. By the latter claim, I mean that literally explaining my judgment that I have an F experience by something extraordinarily simple – the mere occurrence of an F experience – requires an acceptance of mysterious connections; and no such mysterious connections are needed. Instead of mysterious simplicity, we can, and should, bring to bear the science that investigates the dependence of psychological states upon brain states, and the philosophy of Wittgenstein and many others who have shown us the complex setting that is required if there is to be meaning, concepts, and judgments.

It is important in reading the last few paragraphs to keep firmly in mind that "justification" is being used to refer to the logical relation between premises and conclusions. The view I have been developing is that our judgments that we have an experience of a certain phenomenal kind are not justified by being inferred as conclusions from some other judgments that function as premises. In another sense, however, we may well be "justified" in judging that we have an F experience whenever we do so judge. Namely, in a quasi–moral sense, we are not doing something that is "unjustified" if we judge that we have an F experience – i.e., we are not eligible for criticism as being careless reasoners or uncritical believers if we so judge. But, again, these facts depend on a large number of other facts that do not lie on the surface and are not available to introspection or casual thought.[13]

These reflections are bound to bring to mind Russell's (1912, for example) phrase "knowledge by acquaintance". Strictly speaking, this phrase is acceptable, *provided* that it is regimented to have no other sense than "knowledge of phenomenal qualities". Such knowledge is *knowledge*, but it is not knowledge that rests on premises; it is noninferential, or direct, knowledge. This makes it a distinctive case of knowledge, and therefore one may, if one wishes, introduce a technical term for it. Having said that, however, we should also be careful to note that "knowledge by acquaintance" is a dangerous phrase, i.e., it is a phrase that is likely to suggest a misleading picture. (a) It may suggest that "acquaintance" is a special and simple relation that holds between our judgments (or ourselves) and our qualitative events. The account given previously, however, embraces several ordinary relations but no special, simple one. (b) "Knowledge by acquaintance" may suggest that there is something special about the type of *belief* involved in knowing that we are having experiences of a certain phenomenal kind. This idea too finds no place in the foregoing account. (c) Worst of all, the phrase may suggest that *having qualitative events* is *in itself* having a kind of knowledge. This suggestion would, of course, plunge us straight back into the dilemma from which the discussion of this section has enabled us to escape.

Finally, it is important to keep in mind that the topic at hand is knowledge of phenomenal consciousness (or, once we have accepted QER as developed here, our knowledge of qualitative events). I have dwelt on this topic because it is the focal point of an objection to epiphenomenalism, and not because knowledge of qualitative events is so important in itself. Most of the time, we just take it that there are ordinary objects

---

13 Here too, I believe I am following one strand of Wittgenstein's thought. The point being made, however, stands independently of the question of correct interpretation of Wittgenstein.

of various kinds before us, and if nothing problematic occurs, it never crosses our minds to justify these takings by appealing to judgments about the qualities of our perceptual experience. There is no suggestion in the foregoing account that we could, even in principle, justify all our knowledge of ordinary things by deduction (or "construction") from premises about our phenomenal qualities. I have been concerned only to defend the claim that we do have knowledge of our qualitative events and their phenomenal qualities, and to explain how that knowledge is related to the events it is about.[14]

LOSS OF CONTROL

If the foregoing discussion has been as clear as intended, it will have produced a strong impression of our dependency upon our brains. Our attention will have been directed to and held upon the fact that our phenomenal consciousness, just as much as our intelligence and our ability to coordinate our movements, rides upon brain processes of which we have no introspective knowledge, and only lately acquired and still sketchy knowledge through scientific means.

This sense of dependence can make us uncomfortable. The nature of the discomfort is similar to what is sometimes produced by reflection on unpleasant medical facts. How thin are the vessel walls that stand between us, as we now know ourselves, and distressing conditions such as inability to recognize one's wife; how tenuously do we hold our ability to recognize the difference between modus ponens and affirming the

---

14 This paragraph offers a sketch toward responding to some of the issues raised by McDowell (1994). In particular, it allows that ordinary perception is constitutionally a capacity that involves the use of full-blown concepts. Having said that, I believe it is necessary to explicitly resist part of McDowell's treatment of nonconceptual content. (i) McDowell (1994, pp. 57–58) holds that experience is conceptual because it involves short-lived recognitional capacities. But while some concepts require recognitional capacity (have such capacity as a necessary condition of their possession), recognitional capacity is not sufficient for full-blown concept possession. In particular, a (mere) short-lived recognitional capacity does not provide an ability to use the "concept" it allegedly involves in inference. (ii) McDowell (1994, p. 61) considers a case in which one might make a judgment about an ordinary thing, or might only have an inclination to make such a judgment, which one suppresses (because one suspects illusion of some sort). He says, "If one does make a judgement, it is wrung from one by the experience, which serves as one's reason for the judgement." On the view I have been articulating, this is not quite right. Strictly speaking (which would be merely pedantic in any context other than the present one), it is rather the judgment *about* one's experience that (perhaps) justifies one's judgment about what ordinary things are present, not the experience itself.

consequent! Spinoza rightly asserted that the free think of nothing less than of death. Were he alive today, he might well add that they also refrain from dwelling on the fragility and vulnerability of the brain, and the many varieties of mental incompetence to which the technology of keeping the body alive makes us ever more exposed.

It seems possible that the discomfort produced by focusing on our dependence provides a motivational goad that leads many to react to epiphenomenalism with derision, dismissal, and abuse.[15] It is, however, possible to see in this reaction not strength but irony, for resistance to epiphenomenalism may be the last gasp of Cartesianism. It may, that is, be an effort to maintain a vestige of the conception of a self in control, in the face of the fact that we are ineluctably parts of the natural world; and the irony is that it is often the most avid pursuers of naturalizing the mind who are most eager to reject epiphenomenalism. In contrast, epiphenomenalism *can* be seen as the inevitable result of a naturalistic stance, and as a view that both preserves our legitimate scientific interests and – figuratively and literally – saves the phenomena.

15 Dennett (1991, pp. 405–406) provides a stellar example.

Part II

11

Unified Dualism

In Part I of this book, I examined many versions of materialism and found them wanting. Some of them cannot be demonstrated to be false, but they fail to be good theories for other reasons, such as vacuity, unjustified skepticism, introduction of special terms that are not known to be naturalistically definable, and failure to provide advertised explanatory value. It is not good intellectual practice, scientific or otherwise, to give our assent to views that have such grievous faults.

"Materialism" suggests naturalism and respect for science. There is thus some danger that the claim that phenomenal consciousness is material will carry with it the suggestion that it has been brought safely within the orbit of scientific explanation. Since that is very far from being the case, it would be better not to suggest it. It would be better to record the existence of an explanatory gap in a terminology that keeps that fact clearly before our minds. We should say that dualism is our best theory, because we cannot plausibly deny phenomenal consciousness and we cannot give an account of it within our sciences. We know what it is to give a materialist account of life, and we have very promising ideas for further research on purely materialist theories about how our brains make us intelligent. But we do not have any comparable account of or research program about phenomenal consciousness. We ought to face up to this fact, and the straightforward way to do that is to say that as far as we can see, dualism is our best theory, even though, as explained in Chapter 3, we cannot give a demonstrative argument that it is true.

Accepting dualism leaves many questions open about the best form for such a theory to take. I have proposed a particular version, QER, and have given reasons in several places for adopting this form of dualism rather than various alternatives. In the remainder of this book, I shall further develop this version of dualism.

Holding dualism for the reasons just summarized is perfectly compatible with having an interest in discovering a satisfying view of the relation between phenomenal qualities and their causes. Scientific accounts of perception and of the causes of bodily sensations give us overwhelming reason to believe that qualitative events are caused by physical events in the brain, and we can hardly fail to ask what kind of connection this can be or how it can work. Part II is concerned with the prospects for developing a theory of this kind, that is, a theory in which qualitative events will be regarded as being as fundamentally real as quarks or quasars, and in which we will have a satisfying explanatory understanding of the relations among all of the things we regard as real. It will be convenient to have a name for the kind of theory just indicated, and I shall adopt the term "unified dualism" for this purpose.[1]

Because the idea of satisfactory, explanatory understanding is essential to understanding the point of unified dualism, it is important to face up to the fact that we have no theory of what is, in general, required in order to provide explanatory understanding. We should make no apology for this lack of theory, for no such theory is possible. One point to note here is that many of our models of satisfying explanatory understanding come through understanding construction and relations among parts. For example, we explain why some plants turn their leaves toward the sun by reference to the shape of the cells in their leaf stems, and we explain why water is a good solvent by reference to the behavior of H_2O molecules and their interaction with molecules of soluble substances.[2] It

1 The substance of the view here expressed is similar to the one found in Strawson (1994), chap. 4. But Strawson insists that he is some kind of materialist, even though he is as acute and as insistent as anyone in pointing out how little we understand of *how* experiential properties could be material. Strawson suggests the phrase "agnostic materialism", but I find this as confusing as "agnostic theism". "Agnostic monism" would be better – if, as I believe would be natural, it were taken to mean a belief that the world is in principle intelligible, and so all that is real fits together somehow, but we are ignorant, at present, of how that can be. The pull of "monism" toward materialism is, however, so strong that the best choice of term for the unified view we should ultimately desire must include "dualism" if it is not to be misleading in the present conceptual climate.

2 Replying to McGinn's (1991, p. 118) expression of a "brutish feel" of psychophysical connections, Flanagan (1992, p. 119) says, "But it is hard to see why the accounts of the nature of water in terms of its molecular structure, of life in terms of DNA, and so on, aren't also brute." This remark misplaces the bruteness. What is brute are *basic* facts, e.g., that there is charge that comes in two forms, of which likes repel and opposites attract. Out of such brute basic facts, one can *construct* the behavior of H_2O molecules under various conditions of

seems extraordinarily unlikely that we are going to understand the relation between qualitative events and brain events on any such model. One might worry that this unlikelihood implies that we will not be able to achieve explanatory understanding in this area at all. But consider: Newton did not explain motion by construction from materials supplied by Aristotelian physics, and Einstein did not explain motion by construction from Newtonian motions. Fields and wave packets are truly odd if one starts from a billiard ball conception of mechanism, yet we accept electromagnetism as supplying explanations. Waves without a medium were once hardly thinkable but are now incorporated in explanatory accounts. The lesson of these examples is that explanatory understanding is not backward-looking. One is satisfied when one is satisfied; the fact that one's forebears could hardly have imagined *this* sort of explanatory satisfaction is irrelevant. In light of these examples, it is in no way irrational to hope for an explanatorily satisfying unification of our understanding of all that we regard as real, even though it is palpable to us that at present we have no models that show us what this understanding will look like.

It is sometimes argued that the progress of science shows that materialism will triumph in the end. But at best, progress in science shows advancement toward unification – i.e., it shows that later views provide a wider range of explanatory understanding. There is no historical reason to think that our present views will become more and more secure; if anything, the reverse is the case. Thus, we may reasonably hope for progress toward unified dualism, but this is no reason at all to suppose that we will find out how to explain why or how qualitative events arise in a world that remains conceived of as a system of things that are physical, in a sense that remains close to the way we now conceive of physical things and qualitative events.

---

temperature and presence of other molecules, e.g., NaCl. (Strictly, we can do the construction for some very simple cases, and we have strong reasons to believe that, in principle, the same kind of construction could be given in more complex cases, even though the complexity soon outstrips our ability to calculate.) Similarly, DNA enters into processes that we do not yet fully understand, but in which we can already see the outline of a stepwise process that leads from DNA in the presence of other molecules to cell formation, differentiation, repair, adhesion, organ formation, organ interactions, absorption, nutrition, growth, and other life functions. It is exactly such stepwise, constructive processes that we *cannot* provide when we try to connect neural events with phenomenal qualities. Flanagan's remark submerges the genuine fruits of centuries of science and, unfortunately, dismisses the absolutely crucial difference between the achievements of biology and the lack of understanding of the relation between neural events and qualitative events.

An alternative formulation of this point is that while we may hope for explanatory understanding of all that we regard as real, we do not yet have the conceptual scheme within which this understanding can be expressed. In our present conceptual scheme, epiphenomenalist dualism is the least misleading position; but holding that view is compatible with envisaging a revised conceptual scheme in which a unified understanding will be obtainable. When we describe our present position in this way, it will come as no surprise that this book will not offer claims to have proved unified dualism or even to have advanced it very significantly. Conceptual revision takes time and the efforts of many. What can be done is to give reasons for moving in a certain direction, and I shall pursue this effort as far as seems possible.

Rational changing of our conceptual scheme happens not by abandonment but by revision. A useful way of thinking of such change is provided by Sellars's (1981) idea of "successor concepts". Rejection of phlogiston, for example, does not lead us to say that there is no such thing as combustion; instead, our conception of what combustion is changes as we come to regard it as a process in which something (oxygen) is added rather than lost. Applying this background to present concerns leads to the idea that a satisfying view of consciousness will be thinkable only in concepts that are successors to our present ones. Our present division of "materialism" and "dualism" may be superseded by successor concepts in a total view that is more explanatorily satisfying than any we can now so much as imagine.[3]

Several current proposals contain embryonic suggestions for the kind of conceptual revision I have just been describing. Since some of the ideas I will be developing in Chapters 12 and 13 are in conflict with these suggestions, it will be necessary to say why I do not accept them. In explaining these reasons, I will not be aiming at decisive refutations. Many of the views to be considered are not yet fully worked out, and may in the end provide more than can now be seen. When we know that many assumptions must be questioned, it is not possible to be certain which ones we may rely on in supporting one direction of development rather than another. The best we can do is to identify apparent problems, say why some alternatives do not seem promising, and spend most of our

---

3 Other ways of expressing similar ideas about future development of our thought can be found in Nagel (1998). (The particular content of Nagel's suggested direction for the future of our conceptual development is, however, different from what the remainder of this book will propose.)

time trying to find promising steps at places where progress does not seem to be clearly blocked.

KNOWING MATTER FROM INSIDE

Bertrand Russell (1912, 1927b) suggested that in phenomenal consciousness we have our only way of knowing the intrinsic nature of something physical.[4] The negative half of this claim — that we do not know the intrinsic nature of the physical through any way *other* than phenomenal consciousness — flows from the structural nature of our knowledge in physics. Consider, for example, the nature of electrical charge. We investigate this property in physics by examining its causes and effects. For example, charged particles move differently from uncharged particles when placed in magnetic fields, accumulated charge produces visible sparks under certain conditions, current passed through thin wires produces heat, particles that are similarly charged repel each other, and so on. All these facts are relational facts — facts about how charge is related to other physical properties. These other properties are, in turn, known in the same way; for example, heat is known by its tendency to produce expansion, to be radiated, to be transferred by conduction or convection, and to be generated by certain chemical reactions. Mass is known by its gravitational effects, spin by its effects on certain instruments, and so on. If we make our lists of physical causes and effects complete, we can express what we know of physical quantities through descriptions of the form: the property that has such-and-such causes and effects. As to the intrinsic nature of such properties — what they *are* as opposed to what they *do* — physics tells us nothing at all.

This silence of physics about the intrinsic nature of physical reality implies that no theory of the intrinsic nature of physical reality will contradict our physics. Thoughts in the minds of deities can serve as the inner nature of electrons, provided that such thoughts stand in a system of relations of the kind physics discovers. So can any intrinsic properties that we know of under the same proviso. Now, if we ask ourselves what are the properties of which we *do* have intrinsic knowledge, the answer seems to be that phenomenal qualities, and these alone, fill the bill. The redness of our red experiences, for example, does not seem to depend on relations to other things. While red is related to other qualities, most

4   Helpful discussions of the ideas in this section occur in Chalmers (1996) and Stubenberg (1998). See also Maxwell (1978), Feigl (1958), and Lockwood (1989).

187

obviously by being distinct from them, its set of relations to other qualities is not simply all that there is to being red.[5] And it would seem that, since all the properties encountered in physics are merely relational, the only properties left, of which we can know the intrinsic (nonrelational) nature, are phenomenal qualities. These observations create a space for the idea that our knowledge of phenomenal qualities is knowledge of the intrinsic nature of the same physical reality, the relational structure of which is the subject of investigations in physical science.

Intriguing though this idea is, it seems unlikely that it can be satisfactorily worked out. To see why, let us consider just what it is that our phenomenal qualities might be thought to be the intrinsic nature of. One possibility is that they are the intrinsic nature of physical things or properties. There are several candidates here, differences among which do not make a difference to the argument to come. Examples are (a) basic things, e.g., electrons or quarks; (b) basic properties, e.g, charge or mass; and (c) complex things, e.g., brains. Now a key difficulty in all these cases is that our phenomenal qualities are ephemeral, while the things or properties are (at least relatively) permanent. Phenomenal redness, for example, qualifies my consciousness from time to time; but I am always composed of electrons and quarks, which always have their charge, mass, and so on, and I have had my brain for several decades. If phenomenal red is the intrinsic nature of any of the things listed, we would need an explanation of why we have phenomenally red experiences only from time to time. Worse, if phenomenal red is the intrinsic nature of someone's brain, the same reasoning would lead to the same conclusion for phenomenal blue – and for all phenomenal colors, phenomenal sounds, phenomenal tastes, and so on. It does not seem possible that a brain can be all these colors, and so on, all of the time.

---

5   This remark will offend those who understand "all determination is negation" in a certain way. But let us note that we can understand that a quality is different from another quality as a metaphysical claim; there is no need to try to make it into a claim about the meaning of the terms that refer to the qualities. Moreover, there is good reason not to make such a move. Consider red and blue, and consider the set of properties one obtains by substituting for "Q" in the following rubric any quality except red or blue: _____ is different from Q. Properties in the indicated set are all properties that red and blue share. Moreover, being different from red would be the same property as being different from blue if red and blue were not already different, i.e., different apart from the facts about what they differ from. So, unless we admit something as red, and something as blue, that are different apart from considerations of what they are *not*, there would be no difference at all between red and blue. I take this result to be a reductio of ways of taking "all determination is negation" that would conflict with the view expressed in the main text.

It could, of course, be held that various *parts* of physical reality are each intrinsically phenomenal qualitied all of the time, and that a qualitative event is a case of being "exposed" to one or another of these parts. Neural events that may be correlated with experiences of a particular kind could then be regarded as events that amount to "observations" of some part of physical reality. However, the large number of phenomenal qualities prevents the alleged phenomenal qualitied parts of reality from lining up in any plausible way with the physical properties whose intrinsic nature seemed hidden from us. There are four forces (possibly unifiable) and some dozens of particles. Perhaps an exquisitely developed physics will provide us with hundreds of irreducibly distinct physical properties. But there are tens of thousands of phenomenal qualities. If some shade of blue is what charge intrinsically is, and some shade of red is what spin-up intrinsically is, where shall we find physical properties that intrinsically are all the other shades, tastes, and so on?

This problem could, perhaps, be solved by holding that each elementary physical property is intrinsically a combination of parts, each having a different phenomenal quality. We would then be committed to supposing that particular neural events "expose" us to these parts individually. That is, there would be some relation, R, such that a neural event of a certain kind, K, stands in R to x, where x is a part of reality that has phenomenal quality Q; for example, having a phenomenally red conscious event would be having a neural event that stands in R to some part of reality, x, that is intrinsically red.

I doubt that a formal contradiction can be drawn from this view, but if not, that is only because the view says so little. The nature of R is unspecified, and so is the relation between phenomenal qualitied parts of reality and the properties (e.g., charge, mass, spin) to be found in physics. QER as so far developed says that neural events cause phenomenally qualitied, conscious events. This is not all we would like to hear, but it seems we must say at least that much. The theory under consideration says that neural events "expose" us to the properties of parts of reality that combine in some unspecified way to make up charge, mass, and so on. Since we don't know what R is, we don't know *which* part of reality a neural event is supposed to "expose" us to, and this fact seems to preclude our ever making any advance on the question of *which* combinations of phenomenal qualitied parts of reality constitute the intrinsic nature of any physical property. The theory thus appears to introduce a great deal of complexity that has no prospect of paying off in further understanding.

Part of the problem of the view just discussed arises from the mismatch between the ephemerality of our qualitative events and the relative permanence of properties of physical things. Perhaps we can improve the prospects of the "intrinsic nature" view by considering physical realities that are as ephemeral as our qualitative events – namely, our sensory brain events. Thus, for example, from an external point of view, when Eve sees a ripe tomato, a certain set of neural firings occurs. Eve, however, knows this event as it were from the inside, and what she knows about it is that it is phenomenally red.

This view is irrefutable, but it should be avoided. The reason is that it is equivalent to QER as already developed, but is stated in a way that is likely to mislead us about our understanding (or lack of understanding) of consciousness. The key point is that it is just as much of a problem to explain how a set of neural firings could be, in its intrinsic nature, red as it is to explain how a set of neural firings could cause a red conscious event. It seems, indeed, the same *sort* of problem. In fact, we can systematically translate between this view and QER just by switching between grammatically and stylistically appropriate variants of causation and constitution. Thus, consider the following pairs.

(1Q) Neural events of kind K cause phenomenally Q conscious events.
(1I) Neural events of kind K are intrinsically phenomenally Q.

(2Q) Phenomenal qualities exist only in conscious events, which are produced by certain neural events.
(2I) Phenomenal qualities exist only as the intrinsic nature of certain neural events.

(3Q) Phenomenal qualities are epiphenomenal.
(3I) What neural events are intrinsically does not add anything to explanations of the occurrence of the neural events that they cause; the neural properties of neural events are sufficient to explain the neural properties of their neural effects.

(4Q) We do not understand why neural events cause conscious, phenomenally qualitied events.
(4I) We do not understand why neural events have phenomenal qualitied intrinsic natures.

With this list of equivalents in hand, it is easy to see that any statement in QER has an equivalent in the present version of "intrinsic nature" theory, and conversely; and – most importantly – that these equivalents preserve the same structure of problems. They are, in all substantive respects, the same theory. But there is a reason to prefer the qualitative event realist formulation, namely, that it is less likely to mislead. "In experience, we confront the intrinsic nature of our brain events" is apt to sound like a theoretical advance for materialism; but since all the substantive questions remain unresolved, the "intrinsic nature" formulation actually makes no such advance.

It might be suggested that the "intrinsic nature" view offers an account that is meaningfully simpler than QER on the ground that we have independent reason to think that what has relational properties must have some intrinsic properties.[6] If we have already gotten this far, then the choice seems to be between a view that includes three things (i.e., physical relational properties, physical intrinsic properties, and phenomenal qualities) and a view that requires only two things (i.e., physical relational properties and physical intrinsic properties that are identical with phenomenal qualities). In fact, however, both views require three kinds in their ontologies. The apparently simpler second view actually must recognize physical relational properties, physical intrinsic properties *of physical elements*, and physical intrinsic properties *of events* (which are, according to this view, identical with phenomenal qualities). The relation between the last two items on this second list is nontrivial, and raises the same kinds of problems that are familiarly raised by asking what the relation is between brain events and consciousness.

I turn, finally, to a third way of explicating the "intrinsic nature" view, namely, the neutral monism of Russell (1927a). According to this view, phenomenal qualitied events are in themselves neither mental nor physical. They are basic materials for construction. In one kind of construction, they are items of a series composing a mind, and in such a construction they may be regarded as mental. In another kind of construction, they are items in a series from which the physical is constructed, and in such a construction, they may be regarded as elements of physical reality.

Neutral monism is not a view that is easy to understand, but nonetheless, it is possible to see that it suffers from a crucial ambiguity in its idea of "construction". In ordinary uses of this term, elements of construction are *parts* of the constructed whole, and the constructed whole is a whole in virtue of its elements being in certain relations to each other. But Russell seems to be thinking of *logical* construction, which does not make its elements into parts of the constructed whole. Logical construction is

6 I thank Brad Thompson for pointing out the need to respond to this suggestion.

191

inseparable from epistemological concerns. We "construct" a concept by considering what kinds of series of experiences could correctly lead us to infer that an instance of the concept occurs. We know of subatomic particles, for example, by first having a series of experiences involved in our setting up of an accelerator experiment, and then adding to the series by having further experiences when we examine the tracks in the emulsified plates that serve as targets. Certain kinds of series of experiences lead us to say that a proton was detected, and other kinds of series may lead us to declarations of detection of other kinds of particles. Still other kinds of series might have led us to a physical theory very different from the one we now accept, and even one that used concepts different from any that we now have.

These remarks sketch a certain understanding of the "construction" of protons from series of sense experiences in Russell's theory. If this understanding is correct, however, then the view should be considered unpromising. This judgment relies on half a century of philosophy of science, the burden of which is that logical construction cannot provide an adequate account of our physical concepts. Theory always outruns observation; observation provides evidence, but the claims for which observation provides evidence are richer than the sum of our actual, and even our possible, observations. Even our observations need to be couched in terms of ordinary objects and cannot be replaced by records of series of sense experiences.[7] We cannot even get as far as "This is a photographic plate" without exceeding the logical consequences of what is in our sense experience.

It is, of course, possible that there is some deep mistake in this criticism of logical construction. It is, however, very widely accepted, and it decisively undercuts the view that Russellian neutral monism can be a promising line of pursuit for improving our understanding of consciousness.

I close this section with a speculation about the idea of consciousness as giving us access to the intrinsic nature of physical properties – namely, that this idea is a subtle version of the assimilation of consciousness to knowledge. In this case, the structure of the view is that having a conscious event that is an occurrence of phenomenal quality Q is ("really") a knowing of the intrinsic physical property Q. If this suspicion is correct, then the view will not recommend itself to anyone who has accepted the distinction between having a certain kind of conscious experience and

---

7   See, e.g., the article on phenomenalism in Sellars (1963), Chisholm (1948), or Quine (1992).

having knowledge of the kinds of one's conscious experience, on which I have taken pains to insist in the previous chapter.

QUANTUM MECHANICS

Quantum mechanics offers us a field that is paradigmatically physical and testably scientific, and in which there are many strange and still developing ideas. Anyone who is tempted by the idea that we may need a new conceptual scheme in order to achieve explanatory satisfaction about what we now think of as phenomenal consciousness should surely be interested in this territory. Moreover, widely accepted interpretations of the formalisms of quantum mechanics give a special role to experience, or knowledge, or information.[8] Since these concepts are clearly needed in a viable theory of mind, it seems likely that there should be a deep connection between understanding quantum mechanics and understanding phenomenal consciousness. Finally, Hameroff and Penrose (1995–1997) have argued that microtubules and their surrounding conditions allow for effects that are understandable only through the ideas of quantum mechanics. Microtubules seem to be connected with synaptic operations, and they are affected by drugs used in anesthesia. These facts are strongly suggestive of a connection between quantum mechanical understanding of microtubules and understanding of consciousness itself.

Despite these positive indications, there are reasons for doubting that quantum mechanics will be the locus of the kind of conceptual revision that will lead to explanatory understanding of phenomenal consciousness. The first one is that "experience" seems to be equivocal: in philosophy, "experience" is often (though not by any means always) used as a synonym for "phenomenal consciousness", whereas in quantum mechanics, "experience" enters only in connection with the idea that the rules of calculation apply to our states of knowledge, not to what our knowledge is about. Our state of knowledge is a state that contains certain information; but this information is information about a physical state and has little to do with phenomenal consciousness.

This last claim can be supported by an argument that can be conveniently stated in terms of the two-slit experiment. In this experiment, an

---

8   For an explanation of the role of experience see, e.g., Stapp (1993). For a discussion of the special role of information in quantum mechanics, and its distinctness from causation, see Seager (1999).

opaque barrier stands between an emitter and a detector screen. If one slit is opened in the barrier while the emitter is on, the detector screen will record a pattern of hits that is most intense near the point where a line from the emitter through the slit intersects the screen and that falls off with increasing distance from that point. If the first slit is closed and the second slit is opened, the same statement applies. If, however, both slits are opened, the result is not a pair of blobs but, instead, an interference pattern with low intensity where the concentration was highest in the single-slit conditions.

If additional detectors are added so that it can be recorded, for each particle that is emitted, which slit it went through, the interference pattern is destroyed and a mere sum of the two single-slit conditions results. Or, as we may also put it, if we gain information about the trajectories of individual particles in the two-slit condition, the interference pattern is destroyed. Thus, information – or observation, knowledge, or experience – would seem to have an effect on what transpires on the detector screen.

The facts just described, however, have very little to do with phenomenal consciousness. This point is shown by the fact that it does not matter in the least *how* the information comes into our knowledge. It is true that the additional detectors must be readable in some way. Perhaps, for example, there is a light that flashes on if a particle has just passed through slit 1. But it matters not at all whether this light is red, green, or any other color. It matters not at all that the reading is visible; a click or a mild shock would do just as well. The experience could be of any sort whatever, so long as it carries information, i.e., so long as it varies in a way that depends on the trajectory of the particle. This fact implies, however, that the informational content of the reading has nothing particularly to do with the kind of phenomenal consciousness that carries the information. In light of this consequence, it is difficult to see how the connection that quantum mechanics provides between information, or observation, and the existence or nonexistence of the interference pattern can offer any explanatory assistance in understanding how or why neural events give rise to phenomenal qualities.

It might still be thought, however, that there is some intimate connection between consciousness (per se, even if not of any particular kind) and resolution of superpositions into nonsuperposed states. This idea arises in those interpretations of quantum mechanics that hold certain physical states to be intrinsically no more determinate than the descriptions they can be given in quantum mechanics, where the descriptions assign probabilities to a number of incompatible states. For example, in a half-silvered mirror experiment, we may describe the state of a photon as a superposition of the (equiprobable) states (1) passing through the mirror and (2) being reflected. In the absence of actual measurement, we are not allowed to regard the trajectory of the photon as being definitely one of these rather than the other. Any actual measurement, however, produces a definite result, i.e., the photon is measured as having passed through the mirror, or it is measured as having been reflected. In certain interpretations, this "collapse" of the superposition is associated with the fact that an observation is actually made. This conception naturally leads to the question of what, exactly, is an "observation"; and some interpretations answer by making the presence or absence of consciousness essential to the occurrence or nonoccurrence of an observation.

To see why this view is not a promising way of advancing our understanding of consciousness, it will be useful to consider a pair of thought experiments.[9] The first of these experiments involves isolating a group of physicists. Let us lock them up in the Biosphere, remove all devices capable of communicating with the outside, and build a high, well-guarded wall that prevents us from looking in. The physicists are to set up and run a half-silvered mirror experiment with a single photon. Detectors are to be placed at the straight-through and reflected-angle positions. The time for running the experiment is agreed upon before isolation.

Between emission and a change in a detector, the emitted photon is in the superposition of states described earlier. When our isolated physicists have made the observation (of which detector has detected a photon), there is no longer a superposition. Let us ask, however, how physicists on the outside must view this situation. They do not know the states of the detectors; if they have to write down what they know of the state of the photon, they must represent it as a superposition of the two possible trajectories. If some further developments depend on the state of the photon, the physicists on the inside can make an accurate prediction on the basis of their knowledge of a single state; but the physicists on the outside can only project a superposition of consequences of a superposed state of the photon.

---

9   I have constructed these thought experiments to bring out a point of particular relevance
    to the theme of this chapter. It will be evident that they are mere variants of Schrödinger's
    famous cat experiment, and involve ideas that occur in many discussions of the measurement
    problem in quantum mechanics. See Hodgson (1991) for an accessible review of many
    responses to this problem.

Now let us imagine that instead of having isolated a group of physicists, we isolate only a few devices. One of these will be a timer that is set to turn on the experiment at the same time that the physicists would have begun it. Another is a video camera, which is set to be on during the experiment and which records the states of the detectors. Finally, let us include a computer that has an input device that can read the videotape (i.e., that can tell from scanning it which detector detected a photon) and that makes whatever calculations the physicists would have made on the basis of their reading.

We may suppose that our video camera has a timing device and that times are printed on the tape. We may suppose further that the computer makes a record of its calculations, and that the time at which they occur is part of its record. We may suppose, finally, that whenever these records are observed (by outside physicists who have finally opened the wall and unlocked the Biosphere), they will show the same times that the inside physicists would have recorded in the case where they were present and doing the observing and the calculating.

In the case of the (mere) equipment setup, we have the same calculations being done on the inside as we did in the case of the inside physicists. The condition of outside physicists is likewise the same in the two cases: despite their knowledge of the setups, they can only project superposed states of the emitted photon. The moral that it is tempting to draw is that consciousness makes no difference: what happens inside is the same and what can be done on the outside is the same, whether consciousness is present or not.

This conclusion can be resisted without contradiction. One may hold that consciousness, and only consciousness, *cannot* exist in a superposed condition. Thus, the inside physicists' consciousness of detector states cannot be superposed, and collapse must happen when they make the observation. But the mere equipment exists in a superposed state until the outside physicists come inside and observe the records (which, strictly, existed only as states superposed with states corresponding to alternative records until the superposition was collapsed by the outside physicists' late observations).

However, although such a view is not self-contradictory, it rules out any possibility of *explaining* the connection between collapse and consciousness. The reason for this claim is that it has to be simply *assumed* that consciousness cannot exist in a superposed condition; this crucial fact is not the result of some understanding of how consciousness, or how superpositional collapse, works. Such a view does indeed preserve a correlation between consciousness and collapse of superpositions; but this correlation is no more explained than is the (presumed) correlation between neural states and phenomenal qualities of conscious events. Moreover, if we were to suppose that there can eventually be an explanation, in quantum mechanics, of why collapses happen when they do, we would be supposing that we could give a purely physical description of the cause of collapse. If we could do that, we might still find that we have a correlation between such physically described events and conscious events; but this correlation would be no more explanatory than the familiarly hypothesized classical correlation between neural events and conscious events.

This discussion is evidently compatible with the fact that when *we* observe, we are conscious. This fact by itself, however, does not indicate any special connection between quantum mechanics and consciousness. Human observers are likewise possessors of bone marrow; but the fact that our observations are done by possessors of bone marrow shows no special connection between physics and bone marrow.

It may be felt that this discussion leaves out of account the fact that quantum mechanical rules connect observations rather than physical processes. But if we are careful not to equivocate on "observation", we may express the crucial facts by saying that quantum mechanical rules connect experimental setups with probabilities of detector states. There is no *need* to describe detector states in terms that imply consciousness. It is, of course, true that we will not be able to calculate on the basis of a detector state unless we look at the detector; but this fact holds equally for classical cases. This last point should dispel the idea that there is anything special in the connection between our knowing and the world as understood in quantum mechanics.

Before turning to a different kind of connection between consciousness and quantum mechanics, I should emphasize that not all interpretations of quantum mechanics recognize collapses of superpositions. The foregoing discussion, however, does not saddle quantum mechanics *tout court* with ideas that pertain only to some of its interpretations. It applies only to those interpretations that purport to find a deep connection between quantum mechanics and consciousness.

The view considered so far in this section is a somewhat abstract one that attends to the structure of physics and not at all to the structure of brains. It might be thought that a more intimate involvement with brains will lead to a different kind of appreciation for the possible role of quantum mechanics in understanding phenomenal consciousness. This idea has been worked out in considerable detail by Hameroff and Penrose

(1995–1997) in connection with microtubules. These minute structures are found inside neural cells and are, as their name implies, hollow-centered cylinders. Along with connecting proteins (microtubule-associated proteins, or MAPs), microtubules may have a quasi-skeletal function in neural cells, and they may play a role in conduction of molecules from one place to another within them. Microtubules are composed of elements called "tubulins", which can exist in either of two conformations. The conformational state of a tubulin can be influenced by neighboring tubulins and, as a result, microtubules are also able to transmit information along their lengths. Tubulins are known to interact with molecules of substances used in anesthesia in a way that interferes with change of conformation and thus inhibits the information-transferring capacity of microtubules.

The minuteness of microtubules, and their ability to be affected by anesthetics, suggests the possibility that microtubules can be in superposed states, and that collapse to a nonsuperposed state produces phenomenal consciousness. Hameroff and Penrose (1995–1997) hold that "**Orch OR** [Orchestrated Objective Reduction] in microtubules is a model depicting consciousness as sequences of non-computable *self*-selections in fundamental space time geometry. If experience is a quality of space-time, then **Orch OR** indeed begins to address the 'hard problem' of consciousness in a serious way" (p. 193; emphasis in the original). "Reductions" are collapses from superpositions to unsuperposed states. "Objective" signifies that reductions are regarded as real physical processes and not (as in the case of some other theorists) some sort of illusion. Hameroff and Penrose theorize that some objective reductions take place in systems that are isolated from their environments. In these cases, the reduction is self-induced, that is, it comes about because the divergence in the space-time values of the superposed states exceeds a threshold. Systems that are large enough to fit both plausible timing constraints and isolation requirements are argued to be obtainable through orchestration of events in microtubules by means of the connecting proteins. It is these large-scale orchestrated objective reductions that constitute consciousness on the Hameroff–Penrose theory. "We consider each *self*-organized **Orch OR** as a single conscious event; cascades of such events would constitute a 'stream' of consciousness" (p. 190; emphasis in the original).

Many aspects of this theory have been challenged on purely physical grounds. Getting the timing and isolation within plausible limits depends on a host of assumptions, and it is debated whether the required assumptions can be satisfied compatibly with what is known in physics. I shall leave this part of the discussion to the physicists. That is, I shall suppose that the physical assumptions of the Hameroff–Penrose account can be sustained and I shall ask whether, or in what way, this account holds out the promise of explanatory satisfaction regarding phenomenal consciousness. In discussing this question, the only reductions that will be of concern are orchestrated objective reductions as understood by Hameroff and Penrose; thus, I shall adopt the stylistic expedient of abbreviating "**Orch OR**" to "reduction".

A difficulty in the Hameroff–Penrose account can be raised by asking what the difference is between a reduction that is a phenomenal red experience and one that is a phenomenal blue experience. This question may appear to be easily answered by saying that the microtubular state to which a phenomenal red reduction collapses is a different state from the one to which a phenomenal blue reduction collapses. However, this answer gives the difference of reductions only by reference to a difference in what they are related to, not in terms of properties that are intrinsic to reductions themselves.

There is, of course, a property that can be intrinsic to a reduction, namely, the "potentiality property"of being able to collapse to a particular kind of state. But in any case of collapse, there is at least one other, incompatible kind of state to which the collapse might lead, and reductions will always have more than one intrinsic potentiality property. So, if phenomenal qualities are determined by potentiality properties, then consciousness must have more than one phenomenal quality at every time and, indeed, more than one incompatible phenomenal quality at every time. This consequence is directly contrary to the actual character of our experience; thus, intrinsic potentiality properties cannot be identical with or sufficient for producing qualitative events.

There is a further consideration that might be thought to imply that reductions themselves are conscious events, even though the character of a conscious event is determined only by the nature of a nonsuperposed state to which the reduction leads. This consideration lies in the (alleged) property that both consciousness and reductions (on the Hameroff–Penrose model) are *noncomputable*. If consciousness is noncomputable, and if the only physically describable noncomputable items we can find are reductions, then there would be a strong temptation to make the connection between consciousness and reductions as tight as possible.

The claim of noncomputability of consciousness is based on the arguments of Penrose (1989, 1994), which claim to derive their conclusions from the incompleteness of arithmetic established by Gödel (1931). In

Robinson (1992b, 1996b) I have argued that Gödel's results cannot be used to support Penrose's conclusions. I continue to affirm these earlier criticisms, and they form one reason for rejecting the appeal described in the preceding paragraph. Here, however, I want to place these earlier criticisms in suspension in order to raise two other difficulties for applying the noncomputability view in the present context. The first is that the alleged problem raised by incompleteness of arithmetic is a *cognitive* problem. Noncomputability is introduced to enable us to reconcile what we suppose to be our mathematical abilities with a perceived limitation on computable abilities to do mathematics. Now, it is not clear what all this has to do with phenomenal qualities. It is not apparent how supposing that reductions are the loci of phenomenal consciousness would offer any help with the alleged problem we have as mathematicians. If there is no connection between the theory of phenomenal qualities and mathematical needs, however, then the hypothesis that phenomenally conscious events are reductions does no explanatory work, even within the framework of the Hameroff–Penrose view.

The second difficulty is that in many cases, we have apparently continuing consciousness of the same color.[10] Hameroff and Penrose analyze such cases as sequences of events, speculating that the "stream" of consciousness is actually a series of reductions occurring at intervals on the order of tenths of milliseconds to tens of milliseconds (see Hameroff and Penrose, 1995–1997, p. 191). The difficulty here is that in the many cases of apparently continuing consciousness of the same color, reduction after reduction would have to collapse either to the same state or to a state that lies within a class of states so similar that they all have the same phenomenal character. In the first case, the collapses would instantiate the identity function, which is computable (trivially). In the second case, the function from superpositions to (precisely described) collapsed state could conceivably be noncomputable, but there would still be a simple, computable function from superpositions to membership in the class of states with the same phenomenal character. In either case, the idea that reductions are noncomputable would suggest that phenomenal consciousness should not have the kind of continuity over time that it manifestly can have.

This objection can be formally turned aside by appealing to the fact that a noncomputable function may be identical with a computable function

---

10   In the next two chapters, I shall make significant use of continuity and consider important arguments on that topic. I suppress these considerations here in order to follow out a dialectical difficulty in the Hameroff–Penrose account.

for a finite range of arguments. Thus, one might say that repeated collapses to the same state, or similar states, over a finite stretch of time are compatible with noncomputability of consciousness. In the present context, however, this appeal seems ad hoc and unexplanatory. Strictly, the explanatory burden has merely been slightly shifted: instead of being unable to explain why a series of collapses should all go the same way, we now have to explain why a noncomputable function should happen to coincide with a computable function over the particular range during which we have a continuous, unchanging experience.

Again, from a formal point of view, one can maintain noncomputability compatibly with repeated collapses to the same or similar states simply by hypothesizing superpositional states in which the probability of collapse to a given state (or class of similar states) is exceedingly close (but not equal) to 1. The larger the use that is made of this idea, however, the less the idea of noncomputability *explains*. The point of the move, in fact, is precisely to reduce effects that noncomputability might be thought to have in a place where they seem inconvenient.

The foregoing discussion stops short of deriving a contradiction from the attempt to find a place for phenomenal qualities within the fabric of reality as understood in quantum mechanics. But, as in the case of the "intrinsic nature" view, specific and formidable difficulties arise when one tries to work out this idea in detail. These difficulties are strong enough to justify a serious effort to find an alternative approach.

WHY THERE WILL ALWAYS BE ONE KIND OF EXPLANATORY GAP[11]

Physical science respects the principle that the same causes should have the same effects, and this principle entails that different effects have different causes. Wherever, therefore, we can distinguish effects, we can expect a difference in their causes. If an effect is complex, it has distinguishable elements or aspects, which may occur separately from each other on other occasions. A natural expectation, therefore, is that a complex effect will be found to have a cause that also has corresponding distinguishable elements.

Two parallels hold regarding explanation. The first is that when we can explain an occurrence, we can point to various aspects of it and we can relate those various aspects to various aspects of its cause. Bodies can

---

11 The argument of this section was first advanced in Robinson (1996a).

increase their temperature without increasing their mass; we explain this by dividing bodies into small parts and referring mass to the sum of masses of parts while referring temperature to the activity of the parts. Carbon can exist as graphite or as powder or as diamond. Here, we divide carbon atoms into parts and find that the laws of combination permit alternative stable configurations. The second point about explanation is that where we cannot find distinguishable aspects, we cannot find explanation. When we get down to simple properties, e.g., mass or charge, we can have basic laws that we can use to explain other things (namely, complexes), but the basic laws themselves are not explained.

These points hold when we come to explaining our experiences. For example, we can notice similarities of hue, and we can notice that hue remains similar while saturation changes. We can recognize similar degrees of saturation across different hues, as when we classify several different color samples as pastels. We can distinguish brightness levels independently of changes in hue or saturation. Now, our characteristic approach in science is to look for independently variable causes of such independent features; and, indeed, artists and scientists know very well how to mix pigments or light-generating sources in ways that will vary our color experiences in the ways described. The causal connection clearly runs through our neural systems, although we cannot now say just what features of neural events are responsible for preservation of hue across differences of saturation or vice versa. However, no philosopher asserts that there is any unfathomable mystery here; all assume that in the fullness of time, we will be able to identify properties of neural events that systematically covary with hue independently of saturation, other properties that covary with saturation independently of hue, and still other properties that covary with brightness independently of the other two. When we know such properties, we will be in a position to explain why the structure of an experience is what it is by reference to the structure of the neural properties just envisaged. There is no reason to suppose that there is a fundamental explanatory gap here, although there is much we do not know at the present time.

We may apply the same reasoning wherever we find structure in our experience. Thus, for example, we should expect eventually to find analyses of the neural causes of afterimages that explain differences in their shapes as well as differences in their colors. Within hues themselves, it seems that we judge four to be "unique" (or pure, or simple) and the rest to be mixtures (see Hardin, 1988). Details of the neural explanation of these relations among phenomenal qualities may be uncertain, but again, few doubt that a structure of systematic neural differences will be found to underlie, and thus explain, these relations.

Explanations of the kind imagined here, however, lead to further questions that do not have explanatory answers, just as they do in other areas of science. Each of the structures described is a structure *of elements*. Explanation of variance of hue and saturation depends on hues and degrees of saturation. These are elements in these explanations; their relations are expected to be explained by relations in their causes, but those explanations will not explain why the hues are what they are or why saturation is what it is. Explanation of complexity in, say, orange will rely on complexes of neural events – presumably complexes of neural events that have a special relation to the kinds of neural events involved in experiences of unique red and unique yellow. But that explanation will not explain why one neural event causes phenomenal unique-red conscious events or why another causes phenomenal unique-yellow conscious events.

Now, perhaps someone will be able to think of a way in which phenomenal unique red is complex. If so, all parties to the present discussion will expect there to be discoverable (although maybe not easily discoverable) neural events whose structure matches that complexity. But somewhere we will come to qualities that are not further decomposable. Wherever this happens, we will have come to a point where explanation will run out. And the reason for this result will be a familiar one: science explains structure by structure in the causes, but where there is no structure, this kind of explanation cannot be given. The explanatory gap will remain because some phenomenal qualities have no phenomenal structure. For these qualities, the structural complexity of their neural causes will have no corresponding structure in consciousness, and further advances in knowledge of neural structure cannot provide corresponding advances in explanatory force.

To put this conclusion a little more plainly, consider unique red. We cannot rule out the possibility of coming to realize that this phenomenal quality has a complexity of which we are presently unaware. But if it does have such complexity, there will be some further phenomenal qualities that constitute this complexity, and then the foregoing conclusion will apply to those, or to yet further elements of those qualities if they too are complex. This complexity must come to an end somewhere, and for the sake of concreteness I will assume that we have come to the end of possible analysis with unique red itself. Adopting this assumption, it will be correct to say that even though we may hope for some unified view of a relation between brain events and conscious events, we should not expect an explanation of why a *particular* kind of brain event gives rise to *(unique) red*. If we cannot "decompose" unique red – if we cannot define it in terms of some set of elements – then we cannot conclude that red occurs from premises that tell us that its elements occur (and occur in the right relation). But then, unless we already assume something about unique red in our premises, we will not be able to exhibit a statement of the occurrence of unique red as a validly drawn conclusion from any argument we can formulate. "(Unique) red" would be a term that would occur in a categorical conclusion, but not in our premises, and we would not have a valid argument that explains why unique red must be the phenomenal quality that is associated with the kind of brain event that we might well know to be its cause.[12] In this sense, we must expect a limit to our explanatory ability.

Let us consider a possible way around this predicament.[13] Experimental work shows that our color quality space is not symmetrical. There are more distinguishable shades between unique red and unique yellow than there are between unique blue and unique green. Yellow is exceptional in that it darkens to brown, while other colors darken to black. Let us make a plausible "smoothness" assumption, i.e., the assumption that small differences in phenomenal colors of conscious events are caused by small differences in brain events. It may well be that there is only one way of mapping our phenomenal colors onto our brain events that will preserve the smoothness assumption. If this is the case, then there would be a kind of necessity in the fact that a given phenomenal color is associated with the brain event that occupies the corresponding place in the unique mapping.

The assumptions that lead to this kind of necessity, however, still leave open the possibility that our brain events might have been causes of a set of qualities that differ from any we actually experience – a set of qualities that have the same relations among themselves as our colors have, but are as different from the qualities in our experiences as the smell of garlic is from red. That is, it might be true that:

(1) Given that we actually experience the set of phenomenal colors that we do, and that these phenomenal colors stand in the relations that they do, and

---

12 The restriction to categorical (i.e., not disjunctive and not hypothetical) conclusions rules out trivial ways of introducing new terms into the conclusion of an argument. For example, "P, therefore P or Q" is valid whether or not "Q" contains a term that does not occur in "P".

13 For suggestions in this direction, see Hardin (1988) and Clark (1993).

given the smoothness assumption, and given the possibilities for similarities and differences of events in our brains, there is only one way of mapping phenomenal colors onto our brain events, and thus there is a certain brain event, BE1, that must be the one that causes unique red – i.e., *that* event's causing unique red is an unavoidable consequence of the assumptions.

But it might still be false that

(2) BE1 necessarily causes unique red, i.e., there is no possible world in which BE1 occurs and causes a conscious event with phenomenal quality Q, where Q is not unique red.

In a possible world in which BE1 causes Q, where Q ≠ unique red, the causal relations must be different from those in our world. Thus, if we *assume* the causal relations of our world, then we can have a consequent explanation of why we are having a unique red experience on a certain occasion. But the explanatory gap remains with us in this form: we cannot explain why the causal relations between particular brain event kinds and particular phenomenal qualities are what they are.

There is a conceivable way around this conclusion. Suppose it is the case that there is a fixed set of *possible* phenomenal qualities of all sensory types and a fixed set of possible kinds of brain events that might give rise to phenomenal consciousness. Suppose further that some principle analogous to our smoothness assumption is a fundamental metaphysical truth. Then it might be that there is only one way of assigning phenomenal qualities to brain events that is compatible with the fundamental metaphysical truth. In that case, there would be a sense in which a given brain event *must* cause a particular phenomenal quality. Here, however, we should note that we cannot expect ever to have knowledge of phenomenal qualities that our brains do not permit us to experience. It follows that we will never know all of the possible phenomenal qualities, nor will we know what the possible range of these qualities might be. We can thus never expect to be in a position to be able to understand why a particular kind of brain event *must* give rise to a conscious event that has the particular phenomenal quality that it does.

CONCLUSION

This chapter began with some optimism about the possibility of explanatory satisfaction becoming available in a revised conceptual scheme. Since then, I have given reasons for regarding some approaches to conceptual

revision as unpromising, and I have argued that simplicity of a phenomenal quality (to which we must come sooner or later) forces a limitation
on a certain kind of explanation. It would not be surprising if a certain
pall of pessimism were felt to hang over the project of finding a unified
dualism.

It would be gratifying to be able to say that I can now reveal a new
theory that will provide us with the explanatory satisfaction we seek.
Unfortunately, such a theory does not (yet) exist. In the next two chapters,
however, I will describe an approach to understanding the relation of our
brains to phenomenal consciousness that I believe to be more promising
than any alternative of which I am aware.

12

Patterns as Causes of Qualitative Events

In this chapter I introduce *patterns* of neural activity as causes of conscious events. I approach patterns from two directions, once through a thought experiment and once again through the property of homogeneity. The focus in this chapter is to clarify what it is to regard *pattern* – pattern as such – as fundamental to consciousness. Some questions and objections that may be raised regarding the resulting view will be addressed in the following chapter.

A preliminary caveat will save tedious qualifications later and also provide a helpful first step in focusing on the importance of pattern as such. In the thought experiment to follow, I shall assume that the brain events that are at least correlatable with conscious events are neural events. This assumption is both familiar and plausible. It is, however, conceivable that the patterns that are relevant to the occurrence of conscious events are patterns of activity in microtubules, or patterns of activity in glial cells, or patterns of activity in some combination of microtubules, glial cells, and neurons. If any of these possibilities turns out to be actual, the wording of the following discussion would have to be significantly revised. However, since the emphasis is on patterns, in abstraction from the kinds of elements in which patterns may be realized, the main conclusions would remain exactly the same as the ones that will be drawn from the discussion conducted in terms of neurons.

A THOUGHT EXPERIMENT

The motivation for the following thought experiment comes from the idea that neural causes of qualitative events may be approachable by considering neural *differences* in cases that are highly similar except for a

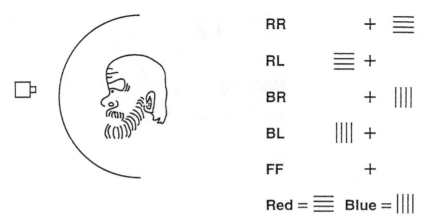

Figure 1.

difference of one phenomenal quality. To follow out this suggestion, let us imagine subjects with normal color vision whose heads are immobilized inside a hollow, uniformly gray hemisphere. (See Figure 1.) A device that cannot be seen directly by subjects can project images visible from inside the hemisphere. In the experiment, only three regions and three colors besides the gray background are used. (a) A black fixation cross is projected in the central region. (b) The remaining two regions used are small but clearly visible rectangular areas, one to the right of the fixation cross and one to the left. These areas are not marked by any visible boundary. Into these areas is projected either a (rectangular) patch of red or one of blue. Only one area receives a red or blue projection at a time. Subjects are instructed to name the color they see on each trial. A trial consists of 500 milliseconds of fixation cross only, followed by 500 milliseconds of fixation cross alone or fixation cross plus one colored rectangle, followed by offset of both fixation cross and colored rectangle (if any). The conditions for a trial can be labeled:

Red conditions:	RR	Red to the Right of fixation
	RL	Red to the Left of fixation
Blue conditions:	BR	Blue to the Right of fixation
	BL	Blue to the Left of fixation
Gray condition:	FF	Fixation cross followed by fixation cross only.

These conditions are to be presented in pseudorandom order, with 2 seconds between subjects' reports and onset of the next trial.

The foregoing setup is quite feasible; but we are now to make the purely imaginary supposition that subjects have each of their neurons impaled with recording electrodes, so that we have a complete record of neural activity during the experiment.

The hypothesis that motivates consideration of this thought experiment is that there ought to be some respect in which the effects of RR and RL in the brain have a commonality that is not present in the other three conditions. There should likewise be a commonality for the brain effects of BR and BL that is not present in the other three conditions. Finally, the brain effects of all of the first four conditions ought to be distinctively different from those of FF. Let us proceed by reflecting on what these commonalities and differences might, or might not, be.

There are numerous logical possibilities here, and it will be helpful to cut down on them if there are neurally plausible ways to do so. One such constraint is embodied in the following Topological Mapping Assumption.

(TMA) Neighboring areas of retinas are mapped onto neighboring areas of primary visual cortex, V1. Neighboring areas of V1 are mapped onto neighboring areas of further visual cortical regions, e.g., V4. Similar neighborhood-preserving mapping is common to our sensory systems.

While there are some discontinuities and metrical distortions in our (roughly) topological mappings, neuroscience supports an approximation to TMA that enables us to suppose there are regions of visual cortical areas that correspond to the regions on which we projected our red or blue rectangles. Which cortical area we should be most interested in is something for neuroscientists to decide; but to fix our ideas for the moment, let us suppose that the area of critical importance will turn out to be V4.[1] Let us label the subareas of V4 that correspond to the left and right rectangular areas on the gray screen "A1" and "A2", respectively. This notation permits the following specification of the questions of interest: What is common to A1 in condition RL and A2 in condition RR that is distinctively different from the other conditions? What is common to A1 in condition BL and A2 in condition BR that is distinctively different from the other conditions? How do these

---

1   The thought experiment I have imagined would generate data from which one could determine the relevant cortical area.

commonalities differ from each other? And how do they both differ from A1 and A2 in condition FF?[2] Let us consider some possible answers.

(a) There is nothing intrinsic to A1 and A2 that distinguishes the red conditions from the blue conditions or from the gray condition.

Since our subjects have normal color vision, some change of state in A1 is brought about by the RL condition, and some change of state in A2 is brought about by the RR condition. Since both of these conditions contain exposure to red rectangles, we are guaranteed to have a commonality of sorts between the indicated events in A1 and A2 – namely, they are both effects of exposure to red.[3] This, however, is an *extrinsic*, or relational, commonality. Likewise, it may be that the indicated events in A1 and A2 both causally contribute to subjects' reporting "red" as the name of the color to which they are exposed. This again is an extrinsic commonality of the two events. The sense of hypothesis (a) is that there is no *other* sort of commonality in the two events – nothing about what goes on in A1 and what goes on in A2 themselves that would lead anyone to classify those events as being of the same kind (strictly, a kind more specific than the generic kind *neural activation event*). And likewise, there is nothing about events in A1 and A2 during blue conditions that would lead anyone who did not already know the commonalities in their causes and their effects to classify them together under any kind more specific than *neural activation event*.

A simple parallel may help to clarify the point being made here. Imagine two automatic doors. One works because an approaching person steps on a movable plate; the other works because an approaching person interrupts a light beam. The cause (an approaching person) is the same and the effect (the opening of the door) is the same, but there can be intermediate stages that are physically quite dissimilar – e.g., one is mechanical, the other electrical. There would be no physical reason to group the mediating processes together if one did not know about their common causes and effects. Now, hypothesis (a) is that this last sentence is true of areas A1 and A2, even when their owner's eyes are being exposed to the same color.

---

2 These questions arise in just the same way if we imagine red and blue to be projected into two different areas on the same side of the fixation cross – near right and far right, for example. The locations in the text were chosen merely for ease of presentation.

3 Strictly speaking, they are effects of exposure to P-red. In the present context, however, it will be simpler and harmless to apply color terms without qualification to external things or light sources.

Hypothesis (a) makes sense if one has already taken a stance that rejects the reality of qualitative events. If there are no such events, then no causes for them are needed. So long as the subject has developed neural connections that allow certain events in A1 and A2 to lead to (correct) reports of "red" and other events in A1 and A2 to lead to (correct) reports of "blue", the skeptic about qualitative events will be satisfied. But from the point of view of QER, hypothesis (a) must be regarded as a premature and unwelcome closing off of any causal explanation of qualitative events.

This remark needs some explanation. Let us begin by noting that while same causes require the same effects, the converse does not hold; that is, it is often possible to bring about the same (kind of) effect by different (kinds of) causes. It is thus not contradictory to suppose that conscious events with the same phenomenal quality can be brought about by different kinds of causes. It follows that hypothesis (a) is not contradictory and does not even contradict QER. However, hypothesis (a) would require a qualitative event realist to accept one of the following two severe explanatory costs.

(1) If a wide variety of different kinds of neural activation events cause qualitative events of the same kind, then there would be no generality of explanation of how a subject learns to correctly report "red" (for example). A particular connection would have to be "learned" from some type of activation in each part of V4 to the correct item in the color lexicon. This might seem acceptable if we consider only two separated areas. But the generalization of hypothesis (a) would apply to all areas, including, for example, an area adjacent to A1. Let us call this area A3; then the generalization of hypothesis (a) would say that completely different kinds of neural activities would be brought about in A1 and A3 by exposure to the same red illumination of adjacent parts of the screen, and both would lead to reports of "red". Presumably, a red illumination that overlapped the areas that cause changes of activation in A1 and in A3 would produce two different kinds of neural activation, namely, one kind in the activated portion of A1 and another in the activated portion of A3. Now, as already noted, these cases are not self-contradictory. But if we take them seriously, and multiply them for other colors from regions that project to the same areas, we will have an explanatory mess, i.e., a set of one-time, brute fact connections from various areas that will offer no opportunity for causal generalizations.

(2) The large collection of brute fact connections could be avoided by holding that common causes (e.g., common illuminations) can explain common effects (i.e., reports using the same predicate) without doing so through a common mechanism or a transmission of common marks through the causal process. However, this view itself proposes a mysterious kind of causation that is not

found elsewhere in the sciences. Moreover, many kinds of external circumstances can cause qualitative events that are indistinguishable in phenomenal color. It is not clear that there is any sense to commonality of cause in these cases, except in the Pickwickian sense that several cases share the ability to bring about qualitative events of the same kind. If this is the right way to look at these cases, then the only real commonality would lie in the effects (i.e., reports using the same predicate). This commonality is genuine enough, but as it comes later than the reported qualitative events, it is ineligible as their cause.

I conclude that while hypothesis (a) does not formally contradict QER, qualitative event realists have good reasons to reject it, that is, they have reasons of the same sorts that are commonly used in science to reject explanatorily unpromising, although not self-contradictory, hypotheses.

Let us briefly turn to a second hypothesis about the relation of events in A1 and A2 to (correct) reports about what is projected on the screen in the thought experiment.

(b) There are distinct neural cell types within A1 and A2. When one type has activation that departs from its gray state, red qualitative events result; when another type has activation that departs from its gray state, blue qualitative events result; and so on.

This hypothesis is logically consistent and is, perhaps, suggested by the fact that there are different types of retinal cells. That is, there are differences among natural chemical kinds present in retinal cells that correlate with differences in sensitivity to light of various frequencies. However, to the best of current neurophysiological knowledge, there are no anatomical differences in cells in the visual cortices that correlate with color differences. Thus, hypothesis (b) is not supported by available evidence.

The most plausible hypothesis is the following one.

(c) There are characteristic temporal *patterns* of neural activity in A1 and A2.[4] There are patterns that are similar in the two regions for red conditions; there are patterns that are similar in the two regions for blue conditions; and the pattern for red is distinctively different from the pattern for blue.

I have stated hypothesis (c) as simply as possible, but it must be borne in mind that there are thousands of distinguishable phenomenal colors.

---

4 Why not spatial patterns? Because it seems doubtful that different brain parts would have the same spatial configuration (at a sufficiently fine level). Synaptic change would not adjust placing of neurons, but would allow for tuning of different brain parts to the same temporal patterns.

I assume that if we have some small set of distinctive color patterns, we can construct other patterns as intermediate cases (on some appropriate measure of gradation) or superpositions (in the Fourier sense, not in the quantum mechanical sense) of the small set of distinctive types. We are not to take it to be an a priori truth that things must work out this way. What is a priori is only that if patterns cause phenomenal colors, there must be enough differences of pattern to correspond to known differences of phenomenal color. It is reasonable to anticipate that the science of neural patterns will make use of a constraint to the effect that colors that are phenomenally regarded as mixed are caused by "mixtures" of patterns that cause unique colors. What kind of mixing this is, in neural detail, is something for brain science to determine.

There is much that is not yet known about temporal coding in the brain. The easiest way to think about pattern is, perhaps, to think of ratios of firing rates among a set of neurons. Peter Cariani (1994) has argued, however, that this description of neural activity may be too crude. If neurons or sets of neurons can respond to more fine-grained properties, e.g., relative times of impulse arrival or ratios of intervals between bursts of high activity, then mean firing rates may hide a multitude of pattern types. For the sake of concreteness and simplicity, I shall speak of patterns as ratios of neural firing rates, but this stylistic practice is not meant to exclude other possibilities. Quite the contrary: it is the business of a science of consciousness to combine knowledge from neuroscience and psychology in order to discover what kinds of patterning occur in brain activity and which kinds of patterns are correlated with which kinds of conscious events.

The large number of possibilities is one source of difficulty in discovering which neural patterns may be causes of particular phenomenal qualities in conscious events. Another source of difficulty here is, evidently, the difficulty of conducting investigations of precise temporal relations among individual neurons. Despite these empirical difficulties, the view that neural activation is the brain correlate of experience is extremely widespread among neuroscientists; and the reasons for this view support hypothesis (c), once that alternative has been clearly distinguished from hypotheses (a) and (b) and the latter have been rejected.

I have approached patterns of activity by considering differences among qualitative events and consequently differences among their causes. This approach has led me to focus, in turn, on what is happening in areas A1 and A2. But it is not to be thought that I mean to suggest that events in A1 and A2 are *sufficient* for qualitative events. There are several lines of

213

thought that converge on the idea that thalamic activity is necessary for consciousness. QER is compatible with such a view. As was pointed out in the discussion of skepticism in Chapter 9, the patterns of neural activity that are sufficient for consciousness may be quite large ones, and distinctive patterns of activity may be required in visual areas, in the thalamus, and perhaps in prefrontal cortical areas as well. The point of the argument so far is only to emphasize the importance of *pattern*, and not at all to identify *which* patterns are required or to determine the size of the region in which patterned activity is necessary if there is to be consciousness.

It will be convenient to have a name for the view summarized in (c) and the surrounding discussion. Let us call it the "Patterns as Causes of Consciousness" (PACC) view.

HOMOGENEITY

A PACC view can be approached in a natural way through reflection on the homogeneity of sensory qualities, which I shall understand to be the "spread-outness" of sensory qualities in time and, sometimes, in space.[5] A taste or a smell can last for a few moments, and even if it changes, it can do so in a smoothly varying way, so that there are neither sensible gaps nor sensible discontinuities or "edges" in the gustatory or olfactory content. Again, although there can be beeps and pings, there *can* also be foghorns or sirens that fill our auditory experience in an unchanging or little-changing way over the course of a few seconds. Warmth or coolness, painfulness or itchiness can infuse the space of a hand or other extended body part for a time without sensible change. And, finally, while ordinary

---

5 Sellars (1963) argued that brain science and basic physics offer only discrete, discontinuous elements, and that it is thus exceedingly difficult to locate homogeneous qualities in the world as described by science. This problem has become known as the "grain problem" (or the "grain argument"), and Sellars went to extraordinary lengths to deal with it. A large literature concerned with the grain problem, and with Sellars's attempted solution, now exists. I bypass that literature here because I am not much concerned with homogeneity as an argument against one or another version of physicalism. In my view, homogeneity functions as a positive clue available for use in trying to work toward a substantive unified dualism.

There is, indeed, one way in which I have, in effect, used an aspect of homogeneity as a negative argument. This occurred when I said, in Chapter 4, that, however representational our experience might be, it does not represent things *as* having the complexity that physical science tells us is there in the external causes of phenomenal consciousness. For example, there is nothing tripartite about our representation of colored surfaces, even though it may well be that triples of reflectance percentages determine what kind of color will characterize our consciousness. This point will, I believe, stand quite robustly on its own, independently of the formulations of Sellars, his interpreters, or his critics.

perceptual scenes are complex and apt to contain movement, we can have a visual experience in which a single color is spread out over some sensible area, and remains so spread out over a sensible duration of at least a few seconds.

Although the examples just noted have been chosen in order to highlight the temporal and spatial continuity of our phenomenal consciousness, it is important to be clear that we are not merely exhibiting a few exotic specimens that we can safely ignore until the last stages of a science of consciousness. Tastes and smells are rarely pointlike at all. Even pings and beeps have a small but noticeable temporal extent. A few pains are jabs or stings; most, alas, stretch out over a bodily region and a period of time. Typical visual experiences, even ones in which many events are occurring, are filled with colors that have both extent and duration. In sum, homogeneity is a pervasive feature of our phenomenal consciousness.

Because homogeneity is a pervasive feature of phenomenal consciousness, an interest in achieving a unified view of brains and consciousness should lead us to look for features of brain events that are like homogeneity in some respects or that might be natural candidates for causing homogeneity. Patterns of neural activity answer to this desideratum. They can extend over a region of space. It is essential to them that they be extensive in time; for example, a ratio of neural firing rates cannot exist without there having been several neural firings at different times. Thus, there is a minimum time for a pattern to occur, and it may last for various periods beyond the minimum. The neural events of which patterns are patterns are, of course, pointlike (although not strictly instantaneous). They may be repeated, but once they have occurred, they are over. By contrast, patterns are the kind of thing that *can* literally last for a stretch of time and are not thereby repeated (unless, of course, they are interrupted, in which case they can be repeated). Further, patterns can change into other patterns by degeneration or gradual replacement; and, of course, they can also change suddenly, as phenomenal qualities sometimes do. Thus, while patterns are not themselves homogeneous, they do share some of the properties that are possessed by events in phenomenal consciousness that exhibit homogeneity.

It may be suggested that there are better candidates for physical properties that may cause homogeneous phenomenal consciousness, namely, waves or fields. Waves and fields can extend in a smooth way over temporal or spatial intervals, and they can change gradually. They can genuinely endure for a time, and their enduring is not merely frequent repetition. Despite these attractive properties, I shall not pursue this suggestion. The reason is that it is difficult to see how waves or fields could be correlated to our experiences or their likely causes by events in sensory neurons. Appropriate correlates might be found in fluctuations in fields caused by ionic movements due to the firings of many neurons. Simple fluctuations, however, would be unlikely to be correlated with phenomenal qualities or even with consciousness. But a complex fluctuation would be a pattern of fluctuations, and so we would have a version of a PACC view in this case, albeit in a different medium (i.e., we would have patterns of field fluctuations rather than patterns of neural firings). It may be that an alternative field theory could be worked out, but until one is actually advanced, it seems fruitless to pursue the idea further.

The view that phenomenal consciousness depends on patterns of neural activity must be clearly distinguished from its converse, i.e, the view that all patterns of neural activity result in phenomenal consciousness. Our brain is pervaded with all sorts of patterns of neural activity that are essential for cognitive and behavioral function but that have no correlates in the contents of consciousness. This lack of correlation may seem puzzling if patterns are claimed to be suitable for causes of homogeneity in phenomenal consciousness. It should be noted, however, that homogeneity is only one aspect of phenomenal consciousness and that there must always be some particular content that is homogeneous. Different patterns will be correlated with different phenomenal qualities, and it is up to neuroscience to discover which patterns are correlated with, e.g., green, and which with blue. It is likewise up to neuroscience to discover which properties of patterns are correlated with color experiences and which other properties are correlated with taste experiences, sound experiences, and so on. If these discoveries are matters for science, it should also be a matter for science to tell us which very general properties of patterns of neural activity correspond to phenomenal consciousness *tout court* (i.e., phenomenal consciousness of some kind or other). The explanation of why some neural event patterns are not correlated with phenomenal consciousness at all will then lie in the types of patterns they exhibit (or fail to exhibit).[6]

Attention to homogeneity provides the basis for an objection to higher order thought theories that is additional to those reviewed in Chapters 6 and 7. Although thoughts are not instantaneous, they do not fill time in a way that matches the ability of phenomenally conscious events to persist

---

6 I thank Michael Pauen for calling my attention to the need to make the clarification contained in this paragraph.

through a duration. When we have (fully) had an occurrent thought, that thought is over.[7] We can have it again, and we can have the related thought that something we have already thought continues to be the case, and we can have the yet further thought that what we have realized to have continued to be the case is *still* the case. But a given thought, once present in complete form, does not endure.

To illustrate this point, consider having a yellow afterimage that gradually fades. This experience does not seem to be a series of thoughts to the effect that now I am having something bright yellow, now I am again (or still) having something bright yellow, now I am having something a little less bright but still yellow, now I am having something a little bit orangey, and so on. Nor does it seem to be a series of thoughts to the same effect, but with one beginning before the next has been completed. We should not, of course, think that we *cannot* have such series of thoughts; the premise is only that afterimages do not seem to have any such serial character, and the conclusion is that such a series is not a plausible candidate for what constitutes phenomenal consciousness.[8]

At this point, one might suggest the view that thoughts about phenomenal qualities differ from other (occurrent) thoughts in having a continuous character. There is, however, a good reason not to make such a move. The point of a higher order thought view is to explain something regarded as problematic – consciousness, including phenomenal consciousness – by analyzing it in terms of something regarded as less problematic – thoughts. If we have to introduce a special kind of "thought" to make the account work, we undercut this alleged explanatory advance. We would merely raise the question of whether introducing thoughts of this special kind is not just introducing another label for phenomenal consciousness.

CONTRAST WITH CHALMERS'S PRINCIPLE OF ORGANIZATIONAL INVARIANCE

Chalmers (1996) raises some of the same questions I have been pursuing here, and some of his answers are superficially similar. For example, I

---

7   The same does not apply, of course, to dispositions to have (occurrent) thoughts. HOT theorists, however, have usually held that mere dispositions cannot serve in an account of sensory consciousness.

8   Historically inclined readers may recognize the roots of this argument in the Aristotelian distinction between activity (*energeia*), which, like seeing, has been done at every time that it continues to be done, and motion (*kinesis*), which, like building a house, has not been done until it is completed (and thus no longer being done).

have said that it is patterns of neural activity that give rise to phenomenal consciousness. Chalmers's account, in one formulation, offers "*functional organization* of the brain" (p. 247; emphasis in the original) as the physical correlate of consciousness; and this phrase is explained as "the *abstract pattern of causal interaction* between various parts of a system, and perhaps between these parts and external inputs and outputs" (p. 247; emphasis in the original). Chalmers's account, like a PACC view, recognizes that pattern can be instantiated in various media; and, again like a PACC view, Chalmers's account takes it to be an empirical question which brain structures instantiate the patterns that are relevant to giving rise to consciousness. A PACC view is, however, different from Chalmers's account, and in light of the similarities just mentioned, it is important to clarify the differences and to explain what can be said in favor of a PACC approach.

There are many ways of dividing any physical object into parts, and consequently, there are many ways of regarding any physical object as a system of causally interacting parts. Chalmers tells us what kind of division of ourselves he has in mind. "In what follows," he says,

the relevant sort of functional organization of a system will always be at a level fine enough to determine behavioral capacities. Call such an organization a *fine-grained* functional organization. For the purposes of illustration, I will usually focus on the neural level of organization in the brain, although a higher level might suffice, and it is not impossible that a lower level could be required. . . .

I claim that conscious experience arises from fine-grained functional organization. More specifically, I will argue for a *principle of organizational invariance*, holding that given any system that has conscious experiences, then any system that has the same fine-grained functional organization will have qualitatively identical experiences. (Pp. 248–249; emphases in the original)

In order to clarify the difference between the commitments of a PACC view and the principle of organizational invariance (hereafter, POI), I shall introduce, and contrast, two ways in which we might imagine building a system that parallels the functional organization of a known subject of consciousness – namely, a human being whom we will call "Jones". To this end, let us imagine a device that we may call a "compuron". A compuron is an extremely small device that takes pulsed inputs and gives pulsed outputs, and that computes an input–output function identical to that of some particular neuron found in Jones's brain. We are to imagine that compurons have 10^3–10^4 input channels, and that they deliver their single output (a series of pulses) through a wire that terminates in many branches. The heart of a compuron is a nanochip, that is, a nonanalog device that calculates the axonal output of the modeled neuron from inputs that represent sets of inputs to that neuron.

To connect compurons to neurons, we will need artificial synapses, or "artisyns". One kind of artisyn takes neurotransmitters and yields electrical impulses as outputs to a compuron; another takes the outputs of compurons and yields neurotransmitters. Input artisyns are designed so that their outputs can be used by the compuron to which they are connected as representations of neurotransmitter input to the modeled neuron. Output artisyns are designed so as to release the same amount of neurotransmitters that the modeled neuron would have released at the output artisyns' locations. Compurons calculate the timing of their pulsed outputs with precision, and output artisyns deliver their packets of neurotransmitter output at the same times that the neuron modeled by the compuron to which they are attached would have delivered them.

Under these stipulations, it is clear that if we replace one of Jones's neurons with a compuron that models it, along with appropriate artisyns, we will have a result that shares Jones's fine-grained functional organization. The result will also share the patterns of activity that are present in the prereplacement, pristine Jones. Thus, on both POI and a PACC view, the altered Jones will be expected to have phenomenal consciousness.

A natural question to ask is, what happens if we replace more of Jones's neurons with compurons? So long as the replaced neurons are widely separated, there is no interesting difference from the simple case just described, and the conclusions are the same. However, if one of the replaced neurons is synaptically connected to another of the replaced neurons, an interesting possibility arises. Namely, instead of having a pair of artisyns (one output artisyn feeding into one input artisyn), we can replace the pair with what we may call a "compusyn". This device has another nanochip that calculates the effect of a pair of artisyns. It takes as input the output of one compuron and delivers to another compuron the same input that that compuron would have received if the connection had been a pair of artisyns instead of one compusyn.

Here again, both fine-grained functional organization and patterns of pulses in compurons match the corresponding properties of the pristine Jones. So, here too, both the POI and a PACC view would conclude that altered Jones has phenomenal consciousness, and, indeed, the same phenomenal consciousness as the pristine Jones.

Let us now imagine that we have replaced most of the neurons in Jones's brain (but not sensory or motor neurons) with compurons and associated interface devices. In this case, a new possibility arises. Imagine that we identify collections of, let us say, 100 compurons in the now extensively altered Jones. Let us stipulate that these collections are to be "connected"; that is, every proper subset of the collection of 100 either receives a connection from or contributes a connection to some compuron that is outside the subset but within the set of 100. Perhaps some members of the set of 100 receive input from and give output to only compurons that are within the set of 100; in general, however, compurons in that set will receive inputs from and give outputs to compurons outside the set, as well as to those inside it.

We are now to imagine that we replace these sets of 100 compurons with new devices, which we may call "compunets". A single compunet replaces the whole set of 100 compurons. It will have as many input channels as the replaced set of 100 compurons had input channels from units outside the set, and it will have as many output channels as the replaced set of 100 compurons had output channels to units outside the replaced set. However, any connections among compurons that are *within* the set of 100 will be only virtual. That is, a compunet does away with internal compusyns; the chip at its heart merely calculates what the mutual effects of compurons within the set would have been, and uses the results to calculate the correct amounts and timing of outputs (for each of its output channels) from the array of its inputs. We may stipulate that compunets are to contain a representation of the function computed by each of the neurons in the set they are replacing, and that they use these representations to generate a representation of the causal transactions among compurons within the replaced set. They track these causal transactions, however, only by computations, not by having internal bits of hardware that individually model single compurons.

Introduction of compunets provides a basis for a conceptual distinction between the POI and a PACC view. Taking the latter first, we can see that compunets (unlike compurons) fail to preserve the patterns of impulses that were maintained when single neurons were replaced by single compurons (and appropriate interfacing devices). The impulses that occurred in any compuron that is connected only to compurons within the set of 100 will simply disappear. (If it is doubted that there will be any such compurons, we can simply do our replacement by compunets on larger sets.) It might be thought that the stipulation that compunets calculate individual transactions among compurons will ensure that original patterns of activity are preserved. But this objection seems ill-motivated. For example, the computation of a firing rate of 50/second in neuron i and 40/second in neuron j, and the further computation of a 5/4 ratio, evidently do not require anything to happen in the computer at a rate of 50/second or 40/second or in a ratio of 5 to 4. The computation will succeed just so long as 50/second and 40/second are *represented*, and these numbers can be represented without there being a physical 50 or a physical 40 of anything in the representations. For example, the numerals in this paragraph represent numbers, but do not do so by containing 50 or 40 physical parts. (Of course, one could divide a printed "50" into 50 parts, each a tiny patch of ink. This fact, however, has nothing to do with the representative function of numerals. On infinitely many principles of division that yield 50 parts for "50", "40" will turn out *not* to have 40 parts.)

According to a PACC view, loss of patterns of activity means loss of the causes of phenomenal consciousness. Thus, while compuron–altered Jones may still have phenomenal consciousness, according to a PACC view, *compunet*-altered Jones does not.[9] But the POI leads to a different result here. Division into sets of the kind described and replacement by compunets will leave us with a being that (i) has a division of parts that will make it isomorphic to the original Jones, (ii) will have causal relations among those parts that are isomorphic to the causal relations among the corresponding parts of Jones, and (iii) will be behaviorally isomorphic to Jones. Satisfaction of these conditions satisfies the demands of organizational invariance. Thus, according to the POI, compunet-altered Jones would be held to have what is required for phenomenal consciousness to arise.

The distinction between the consequences of POI and PACC that I have just drawn may be thought to be unclear in light of some of Chalmers's specifications of what is required for fine-grained functional isomorphism. For Chalmers also envisages brain-simulating devices, and he puts a strong condition on the devices that he claims would exhibit consciousness. Namely, there must be

real causation going on between voltages in various circuits, precisely mirroring patterns of causation between the neurons. For each neuron, there will be a

---

9 I say that compuron–altered Jones *may* still have phenomenal consciousness to allow for the possibility that relevant patterning is at the microtubular level (for example) rather than the neural level. In this case, even compurons would remove the causes of phenomenal consciousness. If, however, neural activity patterns form the causal basis for phenomenal consciousness, then compuron–altered Jones *does* have both the right activity patterns and phenomenal consciousness, while compunet-altered Jones lacks the latter as a consequence of lacking the former.

memory location that represents the neuron, and each of these locations will be physically realized in a voltage at some physical location. It is the causal patterns among these circuits, just as it is the causal patterns among neurons in the brain, that are responsible for any conscious experience that arises. (p. 321)

A superficial reading of this passage might suggest that Chalmers is requiring the same neural activity patterns that are featured in a PACC view. A more careful reading, however, will make it evident that the *causal patterns* to which Chalmers refers are not the same as the *patterns of activity* on which a PACC view focuses.[10] (Unfortunately, use of the word "pattern" seems hardly avoidable for the clear and efficient communication of the main point of each of these distinct views.) The computation that must be paralleled element by element in Chalmers's version of a brain simulator is the passage from neural-state ensemble to neural-state ensemble, beginning with sensory input and ending with behavioral output. The relevant properties are those, and only those, that we must include in order to constrain our computation to the right input–output function. This kind of computation, I have argued (and I believe Chalmers would agree), can be done by devices that convey the right numbers to the right registers in the right sequences and at the right times. Any other causal properties of neural activity are irrelevant and need not be preserved. A PACC view, in contrast, holds that there are causal properties that are relevant to producing conscious experiences that fall outside the set of properties regarded as relevant in Chalmers's theory.

I have described the distinction between POI and PACC as a "conceptual" distinction. The reason for this caution is that compunets are in the far reaches of thought-experiment space. The calculational demand placed on them is severe, and the laws of nature may well be incompatible with supposing that that demand can be met by any device of the required size working under the timing constraints necessary if behavioral isomorphism is to be preserved. The same remarks hold for compurons,

---

10 Chalmers's reference to causal patterns is tied to the idea that a simulation of a brain must reflect "the relevant range of each neuron's states" (1996, p. 321). Which causal patterns are required to be preserved in Chalmers's computational simulation depends on what we take to be the "relevant range". The essential clue to what should count as the relevant range can be found in many places in Chalmers's book. One instance occurs when he says, "What is most relevant to the explanation of the behavior of a complex cognitive system is the abstract causal organization of the system" (p. 320). An implication of this statement is that "relevant" causal patterns are those involved in the production of behavior.

compsyns, or any other imagined neuron-replacement devices. It is even conceivable that laws of physical nature would ensure that any device that met Chalmers's constraints also preserved the patterns of activity required by a PACC view. But for all that, my description of various devices and their differences is *logically* consistent, and this is enough to clarify the difference between POI and PACC views.

Supposing that we accept that POI and PACC views are conceptually distinct, is there any reason to prefer one to the other? It would seem that there is. Patterns of neural events are, no doubt, a somewhat odd kind of candidate for a cause of anything. But they have at least one property that makes them eminently eligible for a causal role, namely, they are occurrents with appropriately definite durations and times of onset and offset. By contrast, the POI makes the causes of qualitative events to consist, in part, of nonoccurrent, conditional facts. This is shown as follows. Qualitative events depend on fine-grained functional organization. Fine-grained functional organization is organization that ensures equivalence of behavioral capacities (equivalence, that is, with a known subject of qualitative events). But behavioral capacities are dispositional facts about subjects — facts that are determined in part by what subjects *would* do under certain counterfactual conditions. It would be too strong to say that it is contradictory to suppose that counterfactual conditionals can be causes, but it would seem that this is a very peculiar view that we should avoid if possible; and the PACC view does avoid this.[11]

Chalmers's thought is complex, and I may be overdrawing his case. But the strand from which I have been distinguishing PACC is certainly

---

11 One could, of course, move to the claim that the causes of qualitative events are the categorical bases of the dispositions that are commonly used to identify occurrences of phenomenal qualities. This is a move in the direction of PACC, but it does not go far enough. It seems clear that one could lose some behavioral capacities without changing one's phenomenal qualities. In fact, we do have occurrences of phenomenal color in dreams, when our behavioral capacities are much reduced. Chalmers (1996, pp. 227–228) discusses this case, and quite correctly locates its peculiarity in the fact that the behavior control mechanisms that are automatically at one's disposal when awake are shut down. But this response drives us in one of two directions. (i) We may narrow our conception of the size of the brain part that is necessary to cause qualitative events, so that actual qualitative events are caused only by actually occurring brain events. That is the direction that a PACC view naturally suggests. (ii) We may reintroduce counterfactuals and hold the causes of qualitative events to be certain actually occurring neural events *plus* the fact that certain other events *would* be occurring *if* certain other conditions were to have obtained. This is the way it seems that Chalmers wants to go; but if we do go this way, we reintroduce counterfactual nonoccurrents as causes of occurrences.

223

present. Consciousness is held (Chalmers, 1996, p. 249) to be an organizational invariant that

remains constant over all functional isomorphs of a given system. Whether the organization is realized in silicon chips, in the population of China, or in beer cans and ping-pong balls does not matter. As long as the functional organization is right, conscious experience will be determined.

But it is hardly conceivable that guaranteeing the right functional organization in the latter materials should entail the occurrence of the kinds of patterns that a PACC envisages.

HOMOGENEITY, COMPUTATION, AND "INFORMATION"

It is often tempting to compare the brain to a computer and thus to regard its operations as essentially the performance of computations. From this point of view, a PACC view may appear dubious, because it proposes the relevance to consciousness of something from which computation abstracts. A PACC approach would thus be supported by any argument that showed a difficulty in relying solely on computation for the cause of consciousness. Reflection on the (temporal) homogeneity of phenomenal qualities supplies such an argument.

A computation is the production of a result. When the result has not been reached, the computation is not complete (although it is ongoing or in process); when the result has been reached, the computation is over. Of course, a computation can be repeated; indeed, it can be repeated many times, yielding a series of identical results. This is quite different, however, from having a continuing cause of the sort that can be supplied by a pattern of activity. For, although there have to be repeated neural firings in order to have a pattern, a pattern of neural firings is by its nature something that continues for a time. There may, indeed, be a minimum time required for a certain neural pattern to occur – the time necessary for each neuron in a set of neurons to establish a firing rate. But there need be no fixed maximum time.

It also makes sense to assign a region of brain tissue over which a given pattern of activity is occurring during a stretch of time. Here again, there is a contrast with computation. Certainly, there are regions of brain tissue that contribute to a computation; but as different regions will in general make their contributions at different times, there need be no region that corresponds to the computation as a whole. We could, of course, consider the sum of involved regions to be the region in which a computation takes place. But no state of that combined region need be contemporaneous with a computation as a whole. By contrast, once again, a pattern of activity may be regarded as taking place throughout the region in which the activated neurons lie, during the whole of a stretch of time in which the pattern is realized. These properties are exactly those that one would expect in a cause of phenomenally conscious events, which can pervade time in a continuous, enduring, and gradually varying way.[12] Here, then, is another reason why we should look to patterns of activity rather than computation for the physical property most closely allied with the rise of consciousness.

Many of the points just made about computation carry over to formulations in terms of "information", as this term is most generally understood.[13] Neural patterns "carry information" in one sense because the probability of their occurrence is not uniform for all times; in another sense because some of them can be correlated with inputs; and in a third sense because descriptions of them can be stored, transmitted, or used in calculations. But correct probability, correlation, and uncorrupted storage and transmission are all achievable with or without preservation of neural activity pattern. Representation of information can be pointlike: there is no need for the representation of information about a pattern to have the same time course as the pattern. Thus, even though patterns contain information in various senses, information is, from the PACC point of

12 These remarks are in apparent conflict with the following statement of Chalmers (1996, p. 332).

> We can see computational formalisms as providing an ideal formalism for the expression of patterns of causal organization, and indeed (in combination with implementational methods) as an ideal tool for their replication. Whatever causal organization turns out to be central to cognition and consciousness, we can expect that a computational account will be able to capture it.

> However, the root of this apparent conflict lies in the difference between POI and PACC that has already been discussed in the previous section. Recalling that patterns of causal organization are not the same as patterns of neural activity, we can see that Chalmers's statement is a consequence of POI, and not a claim that computation is adequate to capture the patterns of activity focused upon by a PACC view.

13 A revealing, if perhaps unguarded, expression of an informational view is given by Crick and Koch (1995, p. 85):

> In order to describe a subjective visual experience, the information has to be transmitted to the motor output stage of the brain. . . . This transmission always involves reencoding the information, so that the explicit information expressed by the motor neurons is related, but not identical, to the explicit information expressed by the firing of neurons associated with color experience, at some level in the visual hierarchy.

view, just the wrong category with which to describe neural events if causation of phenomenal consciousness is the focus of interest.

The inappropriateness of informational description may be difficult to see if one focuses on certain kinds of examples, e.g., the retinal response to a scene in which no changes are taking place.[14] In considering an interval between saccades, one may imagine the "refreshing" of the retinal state by repeated bombardment of retinal cells by photons reflected from the distal scene. Thinking in this way may make it natural to think of the information about the distal causes as being maintained on the retina continuously for the whole intersaccade time. My critique of information as a category of description does not imply that such a way of thinking is objectionable. But it must be noted that the information about the distal scene that is maintained on the retina *can* be represented in ways that do not depend on continual refreshing, e.g., by a statement of what is in the distal scene. Therefore, an informational description of retinal state, on most understandings of "information", does not entail the presence of the features of retinal events that suggest continuity, namely, the maintenance of chemical states in receptors or the maintenance of retinal output patterns. Thus, these features are omitted by (although compatible with) an informational description. In short, the criticism of information as the wrong category for use in describing the neural causes of consciousness is not that it makes a *false* abstraction, but that it is an *abstraction* from that aspect of neural events that is plausibly taken to correspond to homogeneity.[15]

14 Retinal state was introduced by David Chalmers in discussion following a presentation of some of the material in this section, in Bremen in May 1998. In responding to this example, I am, of course, not supposing that it is patterns of *retinal* activity that give rise (directly) to visual consciousness. The virtues of the example are rather that we know quite a lot about retinal activity, and that it is easy to see how an informational description (on many common understandings of "information") would plausibly apply.

15 The foregoing discussion has been qualified so as to apply to most understandings of "information". Chalmers (1996) has explicated "information" in a somewhat different way that is interesting, coherent, and related in fundamental ways to common understandings of the term. Nonetheless, his explication has consequences that differ from those of information as it is most commonly understood. In Chalmers's (1996, p. 293) explication, "we find information everywhere we find causation" – indeed, "information" in Chalmers's explication *precisely* tracks causation. This fact makes it possible to think of neural activity in Chalmersian informational terms (C-informational terms) in a way that does not abstract from neural pattern, and hence does not suffer from the shortcomings of looser uses of "information". However, because most readers will likely not have C-information in mind when "information" is spoken of, it seems best to avoid the concept of information altogether and refer directly to the idea that homogeneous phenomenal consciousness is caused by patterns of neural activity.

13

A Possible Future

The preceding chapter has supported a PACC view with converging lines of argument, one that starts with a thought experiment, and one that is based on homogeneity of phenomenal qualitied conscious events. There is much more that needs to be said in order to connect a PACC view with the possibility of a truly substantive unified dualism. At the same time, serious objections can be raised against what has already been said. Much of the necessary further development of a PACC view can be conveniently provided by stating and responding to these objections, and this will be the strategy I shall pursue in this chapter.

INDEPENDENCE OF PATTERN FROM MEDIUM

The first objection begins by noting a point that PACC theorists must emphatically approve, to wit: taking pattern seriously means distinguishing between pattern and medium and tying consciousness to pattern rather than medium. The objection is that the same patterns that cause consciousness might be realized in media that are extremely implausible as candidates for causes of consciousness. For example, if patterns (of neural activations) are essentially divisions of time into sets of ratios, the same sets of ratios might be producible by careful coordination of a corps of drummers. But no one would think that such a drumming would be sufficient to produce red experiences, for example, no matter how precisely the ratios of intervals between hits on various drum heads might match the ratios of activations in the neurons of a normal experiencer of phenomenal red. There is, of course, no reason why there could not be a synaesthete in whom a drumming produces neural activation patterns that cause a phenomenal red experience. The objection is that if pattern is sufficient for phenomenally conscious events, then a drumming that realized the right pattern would itself be sufficient for phenomenal consciousness, quite apart from any effect that the drumming might have on perceivers; and this is an immensely implausible result.

This objection is a formidable one for at least two reasons. First, a PACC theorist should accept the view that patterns of the kind that can cause consciousness may occur in media other than human brains. One crucial case is brains of other animals. If a PACC approach is not to restrict itself into triviality, it should ultimately be of some use in dealing with questions as to whether, e.g., pigeons or flies have phenomenal consciousness. It is envisaged that there will be some general feature of neural patterns that separates the causes of human conscious events from human brain activity that does not result in consciousness. If patterns with this general feature can be found in other animals, that would be a reason to accept that they have phenomenal consciousness, and lack of such patterns would be a reason against attributing phenomenal consciousness to them. Further, the discussion of replacement scenarios in the previous chapter implies that robots constructed so as to preserve pattern should be credited with phenomenal consciousness. Thus, a PACC theorist who finds the band of drummers intolerable (as a sufficient cause of phenomenal color) needs to find a way of distinguishing pattern realization in some of the media other than human brains (e.g., pigeons, robots) from pattern realization in other media (e.g., bands of drummers). Moreover, such a distinction must be principled, i.e., not drawn in a merely ad hoc fashion so as to exclude the "right" set of implausible cases.

The second reason why the drummer case is a formidable objection is that although we have good clues as to how to look for the patterns of activity that cause phenomenal consciousness, we do not now know what any of these patterns actually are. This fact puts severe limits on our ability to give the principled distinction that we have just seen to be required of PACC theorists. It would, in fact, seem clear that a PACC theorist cannot now make good on this crucial desideratum. Does this mean that a PACC view must be given up? No. It does mean, however, that further defense of a PACC view must be essentially speculative. That is, the best a PACC theorist can do in the present circumstances is to argue that the required principled distinction among pattern realizations *might* be discoverable. The only plausible way that a PACC theorist can do this is to outline a course of development in science, and argue that this is a *possible* (i.e., consistently describable) future development and that it could in due course provide the kind of principled distinction that

228

a PACC theory requires. "Possible" here cannot mean merely "logically possible"; it must imply not only internal consistency, but also consistency with what we already know in science and with what we know about the structure of scientific theories and the ways in which scientific theories can develop.

A clue that is available to PACC theorists comes from temporal and spatial considerations. We can be conscious of the contents of backward-masked tachistoscopic presentations of less than 100 milliseconds, and under some conditions we can reliably react to such contents within 800 milliseconds. A very conservative estimate would hold that neural patterns sufficient to cause phenomenal consciousness can establish themselves within 400 milliseconds. A lower temporal bound is harder to discern, but is plausibly in the low millisecond range and not plausibly lower than the tenths of millisecond range. The spatial extent required for consciousness-causing patterns cannot be greater than the size of a human brain, and since, plausibly, those who have lost significant parts of their brains are still phenomenally conscious, the required spatial extent is presumably smaller than the whole brain. I have already mentioned the fact that patterns that cause phenomenal qualities should be sortable into genera and species corresponding to differences between, e.g., vision and sound. This fact provides a constraint that should be usable for the purpose of getting more definite about the temporal and spatial boundaries of the patterns of neural activities that can cause conscious events.

A corps of drummers would exceed such boundaries by at least two orders of magnitude. It is not evident that this fact must make a significant difference, but neither is it evident that it could not. The possibility that spatiotemporal size could be relevant is suggested by the likelihood that patterns combine (or interfere) in some ways. We can illustrate this possibility by reflecting on nonunique colors, e.g., orange. PACC holds that this phenomenal quality of conscious events occurs when some pattern is realized; let us call this pattern "P(o)". It seems likely that P(o) is related in some systematic way to patterns P(r) and P(y), i.e., to the patterns that yield unique red and unique yellow, respectively. It is not at present clear just what kind of combining this is, but it seems possible that the larger a region we consider, the more possibilities for combination there may be. Combination, however, is a type of alteration; and some alterations would be destructive of patterns of any particular type. It is thus conceivable that large spatiotemporal regions would entail combinations of patterns that would take us out of the set of consciousness-causing patterns, even in cases where some *part* of the total occurrences in those regions exhibited a pattern that in other circumstances would cause a qualitative event. In that case, a PACC view might consistently hold the principle that phenomenal qualities (or their absence) depend on the whole character of a pattern in a given region. Such a principle, together with the other assumptions just indicated, would explain how the size of the spatiotemporal region of a pattern of activity could make a difference to the causation of qualitative events.

The suggestion just outlined may be more intelligible in the light of a very imperfect analogy. The patterns in an Asian carpet may often be broken down into a pattern of, say, reds and yellows and another pattern of blues and browns. One could, for example, note that there were three red blobs relatively close together, then a longer separation in which two yellow blobs occur, with blues and browns occurring in another pattern in between the reds and yellows. In this way, we might speak of the whole pattern and several subpatterns. Let one of these subpatterns be P(x). In another context, we might have P(x) without the rest. On the assumption that some class of events E1, E2, ... depends on the whole pattern in a region, we might have E1 when P(x) occurs alone but some other kind of event, perhaps very different from E1, when the whole pattern occurs, even though, in a sense, P(x) is present as a component of the larger pattern.[1]

Neither the analogy nor the ideas it is meant to illustrate can profitably be pursued further in our present state of ignorance about what kinds of neural patterns actually occur in the course of our coming to have phenomenal consciousness. It cannot even be claimed that the suggested scenario is certain to make sense in the light of future discoveries about patterns of neural activation. It follows that PACC theorists can make only the weakest of defenses here. They can say only that the foregoing scenario seems to be possible, and that therefore it is not certain that a

---

1 The last two paragraphs improve on the formulation in Robinson (1999b), where I also dealt with the drummers problem for a PACC view. One of the improvements is the dropping of the term "natural salience". Ulrich Mohrhoff has convinced me (in personal communications) that this was an unfortunate terminological choice. The problem is that patterns are salient, in one very obvious sense, just in virtue of being patterns, and this association of "salience" with pattern obscures its connection with the quite different idea that I intended to convey by its use. Terminology is not the only improvement, however, and I believe that the present formulation is an advance in the understanding of how a PACC view might possibly be developed.

principled division of smaller and larger spatiotemporal regions in which patterns may occur will prove unavailable. Such a conclusion is not as much as one would like; it is, however, enough to support the view that the drummer case is not decisive against a PACC view.

An objection may, however, be raised by the following reflections. A temporal analogue of spatial subpatterns would be simultaneously occurring temporal patterns, as, for example, when a measure in 4/4 time is played against a 3/4 measure in another instrument. There is, however, another way of thinking about pattern combination. A pattern, P1, might occur between t_1 and t_2; a further pattern, P2A, might occur between t_2 and t_3; and the consequence might be that another pattern, P3A, occurs in the whole interval from t_1 to t_3. Suppose that P3A produces qualitative event Q3A. Suppose further that P2B could have occurred instead of P2A (in the interval t_2–t_3) and that, in that case, P3B would have occurred instead of P3A (in the combined interval, t_1–t_3). Suppose, finally, that P3B produces qualitative event Q3B, distinct from Q3A. These suppositions would seem to lead to a problem; namely, what kind of qualitative event should P1 produce? It might seem that it should produce events with different phenomenal qualities, depending on what is to follow it. But that would not be possible unless one were willing to countenance backward causation.

There is, however, no real problem here. If P1 by itself is sufficient to produce a qualitative event, then that event will occur, and it will be *followed* by different qualitative events, depending on whether what follows P1 is P2A or P2B. It is, however, possible that P1 by itself is insufficient to produce any qualitative event, and in that case we may say simply that what kind of qualitative event occurs will depend on whether P3A or P3B occurs. It is essential to recall here the point, made in the discussion of skepticism, that causes of qualitative events should not be assumed to be instantaneous.[2]

Our consciousness can undergo sudden changes or it can evolve gradually from one set of qualities to another. It is certainly possible that this kind of difference corresponds not merely to the rate of succession of patterns, but also to differences in some relation of similarity or overlap.

---

2 The minimum time for a qualitative event-causing pattern to establish itself may vary from case to case. A possibly helpful analogy lies in music. Four notes, for example, are enough to establish the opening of Beethoven's Fifth Symphony. Other melodies might require more notes.

However, in the absence of a hypothesis about what the actual relevant patterns are, it is difficult to generate a more detailed conception of what the relevant relations might be.[3]

It is plain that a PACC view is hostage to future empirical results. But any serious move in the direction of trying to find a unified dualism must envisage a converging of our ways of thinking about consciousness and our ways of thinking about its causes; thus, any such move necessarily commits itself to ways of thinking that court empirical refutation. The reward for accepting this risk is a view that replaces empty protestations of faith with at least a suggestion of where to look for interesting progress in our understanding of the causes of consciousness.

There is a second possible scenario that enables one to envisage a principled rejection of the drummer case. The clue here is that the pattern of drumbeats is maintained in a way that does not make use of the elements of the pattern themselves. That is, the pattern is maintained by the drummers, who need not depend on hearing the results of their activity in order to maintain it. By contrast, although the patterns of neural activation that are the likely causes of qualitative events are initiated and partially maintained by input from the sense organs, their continuation also depends on the reentrant effects of the neural activations that are elements of the pattern.

By itself, this difference does not explain why there should be any difference in the effects of the two instances of pattern. But a further possibility is that phenomenal consciousness depends on what might be called a "meta-pattern", i.e., a pattern of small fluctuations in the basic pattern. And it might turn out that there are *physical* reasons why a sufficiently close match of the meta-pattern would require a dynamical system to produce it – that is, a system in which the fluctuations are under the control of the elements of the pattern itself.

A possible reply to this suggestion is that the corps of drummers *might* work in such a way as to make later activities depend on a reentrant loop – in this case, one that goes through the hearing (or other method of sensing) of the elements of the patterned activity, i.e., the (individual) drumbeats. However, in this case the loop is rather long and depends on many conditions. These facts once again open the possibility that there

---

3 I thank Brad Thompson for prodding me with a question to which the last three paragraphs attempt an answer.

are physical reasons why such a system could not achieve the kind of fluctuation of pattern required for consciousness.

Plainly, it is not necessary that any of these suggestions about the difference of the drummer corps from activations of sets of neurons will turn out to draw divisions where we antecedently expect them. If investigation of neural activation patterns does not turn up *any* principled way of dividing events that produce phenomenal qualities from events that do not, that would be bad, and probably fatal, news for a PACC view. But it is an open possibility that some principle of distinction will emerge naturally from the study of activation patterns, and that such a principle will incline us to make some revisions in our views of where the division between conscious and unconscious subjects falls.

We can hardly say more about the relevant possibilities without knowing more about what patterns of activation cause the phenomenal qualities of our consciousness. This limitation itself might be thought to be objectionable, but in fact it is not. It is doubtful whether a physicist in the 1940s could have come up with our present classification of particles a priori, even as an item on a list of imaginable possibilities. Quantum mechanics almost certainly could not have appeared on an 1880 list of possibilities for future development of physics, even one generated by the best minds working under instructions to be speculative. Science does not merely separate out actualities from a list of already given possibilities. Instead, it increases our knowledge of the worlds that are possible, even as it enables us to eliminate some of the possibilities that we have long entertained. The natural expectation should be that a science of the brain event patterns that cause our consciousness will enable us to form new ideas about the precise character of the pattern properties that are relevant to consciousness and about the nature of the constraints on the realization of these properties.

PANPSYCHISM

The PACC view I have been presenting requires distinctive patterns for consciousness and supposes that such patterns will be caused only in very special circumstances. These features clearly distinguish the view from panpsychism. There are, nonetheless, two aspects of the PACC view that might be thought to raise problems for it that have parallels in problems for panpsychism. In this section, I identify these aspects and explain why they do not undercut the PACC approach.

233

One attractive feature of a PACC view is that patterns can change gradually from one to another. But this means that patterns can also degrade gradually, either into sets of activations that do not differ from noise or into a wide variety of other patterns. Either of these cases of gradual degradation may suggest that a PACC view will be committed to the existence of consciousness-yielding patterned activity quite beyond the range of plausibility, or that it will be able to avoid such a result only by introducing arbitrary, ad hoc boundaries within the range of patterned activities. The same kind of worry arises from allowing that the size of a spatiotemporal region in which activity occurs may be relevant to its relation to qualitative events. The problem is that there can be effectively continuous gradation in the sizes of such regions. Once again, a dilemma threatens: we will either have to extend the range of consciousness implausibly or introduce arbitrary cutoff points.

The solution to these difficulties is the same as that which allows us to speak sensibly of a solar system. In principle, the sun's gravitational effect extends to the entire universe. However, the rate at which this effect decreases is sufficiently steep to make it negligible beyond a certain range, and there is a nonarbitrary reason to regard the solar system as a unit. The solar system is, of course, only an analogy that is not to be pressed very far. In nonanalogous terms, the answer to the dilemmas of the preceding paragraph is that there is a third possibility, namely, nonarbitrary, nondiscontinuous, but steep degradations of pattern that will serve as "natural" boundaries for the set of consciousness-yielding patterns. A search for such steep degradations would be one aspect of plausible approaches to a science of the causes of consciousness.

A second suspicion of a parallel with a problem for panpsychism arises from the assumption that patterns can be combined. In view of this assumption, it may appear that a PACC view is committed to what Seager (1995, p. 280) has called the "combination problem" – "the problem of explaining how the myriad elements of 'atomic consciousness' can be combined into a new, complex and rich consciousness such as that we possess". The problem is that the consciousness of, say, molecules must be a rather primitive consciousness, one that does not reach anything so rich as, for example, a painful conscious experience. But the question of how a collection of nonpains should add up to a painful experience, or how they might sometimes add up to a painful experience and sometimes to a red experience, seems extremely formidable.

A key point that enables a PACC view to avoid the combination problem is that panpsychism attributes some (primitive) form of consciousness to each *part* of the physical world.[4] In contrast, a PACC view implies the presence of phenomenal qualities only where there are patterns of events in small regions. Presumably, patterns of the required kinds would not be found at the level of individual atoms or molecules, or in thermal motions of these, or in the combinations of these in any ordinary inanimate objects. Once this point is clear, it is also clear that the "combination" envisaged by a PACC view is a combination *of patterns*, and that this is quite a different matter from combinations of (alleged) mental properties *of parts* (e.g., atomic or molecular parts) of objects. There is a kind of intelligibility in the idea that a pattern that yields unique yellow and a pattern that yields unique red should form a pattern that yields another color when they are "superimposed" (e.g., by occurring simultaneously). This kind of intelligibility is completely lacking from a panpsychist combination of properties of parts.

ISN'T THIS STILL MERE CORRELATION?

Unified dualism aims at an explanatory understanding of consciousness, an overcoming of the "explanatory gap" or rather, ultimately, a view in which a gap to be bridged never even appears to arise. Sympathetic readers may agree that the PACC approach has provided some small insight about possible correlates or causes of qualitative events, and perhaps even critics will concede that it offers something potentially useful to a science of the causes of consciousness. But it will surely be said that the explanatory gap has not been overcome and that we remain faced with an essentially brute fact of correlation between certain properties of neural events and certain kinds of phenomenal consciousness.

The strategy of this section has two parts. The first requires but one sentence: we should wholeheartedly agree with the objection. The remainder of this section will underwrite the agreement by explaining the reasons for it. In the following section, I will use our understanding of the reasons why we do not now understand consciousness to point to a way of conceiving how we may be able to improve our situation.

Let us begin with a point about explanation. Explaining why something occurs requires ruling out its nonoccurrence. If something, X, *might not*

---

4   The bearers of primitive mental properties, according to panpsychism, are *constituents* (Nagel, 1979, pp. 184–185; 1986, p. 50) or *elements* (Seager, 1995) of physical reality. (Seager's "elements" here are not the elements of the chemist's periodic table, but rather any small constituent of the physical world.)

have occurred, given what one says in one's explanation, then one has not explained why X has occurred.[5] This principle seems to be evident, but it may be challenged in view of certain interpretations of quantum mechanics. For example, it may be said that the decay of a particular radioactive atom, A, at a certain time, t, is explained by its instability. One may even make a *decision* to use "explanation" in such a way that such a claim is to be counted as true. Against such a decision, however, lies the fact that, according to quantum mechanical theory, A could have had that same instability and yet *not* have decayed at t. In fact, a natural way of stating the radical revision that many interpretations of quantum mechanics seem to require in our thinking is to say that, as a matter of deep principle, *there can be no explanation* of why A decays at t.[6] It is compatible with this point that we are able to explain why A *can* decay at t; this, however, is a different explanandum from the original.

If we use "explanation" in a way that respects the principle just enunciated, we can say that explanation of the occurrence of something requires some kind of necessity. Nonoccurrence of the explanandum must be ruled out; it cannot be open that it may not occur.[7] It is precisely here that explanation of consciousness comes to grief, for it seems that there is no necessity that consciousness occur, given that any pattern of neural activation occurs. Let us give this point some detail by considering some candidates for necessity.

The strongest kind of necessity would be logical (or mathematical) necessity, a necessity that would be paralleled by a deduction of qualitative

---

5 For similar views, see Donagan (1959) and Kitcher in Kitcher and Salmon (1989).

6 In contrast, there may well be causes of the winning of a particular race by the mud-running horse (one less affected by a muddy track than most racehorses), even though it does not win all of its muddy-track races (but only a relatively high percentage of them). It seems intuitively plausible that, in the case of a win, we would think that the horse's superior ability on mud is only one causal factor among several. The mud-running ability is not *the* cause of the win; besides the mud-running ability, the skill of the jockey, the position at the gate, the particularities of the competing horses, and the velocity of the wind are all likely contributors to the full cause of the win.

7 A hard case is presented by astronomically minuscule probabilities of, e.g., bodies failing to fall when support is removed. However, (i) removing support does *always* change the probability of falling from extremely low to extremely high. (ii) It seems likely that we are unable to form an *intuitive* difference between necessitating the extreme probability of an occurrence and necessitating the occurrence itself, however well we understand the difference intellectually. (iii) If there were an identifiable causal factor that separated the case of nonfalling unsupported bodies from the normal cases, we would likely include absence of that factor as part of the cause of falling. But the same theory that informs us of the minuscule probability of nonfalling also tells us that there is no such additional causal factor.

events from premises that assert that neural events of some kind occurred. If anyone could so much as imagine how such a deduction might go, the shape of discussions of consciousness in the past 300 years would have been entirely different from what it actually has been. Unfortunately, as explained in Chapter 11, we must sooner or later come to phenomenal qualities that we can no longer regard as structures (or combinations) of phenomenal qualities, and when we arrive at this point, our linguistic representations of phenomenal qualities will be undefined single terms. If these appear in the conclusion of a valid deduction of a categorical statement, they must have already appeared in the premises. In this case the argument will not be an explanation of their occurrence, because it must already presuppose it.

We might seek to introduce a kind of necessity through relations of *meaning*. If having a qualitative event of a certain phenomenal kind, Q, just means to behave in a certain way or to have a certain kind of brain event, then exhibiting that behavior, or possessing that kind of brain event, will guarantee the occurrence of a Q qualitative event. Behaviorism for qualitative events, however, has proven to be a dead end. Pain is the strongest candidate here, but in fact there is no behavior that one has to exhibit if one has a pain or that guarantees that one has a pain if one exhibits it.[8] For qualities other than those of bodily sensations, e.g., blue, the looseness of the relation between phenomenal quality and behavior is perfectly obvious. Also evident is the fact that connection of qualitative events with neural events is not a matter of meaning.

We can get a lively sense of compulsory occurrence of qualitative events if we have already established a correlation with neural events. For example, let us suppose that we know that Jones has normal sensitivity to painful stimuli. If we see that she has suffered some injury and is complaining about it, we will have no doubt that she is in pain. We will feel fully entitled to predict that if her brain gets into the same state at some future time, she will again be in pain. We might express this point by saying that she *couldn't* be in that same neural state again without being in pain again. This kind of necessity, however, is not one that will enable us to explain how or why we have phenomenal consciousness. The reason is that it presupposes the connection to be explained. *Given* that a certain neural state is correlated with being in pain, it must be that if that state occurs, so does pain; but, evidently, this cannot answer the question at

8   For discussion of pain, see Goldstein (1994). For general criticisms of logical behaviorism, see Chisholm (1957) and Geach (1957).

issue, namely, why it is the case that a certain neural state is correlated with being in pain?[9]

An alternative formulation of the point just made can be given in terms of laws of nature. Laws of nature license inferences, and thus, from one set of facts, plus connecting laws, we can infer another set of facts. The critical point can then be formulated this way: to explain a fact from other facts plus laws of nature evidently does not explain why the laws of nature are what they are. But the question that stands in the way of a unified understanding of consciousness and the physical world is exactly why it should be the case that there is a lawful connection between neural events and phenomenally qualitied conscious events.

A special case of necessity inherited from laws is what might be called "constructive" necessity. A body is constructed (or composed) of H_2O molecules, and at temperature T the body is a liquid. Liquidity of the body is explainable by reference to the properties of its constituent molecules and their relations at temperature T. This background gives a very robust sense to saying that the body *must* be liquid at T. This necessity, however, depends on the properties and relations of the constituent molecules and their relations to temperature; and these are contingent matters, that is, laws of nature and not laws of logic. We have already seen that, where there is complexity of structure in phenomenal qualities, we may expect corresponding complexity of structure in causes. Thus, *given* that some patterns of neural activation cause phenomenally conscious events, we may have a constructive science of complexes of phenomenally conscious events. But, evidently, such a constructive explanation cannot be offered for why elementary phenomenal qualities should be caused by just those neural events that do cause them.

---

9 This paragraph undercuts Searle's (1992) attempt to dismiss the mind–body problem by claiming that "given a full understanding of the brain, it seems to me likely that we would think it obvious that if the brain was in a certain sort of state, it had to be conscious" (p. 102). Searle buttresses this claim by observing that we already accept that if we see a screaming man with a foot caught in some machinery, it would be inconceivable that the man was not in pain. "The physical causes necessitate the pain" (p. 102). There is, of course, something right about this: namely, knowing what we do know about almost all people, that is, the generalization that having a body part crushed causes pain, we would unhesitatingly attribute pain to the imagined victim. This evident fact does nothing whatsoever to explain why the generalization is true. Likewise, we may discover generalizations about patterns of neural activity and pains. Such generalizations will enable us to deduce occurrences of pains from the generalizations and the pattern descriptions; but that fact does not show how we might ever be able to *explain* the generalizations themselves.

Perhaps it will be suggested that the necessity we need can be provided by Kripke's discovery that necessities can be known a posteriori. Identities, such as that between water and H_2O, or between heat (of bodies) and mean kinetic energy of molecular motion, have to be discovered by science, but since they are identities stated with rigidly designating expressions, they are necessary truths. It may be argued that the most parsimonious hypothesis is that phenomenally conscious events are identical with neural events, namely, the ones that exhibit patterns that QER unparsimoniously regards as causes of distinct, conscious events. And it may then be further argued that because the postulated identity is formulated with rigid designators, it expresses a necessary truth.

There are two difficulties in this suggestion. First, as is well known, Kripke (1971) has resisted the idea that there is a parallelism between the cases of heat and phenomenal qualities. The identity of heat with mean kinetic energy of molecular motion (hereafter, K) *appears* contingent, and this fact must be explained. A plausible explanation is that there is another fact with which the relation between heat and K can be confused – namely, the fact that the (feeling of) warmth that we have when we are near hot bodies could have failed to have been produced by them or could have been produced by something else. Thus, we have three terms in this case: heat, K, and warmth. The identity of the first two is necessary, but the connections between either of the first two and the third is contingent, and this latter fact explains the appearance of the contingency of the identity of the first two. This kind of explanation, however, is not available to us in the case of patterns in neural events and warmth itself. Warmth is not the cause of a certain feeling: it *is* a certain feeling. "Warmth" is already a rigid designator of that kind of feeling. It certainly does not *appear* that warmth is necessarily identical with (or necessarily connected in any way with) a pattern of neural activity. Thus, if we suppose that it is actually necessarily identical with such a pattern, we will have no explanation of the apparent contingency. The heat–K connection is thus not a good model for the connection between warmth and a pattern of neural activation.[10]

---

10 It might be suggested that there is an alternative explanation for the appearance of the contingency of the relation between warmth and pattern of activation. Namely, if one already has the idea of multiple realization, then contingency might seem to be built into the relation between any X and whatever it is that, in actual fact, realizes it. However, to apply this idea in the present case would presuppose that we think of phenomenal qualities as functional properties that may be multiply realized. While the view that phenomenal qualities are functional properties has its place in the dialectical history of philosophy of

Many materialists will be willing simply to bite the bullet at this point and postulate identity of phenomenal qualities with some properties of neural events without explaining the apparent contingency of the identity.[11] This possibility brings us to the second difficulty in the attempt to use the necessity of identity in the present context. The difficulty is that the materialism that results from the presently contemplated move is a completely empty materialism, and thus a view that is of no use at all in trying to approach a unified view of consciousness and the physical world. The root of the emptiness lies in the difference between the way identity is arrived at in genuine science and in materialist philosophy. In the scientific cases, the identity claim is reached on the basis of an *explanatory* connection. H_2O molecules have electrochemical properties and a natural resonance frequency. The former explain why H_2O molecules cluster around many other molecules and, thus, why the water that is composed of H_2O molecules is a good solvent. The latter explains why water does not absorb electromagnetic radiation with frequencies in the visible spectrum, and thus why water is transparent. Molecular motion of heated bodies helps to explain their expansion and the conduction of heat from one body to an adjacent body. By contrast, the identity proposed by materialist philosophy merely postulates an identity to achieve *parsimony*; but this parsimony does no explanatory work. Its claim that consciousness has been brought within the sphere of the physical, because it is necessarily identical with something in the physical world, merely hides the facts that the identification is merely postulated, unexplanatory, and utterly unlike the identities discovered by genuine scientific activity.[12] Such a view courts the danger of closing off the search for a unified view of

mind (see Chapter 8), it is doubtful that this view of phenomenal qualities is sufficiently plausible to account for our intuitions that such qualities are only contingently related to neural activation patterns.

11   Other materialists will try to explain *away* the appearance that an explanation is needed. Some such attempts depend on higher order representation theories, and are thus indirectly undercut by criticisms of those theories in Chapters 6 and 7. The deepest move in this direction depends on the concept/property distinction, which has already been considered in the section on property identity without explanatory reduction in Chapter 3.

12   QER and identity theory agree that there are brain state similarities and differences that correspond to structural similarities and differences in experience. A consequence of this agreement is that structural similarities and differences get substantively the same explanations (though QER speaks of parallel structures in the causes of qualitative events where identity theory speaks of parallel structures of identicals). So, it is not the *structural* explanations of identity theory that are here being characterized as unexplanatory and empty. It is the identity claim itself.

consciousness and neural activations by promotion of the illusion that such a view has already been achieved.

CONSERVATION

There is just one kind of necessity that remains to be considered, and it may be said to lie between logical necessity and lawful connection. This is the kind of necessity that flows from conservation principles. It is a contingent fact that water does not flow uphill, but once we are able to conceptualize such a case as a violation of conservation of energy, we get a robust sense of necessity of its nonoccurrence. Conservation of energy does not seem to be a logical or mathematical fact.[13] Nonetheless, it seems to be available as a way of providing some genuine explanatory backing to less basic causal facts.

There is, evidently, no reason to think that phenomenal qualities are describable in terms of energy, no reason to suppose that their production diverts energy from other effects of neural activities, and no known way of making it plausible that energy could enter the picture. Conservation of energy is mentioned here only as an aid in focusing on the *kind of necessity* that it confers on some explanations, and the intended suggestion is that we should abstract this type of explanatory backing from its attachment to energy. What we are left with after this abstraction is the form of a very fundamental principle that is not itself a principle of logic, but that stands as a basic principle that confers a kind of necessity on a broad class of explanations that are governed by it.

A conservation principle requires *something* that is conserved. Unfortunately, our present state of knowledge does not support any definite claim as to what this something might be. It does not seem out of the question, however, that such a conserved nature could be discovered. It is possible to *imagine* a candidate here in the form of complexity. To explain this remark, let us note that homogeneity can be regarded as a type of simplicity; it requires what might be called spatial or temporal "extensity", but the phenomenal quality that has extensity is a kind of sameness, and not something that is definable by reference to its parts. It

---

13 This appearance may be deceptive, for perhaps nothing could count as the *energy* of a body unless it was conserved. That properties *essentially* involve laws into which those properties enter is a thesis that has been argued for by Shoemaker (1980) and Swoyer (1982). I shall not go into this controversy here, because I believe that the use I shall make of the idea of conservation principles will survive whether the essentialist thesis stands or falls.

seems possible that homogeneity might be regarded as opposite to some type of complexity. A conservation of complexity principle would then require homogeneity to "offset" an increase in that type of complexity. That is, the total complexity of a system in which both a complexity property of neural activation patterns and its homogeneous (i.e., phenomenal qualitied) effect are included might be the same as the complexity of a less complex neural activation pattern that does not cause a phenomenal qualitied event. In such a case, it could conceivably turn out that conservation of a complexity property would give us a sense that a phenomenal qualitied event *had* to occur.

Let us go a little further down the path of imagination before returning to the sobriety of defensible claims. A clarification is in order concerning the phrase "a complexity property". Complexity is itself a rather complex subject of inquiry and requires recognition of at least two fundamental properties: (i) Kolmogorov complexity and (ii) logical (or computational) depth.[14] Both of these properties are to be included under the concept of a complexity property. We are not in a position to assert that the study of complexity will prove to require further properties that are as fundamental as these two, but neither can we foreclose on the possibility that the study of pattern in neural activations would lead to the introduction of further basic properties that would naturally be grouped with the two just cited. Such properties would also be "complexity properties" in the intended use of this term.

It seems conceivable that the neural activation patterns that cause our qualitative events should exhibit a complexity property that can be measured and that has a high value only in such events. If we can imagine that to be the case, we can also imagine that conceiving homogeneity as offsetting the complexity property of neural activation patterns would offer a striking theoretical simplification. That is, it is imaginable that homogeneity over a region of time, or space and time, may turn out to have a kind of "simplicity" or "negative complexity" that can keep a global measure of complexity near a neutral value. On such a conception, the

---

14 See Bennett (1988) and Juedes et al. (1994) for technically adequate definitions and discussion. Informally, Kolmogorov complexity of a string, S, of 0s and 1s is the length of the shortest program that would enable a standard Turing Machine to generate S exactly. (The longer this program has to be, the less redundant and less compressible S is, and the more randomness and more informational content it has.) Logical depth is the minimal time (measured in operational steps) that it would take a standard Turing Machine to compute S from random input. Greater depth corresponds to less triviality, in the sense in which a random sequence, though high in information, is trivial, or low in interest or usefulness.

complexity exhibited by neural activation patterns and the simplicity of homogeneous phenomenal qualities would be of opposite sign and could be algebraically summed. In that case, it might be very natural to think of phenomenal qualities as "forced upon" the world in something like the sense in which conservation of energy "forces" there to be causal relations among familiar examples of physical events.

Even with all this background, it is not clear how we could imagine understanding why a particular pattern produces a particular phenomenal quality, e.g., red as opposed to blue or as opposed to bitter. Nonetheless, if a system of patterns exhibited a characteristic complexity property and a set of relations among themselves that was isomorphic to phenomenal similarities and differences (e.g., groupings for tastes as distinguished from sounds and as distinguished from colors), it might be possible to conceive of phenomenal qualities as necessitated by the neural patterns with which they are associated.

It will hardly be necessary to point out that the last few paragraphs have been highly speculative. No one should assert that what has been described will be the shape of a future science of the causes of consciousness; at most it provides a glimmer of a possibility of future enlightenment. But in the darkness that otherwise surrounds the subject of consciousness, even a glimmer should be counted as welcome. Less metaphorically, the proposition we are entitled to take away from our flight of fancy is this. We do not know what an investigation of patterns of neural activity will discover, but we do not know that some satisfying advance cannot be made. It would be intellectually unhealthy not to be suspicious, and doubtful that the foregoing imaginings will turn out to be very close to the truth. But it would be intellectually arrogant to suppose that there *cannot* be some progress that is vaguely like what has been imagined. In this situation, the truly scientifically minded will say "Let us investigate; let us see what a detailed understanding of neural activation patterns may eventually suggest to us as a way of organizing our thinking about their properties."

THE NONTRANSITIVITY PROBLEM

The homogeneity of qualitative events was noted in early chapters and has become more and more central as I have explored the possibility of achieving a unified dualism. The final objection I shall consider is one that is particularly important, because it raises a deep and difficult problem for any theory that embraces homogeneity.

Let us state the problem as starkly as possible. Imagine that we have an appearance of a patch of color, and that we have labeled some small regions of this appearance as *a*, *b*, *c*, and *d*. We may assume that there are corresponding regions of some physical color patch, but the letters are to be understood as referring to subregions of the *appearance*, not the patch. Of course, some philosophers will object to talking this way; but we may assume they will agree that qualitative event realists are committed to accepting the sense of such remarks, and they will not hesitate to accept any difficulties such remarks may lead to as potential reductios of QER. Now, let us stipulate that the possessor of the appearance says that *a* and *d* are different but that, when attending to any of the adjacent pairs of regions, the subject says (with sincerity) that they look the same. Finally, let us stipulate that this is a case in which the subject also says that the transition looks smooth, i.e., that there do not seem to be any edges where the color changes. (The possibility of such a case is a familiar datum. The stipulation is not that such a case is possible, but only that it is this kind of case that we are now to consider.)

It seems that we must say in this case that (i) there are real qualitative differences between at least one of the adjacent pairs of labeled regions (and, of course, possibly between each of the pairs). This is forced upon us by the transitivity of identity: if there were no qualitative difference between any of the adjacent regions, then the color of $a =$ the color of $b =$ the color of $c =$ the color of d, and so the color of $a =$ the color of d, contrary to the hypothesis. But now we are talking about the qualities of the appearances, that is, the way things look. So, we must say that there is a real difference in the way some pair of external patches look. Without loss of generality, let us suppose that these are patches that cause subregions a and b. Then we can say that there is a real difference in the qualities of a and b. And since these are qualities of the way things look, this difference is a *phenomenal* difference, i.e., a difference of phenomenal qualities. But it also seems that we must say that (ii) the regions of the external object that correspond to a and b look the same to the possessor of the appearance of the region of which they are both subregions. That is, it seems we must say that a and b are phenomenally the same – they have the same phenomenal qualities. Putting (i) and (ii) together, we have that a and b are phenomenally the same and phenomenally different. This is a contradiction, and if QER really leads to it, it must be rejected.

Briefly stated, the solution to this difficulty is as follows. Qualitative event realists must accept (i), and thus they ought to reject (ii). They *can* reject (ii) by rejecting the move from "looks the same" to "has the same phenomenal quality". "Looks the same" can be thought of as equivalent to "I can't tell any difference"; and inability to tell any difference is not the same as telling that there is no difference.[15]

However formally correct this solution might be, it is not satisfying. Let us ask why. An obvious point is that this answer introduces the possibility of error with respect to our own appearances. *a* and *b* are qualitatively different, but we judge that they are not. This is no problem if we are talking about external objects, but how can our *appearances* differ when we don't think they do?

If one assimilates judging, or knowing, into the very constitution of appearances, there is no good answer available to this question. I have, however, already argued against this assimilation in Chapter 10. If that argument is accepted, and it is agreed that being an appearance is not the kind of thing that entails knowledge, then there is logical space for small differences in appearances to occur without knowledge of them, and even for small differences in appearances to occur compatibly with false belief in their absence.

Even if this point is accepted, however, it still needs to be explained how the required misfires of beliefs are possible. Here is a solution: whether our belief is true or false, it concerns the properties in two regions that we regard as separate. (If we could not be regarding them as separate, we would be judging only that the color at *a* is the color at *a*.) Identifying two regions about which to make a judgment takes a small amount of time – time enough for a shift of attention from one region to another. This time can allow a small deterioration of memory and/or an opportunity for the pattern of neural activity causing the color of region *a* to interact with the pattern of activity causing the color of region *b*. If the patterns are similar enough so that a difference is not preserved in (short-term) memory, then no sense of difference will arise, and the judgment will be made that there is no difference.[16]

---

15 This resolution has some similarity to some ideas in Burgess (1990). Burgess tries to apply his view to underwrite the idea that appearances may not even appear to be continuous; they may merely fail to appear discontinuous. However, while such an idea can be given substance in connection with apparent continuity of external surfaces, it cannot be taken over into appearances, since there is no way to make more than a verbal difference between "appearance in which no discontinuity appears" and "appearance that appears continuous".

16 As an anonymous reviewer has pointed out, we need not shift attention when there are salient differences of quality. But in the case now being considered, one is actively trying to find a difference, and what we do in such cases is to try to compare one region with another. (These regions do not, of course, have marked boundaries, but are identified only as, e.g., "here ... and a little to the right".) Sometimes this works. For example, one can notice

We do not normally dwell on cases where judgments of difference are so difficult, but the explanation just given seems to be a natural extension of a very familiar experience. We may have lived for years surrounded by a wall painted a certain shade of off-white. We know perfectly well what the wall looks like. Our long experience, however, will not serve us as a good guide when we have made some small repair and now want to buy some matching paint. We will, of course, not return from the paint store with red paint, or even pale pink or eggshell blue. But there will be a range around the desired color within which our memory will not preserve a definite template for comparison. Bringing home a set of samples will help, and we will be able to eliminate some colors by looking at the wall, then looking away toward the card in our hand. Several will be left, and we will do best by holding the card against the wall and comparing. The explanation of the previous paragraph holds that even in this case there must be some reliance on memory. Two patches can be in our visual fields without being in our attentional fields, and the comparison process takes a theoretically significant, though practically negligible, time. The explanation of the previous paragraph further holds that the same points apply when we consider attending to different regions of our appearances. This likewise takes time and thus leaves judgment dependent on memory. Again, the time is small, but so are the differences that may be falsely judged. The vagaries of memory that occur for these small times and small differences are well below any practical significance, or even detectability in everyday contexts, but they are sufficient to resolve the problem posed by intransitivity of indiscriminability.

The explanation just sketched crucially depends on the idea of shifts of attention and the fact that these take time. Let us call it the "shift of attention view" (SAV) of the intransitivity of indiscriminability. The SAV will, perhaps, resolve a puzzlement caused by a remark in Jackson and Pinkerton (1973). These authors consider the suggestion that A might look the same as B, and B might look the same as C, but A might not look the same as C. They object that if this is supposed to happen in one person at one time, the case is inconsistent. Since A and C look different, looking the same as one of them must be different from looking the same

what one previously did not notice, namely, the difference in brightness of a uniformly colored carpet at a place near a window and at a place on the other side of the room. But one will fail to judge a difference between the regions at 6 feet and 7 feet from the window.

as the other; thus the supposed B will have to look two different ways at the same time. A possible reaction to this objection is that it simply begs the question. That is, it might seem as if the phenomenon to be accounted for just is the fact that, at one and the same time, A = B, B = C, and A ≠ C (reading "=" as qualitative identity). The SAV resolves the tension between these claims in the following way. There can be a phenomenal color expanse that lasts for a few seconds during which it does not strike us as changing, and in which we do not judge A to differ from B or B to differ from C, even though we judge A to differ from C. These facts explain why we are inclined to accept the phenomenal description. But, strictly speaking at a refined time scale, each of the comparative judgments takes time and occurs at different times; and thus the threatened inconsistency is avoided.

The SAV has a consequence that may be thought to undercut QER. This consequence is that we are in no position to rule out the view that there are discrete changes (or boundaries or bands) in an apparently continuously varying color appearance. Consider again our two appearance regions *a* and *b*. We supposed that *a* and *b* are different in quality, but that the attentional shift required for their possessor to judge about their quality induced a loss of memory that, had it been preserved, might have allowed successful comparison. (Such loss is equivalent to confusion, which can be plausibly traced to deterioration of pattern during the time of the attentional shift.) Now, this account is compatible with strict continuity in the passage of color difference from region *a* to region *b*; but it is also *compatible* with there being a discrete boundary between the color qualities in the two regions, so long as the difference on either side of the boundary is small. The SAV thus deflects an objection to a strict continuity of variability view, but it does not offer support for it in the sense of implying continuity of variability rather than a small discrete change view.

This consequence may be thought to lead directly to a problem for the continuity of spread, and thus to a reason for rejecting the considerable body of appeals I have made to arguments based on homogeneity of phenomenal qualities. The problem will arise, namely, if we take difference of *location* to be just another instance of qualitative difference; for then, we can conclude that the SAV that we needed to account for intransitivity of indiscriminability will also apply to location. But if we must accept this application to location, we will be in danger of undercutting the view that there are homogeneous qualities. If we can fail to distinguish close but discrete locations, then for all we know, phenomenal color is not homogeneous, but instead composed of discrete color points.[17]

There are, however, two reasons why difference of location *cannot* be treated as qualitative difference from the perspective of the SAV. One is that if there is nothing at a location between two other locations, that is a *gap*, which is a large difference, not a small one. Thus, the SAV will not imply that there should be inability to judge the presence of such a gap. The second reason is that the SAV presupposes that attention is shifted from one location to another. It says that in attending to one location and then another (for the purpose of comparing qualities at those locations) there is a small time lapse, and that this allows for memorial deterioration leading to inability to judge a qualitative difference. If we try to apply this idea to location, we get the following: in attending to one location and then another (for the purpose of comparing locational qualities) there is a small time lapse, and this allows for memorial deterioration leading to inability to judge a difference in location. But this attempted application yields *nonsense*. We cannot coherently suppose that we have shifted our attention from one location to another and at the same time suppose that we are mistaken when we judge ourselves to have made such a shift.

It is, however, possible to *think* we have shifted the location of our attention, even though we have failed to do so, i.e., we attend in fact to the same location both before and after what we mistakenly take to be a shift. One might argue that such an error leads to a false impression of homogeneity by leading us to judge qualitative sameness at different places when in fact we are only judging qualitative sameness at the same place. However, occasional errors of this kind would not suffice to undercut the correctness of our judgments of homogeneity. To get that unhappy result, we would have to make the implausible supposition that we pervasively fail to succeed in our apparent shifts of attention.

The conclusion we should draw from the last two paragraphs is that there are, within the SAV, good, principled reasons to distinguish location from qualitative aspects of experience. A further conclusion we should draw on the basis of this distinguishability is that while both strictly continuous qualitative variation and qualitative variation by very small discrete changes are compatible with our experience, we do not have a theory that allows us to understand how color experience could fail to be literally continuously spread out. We do not have a theory that makes the idea

---

17 This objection is a natural application of considerations developed in Clark (1989).

of a color *point* intelligible.[18] As far as we can understand the matter, we must think of color as occupying *regions* (whether it changes over those regions continuously or by small jumps). This conclusion is sufficient to support the appeals to homogeneity that have occurred in this book.

I have followed common practice in using color as an example of variable quality and in conceiving of homogeneity primarily in terms of spatial spread. But I want to make it explicit that the same conclusions are to be applied to changes over time. Here it is, perhaps, even more obvious that comparative judgments require reliance on memory. The arguments of the last few paragraphs will lead us to say that a tone, (or a taste, smell, or feeling of pressure) might insensibly change into another easily distinguishable one over a period of time, even though for pairs of times within the period, we do not have a sense of qualitative difference. Again, the variability could be strictly continuous or it could be a series of small differences. And, again, the argument for the possibility of qualitative variation by small differences cannot be reiterated so as to show the intelligibility of the idea that the sound of a foghorn, the smell of a bakery, and so on are "really" temporal series of sound points, smell points, and so on. Thus, we are entitled to continue to regard phenomenal qualities as *filling* time (and sometimes, space) and to think of consciousness as essentially composed of events that instantiate properties that are homogeneous.

CONCLUSION

Contemporary investigators of phenomenal consciousness must first decide whether to try to explain it or to try to explain it away. In Chapter 9, I have said what can be said in support of the first alternative in a relatively short and direct way. In the long run, however, the best response to skepticism is the possibility of interesting development of a realist view. In Part II of this book, I have sketched some ideas for a possible future. It is evident that we are not yet in that future, but to me the possibilities look exciting.

Realists are rightly called upon to state the content of their realism. I began to do this in Chapter 2 and have added many specifications of QER as the book has progressed. A crucial part of this specification is the choice

---

18 It may be possible to define "color at point *p*" by reference to intersections of colored regions. Such a definition, however, would presuppose color regions, and its possibility thus does not undercut the point being made in the text.

between materialism and dualism. In Chapter 3, I argued that it is vain to look for demonstration on either side of this issue. Since then, I have weighed the merits of various views, and my conclusion is this. When materialism is formulated in ways that have genuine content, it runs into difficulties from which it can escape only by reducing its content. In the end, what remains is an empty shell whose only virtue is that it cannot be shown to be contradictory. Despite historical association with examples drawn from science and despite (unsuccessful) appeals to scientific analogies or alleged principles of simplicity, such empty materialism is not a deliverance of any scientific research, but only a metaphysical preference.

Dualism does not now offer an explanation of consciousness. But – somewhat paradoxically – by facing up squarely to the reality of the explanatory gap, it offers the possibility of a research program that can conceivably lead to a reduction of puzzlement about the relation between our experiences and our brains. We should not let idle assurances that everything is material interfere with our pursuit of a conceptual revision that may permit that kind of advance in our understanding. As far as we have any reason to believe, the qualitative events that do not seem to be material really are not material. Instead of resting with an identity about which nothing further can be said, we should bend our intellectual efforts toward understanding how the phenomenally qualited events that constitute our conscious experiences are related to the properties of events in our brains.

References

Anscombe, G. E. M. (1963/1981) "The Intentionality of Sensation: A Grammatical Feature", in *The Collected Philosophical Papers of G. E. M. Anscombe, vol. 2: Metaphysics and the Philosophy of Mind* (Oxford: Blackwell), pp. 3–20. Given as the Howison Lecture in 1963.

Aristotle, *De Somniis (On Dreams)*, 458b–462b.

Armstrong, D. M. (1968) *A Materialist Theory of the Mind* (New York: Humanities Press).

Baldwin, T. (1992) "The Projective Theory of Sensory Content", in T. Crane, ed., *The Contents of Experience* (Cambridge: Cambridge University Press), pp. 177–195.

Bennett, C. H. (1988) "Logical Depth and Physical Complexity", in R. Herken, ed., *The Universal Turing Machine: A Half Century Survey* (Oxford: Oxford University Press), pp. 227–257.

Berkeley, G. (1734/1948) *Three Dialogues Between Hylas and Philonous*. In A. A. Luce and T. E. Jessop, eds., *The Works of George Berkeley, Bishop of Cloyne* (London: Nelson & Sons, 1948). Page references are to volume ii of the Luce–Jessop edition.

Block, N. (1995a) "On a Confusion about a Function of Consciousness", *Behavioral and Brain Sciences*, 18:227–247.

Block, N. (1995b) "How Many Concepts of Consciousness?" (Author's response to commentaries on the target article), *Behavioral and Brain Sciences*, 18:272–287.

Boghossian, P. A. and Velleman, D. J. (1989) "Color as Secondary Quality", *Mind*, 98:81–103.

Burgess, J. A. (1990) "Phenomenal Qualities and the Nontransitivity of Matching", *Australasian Journal of Philosophy*, 68:206–220.

Byrne, A. and Hilbert, D. (1997) *Readings on Color* (Cambridge, MA: MIT Press).

Cariani, P. (1994) "As If Time Really Mattered: Temporal Strategies for Neural Coding of Sensory Information", in K. Pribram, ed., *Origins: Brain and Self Organization* (Hillsdale, NJ: Erlbaum), pp. 208–252.

Carruthers, P. (1989) "Brute Experience", *Journal of Philosophy*, 86:258–269.

Chalmers, D. J. (1996) *The Conscious Mind: In Search of a Fundamental Theory* (Oxford: Oxford University Press).

251

Chisholm, R. (1948) "The Problem of Empiricism", *Journal of Philosophy*, 45:512–517.

Chisholm, R. (1957) *Perceiving: A Philosophical Study* (Ithaca, NY: Cornell University Press).

Chisholm, R. and Sellars, W. (1958) "Chisholm–Sellars Correspondence on Intentionality", in H. Feigl, M. Scriven, and G. Maxwell, eds., *Concepts, Theories, and the Mind–Body Problem, Minnesota Studies in the Philosophy of Science*, vol. 2 (Minneapolis: University of Minnesota Press), pp. 521–539.

Churchland, P. M. (1979) *Scientific Realism and the Plasticity of Mind* (Cambridge: Cambridge University Press).

Churchland, P. S. (1998) "Brainshy: Nonneural Theories of Conscious Experience", in S. R. Hameroff et al., eds. (1998), pp. 109–126.

Clark, A. (1989) "The Particulate Instantiation of Homogeneous Pink", *Synthese*, 80:277–304.

Clark, A. (1993) *Sensory Qualities* (Oxford: Oxford University Press).

Clark, A. (2000) *A Theory of Sentience* (Oxford: Oxford University Press).

Cohen, J. D. and Schooler, J. W., eds. (1977) *Scientific Approaches to Consciousness* (Mahwah, NJ: Erlbaum).

Cottrell, A. (1999) "Sniffing the Camembert: On the Conceivability of Zombies", *Journal of Consciousness Studies*, 6:4–12.

Crick, F. and Koch, C. (1995) "Why Neuroscience May Be Able to Explain Consciousness", *Scientific American*, December, pp. 84–85.

Dark, V. J. (1988) "Semantic Priming, Prime Reportability, and Retroactive Priming Are Interdependent", *Memory and Cognition*, 16:299–308.

Dark, V. J. and Benson, K. (1991) "Semantic Priming and Identification of Near Threshold Primes in a Lexical Decision Task", *Quarterly Journal of Experimental Psychology*, 43A:53–78.

Dennett, D. C. (1978) *Brainstorms* (Cambridge, MA: MIT Press/Bradford).

Dennett, D. C. (1985) "Can Machines Think?", in M. Shafto, ed., *How We Know* (San Francisco: Harper & Row), pp. 121–145.

Dennett, D. C. (1988) "Quining Qualia", in A. Marcel and E. Bisiach, eds., *Consciousness in Contemporary Science* (New York: Oxford University Press), pp. 42–77.

Dennett, D. C. (1991) *Consciousness Explained* (Boston: Little, Brown).

Descartes, R. (1641) *Meditations on First Philosophy.*

Descartes, R. (1644) *The Principles of Philosophy.*

Donagan, Alan (1959) "Explanation in History", in P. Gardiner, ed., *Theories of History* (New York: Free Press of Glencoe), pp. 428–443.

Doxiadis, A. (1992) *Uncle Petros and Goldbach's Conjecture* (New York and London: Bloomsbury).

Dretske, F. (1988) *Explaining Behavior* (Cambridge, MA: MIT Press).

Dretske, F. (1995) *Naturalizing the Mind* (Cambridge, MA: MIT Press).

Feigl, H. (1958) "The 'Mental' and the 'Physical' ", in H. Feigl et al., eds. (1958), pp. 370–497.

Feigl, H., Scriven, M., and Maxwell, G., eds. (1958) *Concepts, Theories, and the Mind–Body Problem, Minnesota Studies in the Philosophy of Science*, vol. II (Minneapolis: University of Minnesota Press).

Flanagan, O. (1992) *Consciousness Reconsidered* (Cambridge, MA: MIT Press).

Fodor, J. (2000) *The Mind Doesn't Work That Way: The Scope and Limits of Computational Psychology* (Cambridge, MA: MIT Press/Bradford).

Gallistel, C. R. (1990) *The Organization of Learning* (Cambridge, MA: MIT Press).

Geach, P. T. (1957) *Mental Acts: Their Content and Their Objects* (New York: Humanities Press).

Gödel, K. (1931) "Über Formal Unentscheidbare Sätze der *Principia Mathematica* und Verwandter Systeme, I", *Monatshefte für Mathematik und Physik*, 38:173–198.

Goldman, A. I. (1971) "The Individuation of Action", *Journal of Philosophy*, 68: 761–774.

Goldstein, I. (1994) "Identifying Mental States: A Celebrated Hypothesis Refuted", *Australasian Journal of Philosophy*, 72:46–62.

Grisham, J. (1991) *The Firm* (New York: Doubleday).

Haldane, E. S. and Ross, G. R. T., trs. (1931) *The Philosophical Works of Descartes* (Cambridge: Cambridge University Press).

Hameroff, S. R., Kaszniak, A. W., and Scott, A. C., eds. (1998) *Toward a Science of Consciousness II: The Second Tucson Discussions and Debates* (Cambridge, MA: MIT Press/Bradford).

Hameroff, S. R. and Penrose, R. (1995–1997) "Conscious Events as Orchestrated Space-Time Selections", in J. Shear, ed., *Explaining Consciousness – The 'Hard Problem'* (Cambridge, MA: MIT Press/Bradford), pp. 177–195.

Hardin, C. L. (1988) *Color for Philosophers* (Indianapolis: Hackett).

Harman, G. (1990) "The Intrinsic Quality of Experience", *Philosophical Perspectives*, 4:31–52.

Hill, C. (1991) *Sensations: A Defense of Type Materialism* (Cambridge: Cambridge University Press).

Hobbes, T. (1651) *Leviathan*.

Hodgson, D. (1991) *The Mind Matters: Consciousness and Choice in a Quantum World* (Oxford: Oxford University Press).

Hume, D. (1748) *An Inquiry Concerning Human Understanding*.

Jackson, F. C. (1982) "Epiphenomenal Qualia", *Philosophical Quarterly*, 32:127–136.

Jackson, F. C. and Pinkerton, R. J. (1973) "On an Argument Against Sensory Items", *Mind*, 82:269–271.

Juedes, D. W., Lathrop, J. I., and Lutz, J. H. (1994) "Computational Depth and Reducibility", *Theoretical Computer Science*, 132:37–70.

Kandel, E. R., Schwartz, J. H., and Jessell, T. M., eds. (1995) *Essentials of Neural Science and Behavior* (Stamford, CT: Appleton & Lange).

Kihlstrom, J. F. (1999) "Conscious versus Unconscious Cognition", in R. J. Sternberg, ed., *The Nature of Cognition* (Cambridge, MA: MIT Press/Bradford), pp. 173–203.

Kim, J. (1973) "Causation, Nomic Subsumption, and the Concept of Event", *Journal of Philosophy*, 70:217–236.

Kim, J. (1976) "Events as Property Exemplifications", in M. Brand and D. Walton, eds., *Action Theory* (Dordrecht: Reidel), pp. 159–177.

Kim, J. (1993) *Supervenience and Mind: Selected Philosophical Essays* (Cambridge: Cambridge University Press).

Kitcher, P. and Salmon, W. (1989) *Scientific Explanation* (Minneapolis: University of Minnesota Press).

Kripke, S. (1971) "Identity and Necessity", in M. K. Munitz, ed., *Identity and Individuation* (New York: New York University Press), pp. 135–164.

Levine, J. (1983) "Materialism and Qualia: The Explanatory Gap", *Pacific Philosophical Quarterly*, 64:354–361.

Levine, J. (2001) *Purple Haze* (Oxford: Oxford University Press).

Lewis, C. I. (1929) *Mind and the World Order* (New York: Charles Scribner's Sons).

Loar, B. (1990) "Phenomenal States", *Philosophical Perspectives*, 4:81–108.

Locke, J. (1690) *An Essay Concerning Human Understanding*.

Lockwood, M. (1989) *Mind, Brain, and the Quantum* (Oxford: Blackwell).

Lormand, E. (1996) "Nonphenomenal Consciousness", *Noûs*, 30:242–261.

Lycan, W. G. (1987) *Consciousness* (Cambridge, MA: MIT Press).

Lycan, W. G. (1996) *Consciousness and Experience* (Cambridge, MA: MIT Press).

Maxwell, G. (1978) "Rigid Designators and Mind–Brain Identity", in C. W. Savage, ed. (1978), pp. 365–403.

McDowell, J. (1994) *Mind and World* (Cambridge, MA: Harvard University Press).

McGinn, C. (1991) *The Problem of Consciousness* (Oxford: Blackwell).

Metzinger, T., ed. (1995) *Conscious Experience* (Thorverton, UK: Imprint Academic).

Millikan, R. G. (1984) *Language, Thought, and Other Biological Categories: New Foundations for Realism* (Cambridge, MA: MIT Press).

Moore, G. E. (1903/1922) "The Refutation of Idealism", *Mind*, 12:433–453. Reprinted in G. E. Moore, *Philosophical Studies* (London: Routledge and Kegan Paul, 1922). Page references are to the 1922 volume.

Moore, G. E. (1953/1966) *Some Main Problems of Philosophy* (London: Allen & Unwin). Page references are to the 1966 edition.

Muter, P. (1980) "Very Rapid Forgetting", *Memory & Cognition*, 8:174–179.

Nagel, T. (1979) "Panpsychism", in T. Nagel, *Mortal Questions* (Cambridge: Cambridge University Press), pp. 181–195.

Nagel, T. (1986) *The View from Nowhere* (Oxford: Oxford University Press).

Nagel, T. (1998) "Conceiving the Impossible and the Mind–Body Problem", Royal Institute of Philosophy Lecture for 1998, *Philosophy*, 73:337–352.

O'Shaughnessy, B. (1980) *The Will: A Dual Aspect Theory* (Cambridge: Cambridge University Press).

Peacocke, C. (1983) *Sense and Content* (Oxford: Oxford University Press).

Peirce, C. S. (1935) *Collected Papers of Charles Sanders Peirce*, vol. VI, *Scientific Metaphysics*, C. Hartshorne and P. Weiss, eds. (Cambridge, MA: Harvard University Press).

Penrose, R. (1989) *The Emperor's New Mind* (Oxford: Oxford University Press).

Penrose, R. (1994) *Shadows of the Mind* (Oxford: Oxford University Press).

Putnam, H. (1965) "Brains and Behavior", in R. Butler, ed., *Analytical Philosophy*, second series (Oxford: Oxford University Press), pp. 1–20.

Quine, W. V. O. (1992) *The Pursuit of Truth*, 2nd ed. (Cambridge, MA: Harvard University Press).

Raffman, D. (1995) "On the Persistence of Phenomenology", in T. Metzinger, ed., (1995), pp. 293–308.

Rensink, R. A., O'Regan, J. K., and Clark, J. J. (1997) "To See or Not to See: The Need for Attention to Perceive Changes in Scenes", *Psychological Science*, 8:368–373.

Robinson, W. S. (1982) "Causation, Sensations, and Knowledge", *Mind*, 91: 524–540.

Robinson, W. S. (1988) *Brains and People* (Philadelphia: Temple University Press).

Robinson, W. S. (1992a) *Computers, Minds, and Robots* (Philadelphia: Temple University Press).

Robinson, W. S. (1992b) "Penrose and Mathematical Ability", *Analysis*, 52:80–87.

Robinson, W. S. (1994) "Orwell, Stalin, and Determinate Qualia", *Pacific Philosophical Quarterly*, 75:151–164.

Robinson, W. S. (1996a) "The Hardness of the Hard Problem", *Journal of Consciousness Studies*, 3:14–25. Reprinted in J. Shear, ed., *Explaining Consciousness – The 'Hard Problem'* (Cambridge, MA: MIT Press, 1995–1997), pp. 149–161.

Robinson, W. S. (1996b) Review of Roger Penrose, *Shadows of the Mind, Philosophical Psychology*, 9:119–122.

Robinson, W. S. (1997a) "Some Nonhuman Animals Can Have Pains in a Morally Relevant Sense", *Biology and Philosophy*, 12:51–71.

Robinson, W. S. (1997b) "Intrinsic Qualities of Experience: Surviving Harman's Critique", *Erkenntnis*, 47:285–309.

Robinson, W. S. (1998) "Could a Robot Be Qualitatively Conscious?", *AISB Quarterly*, No. 99:13–18. ("AISB" abbreviates "Artificial Intelligence and Simulation of Behavior".)

Robinson, W. S. (1999a) "Epiphenomenalism" in the *Stanford Encyclopedia of Philosophy*, electronic publication by CSLI, Stanford University, archive edition of March 31, 1999. Available at http://plato.stanford.edu/entries/epiphenomenalism/

Robinson, W. S. (1999b) "Qualia Realism and Neural Activation Patterns", *Journal of Consciousness Studies*, 6:65–80.

Robinson, W. S. (forthcoming) "Thoughts without Distinctive Non-Imagistic Phenomenology", *Philosophy and Phenomenological Research*.

Rosenthal, D. (1986) "Two Concepts of Consciousness", *Philosophical Studies*, 94: 329–359.

Rosenthal, D. (1990) *A Theory of Consciousness*, Report No. 40/1990 (Bielefeld, Germany: Research Group on Mind and Brain, Center for Interdisciplinary Research, University of Bielefeld).

Rosenthal, D. (1991) "The Independence of Consciousness and Sensory Quality", in E. Villanueva, ed., *Consciousness: Philosophical Issues*, vol. 1 (Atascadero, CA: Ridgeview), pp. 15–36.

Rosenthal, D. (1993) "Thinking That One Thinks", in M. Davies and G. W. Humphreys, eds., *Consciousness: Psychological and Philosophical Essays* (Oxford: Blackwell), pp. 197–223.

Russell, B. (1912) *The Problems of Philosophy* (Oxford: Oxford University Press).

Russell, B. (1927a) *An Outline of Philosophy* (London: Allen & Unwin).

Russell, B. (1927b) *The Analysis of Matter* (London: Kegan Paul).

Ryle, G. (1949) *The Concept of Mind* (London: Hutchinson).

255

Savage, C. W., ed. (1978) *Perception and Cognition: Issues in the Foundations of Psychology, Minnesota Studies in the Philosophy of Science*, vol. IX (Minneapolis: University of Minnesota Press).

Seager, W. (1995) "Consciousness, Information and Panpsychism", *Journal of Consciousness Studies*, 2:272–288.

Seager, W. (1999) *Theories of Consciousness* (London and New York: Routledge).

Searle, J. R. (1992) *The Rediscovery of the Mind* (Cambridge, MA: MIT Press/Bradford).

Sellars, W. (1956) "Empiricism and the Philosophy of Mind", in H. Feigl and M. Scriven, eds., *The Foundations of Science and the Concepts of Psychology and Psychoanalysis, Minnesota Studies in the Philosophy of Science*, vol. 1 (Minneapolis: University of Minnesota Press), pp. 253–329.

Sellars, W. (1963) *Science, Perception and Reality* (London: Routledge & Kegan Paul).

Sellars, W. (1971) "Science, Sense Impressions and Sensa", *The Review of Metaphysics*, 24:391–447.

Sellars, W. (1981) "Foundations for a Metaphysics of Pure Process" (The Carus Lectures for 1977–1978), *The Monist*, 64:3–90.

Shaffer, J. (1968) *Philosophy of Mind* (Englewood Cliffs, NJ: Prentice-Hall).

Shiffrin, R. M. (1997) "Attention, Automatism, and Consciousness", in J. D. Cohen and J. W. Schooler, eds. (1997), pp. 49–64.

Shoemaker, S. (1980) "Causality and Properties", in P. van Inwagen, ed., *Time and Cause* (Dordrecht: Reidel), pp. 109–135.

Simons, D. J., Franconeri, S. L., and Reimer, R. L. (2000) "Change Blindness in the Absence of a Visual Disruption", *Perception*, 29:1143–1154.

Simons, D. J. and Levin, D. T. (1997) "Failure to Detect Changes to Attended Objects", *Investigative Ophthalmology and Visual Science*, 38:S707.

Skarda, C. and Freeman, W. (1987) "How Brains Make Chaos in Order to Make Sense of the World", *Behavioral and Brain Sciences*, 10:161–195.

Stalnaker, R. (1996) "On a Defense of the Hegemony of Representation", in E. Villanueva, ed., *Perception: Philosophical Issues*, vol. 7 (Atascadero, CA: Ridgeview), pp. 101–108.

Stapp, H. (1993) *Mind, Matter, and Quantum Mechanics* (Berlin: Springer-Verlag).

Strawson, G. (1994) *Mental Reality* (Cambridge, MA: MIT Press/Bradford).

Stubenberg, L. (1998) *Consciousness and Qualia* (Amsterdam and Philadelphia: John Benjamins).

Sturgeon, S. (2000) *Matters of Mind: Consciousness, Reason and Nature* (London and New York: Routledge).

Swoyer, C. (1982) "The Nature of Natural Laws", *Australasian Journal of Philosophy*, 60:203–223.

Turing, A. (1950) "Computing Machinery and Intelligence", *Mind*, 59:433–460.

Tye, M. (1995a) *Ten Problems of Consciousness: A Representational Theory of the Phenomenal Mind* (Cambridge, MA: MIT Press/Bradford).

Tye, M. (1995b) "Blindsight, Orgasm and Representational Overlap", (open peer commentary on Block, 1995a), *Behavioral and Brain Sciences*, 18:268–269.

Tye, M. (2000) *Consciousness, Color and Content* (Cambridge, MA: MIT Press).

Velmans, M. (2000) *Understanding Consciousness* (London and Philadelphia: Routledge).

Wegner, D. M., and Wheatley, T. (1999) "Apparent Mental Causation: Sources of the Experience of Will", *American Psychologist*, 54:480–492.

White, S. L. (1986) "Curse of the Qualia", *Synthese*, 68:333–368.

Wittgenstein, L. (1953) *Philosophical Investigations* (New York: Macmillan).

Wolfe, J. M. (1999) "Inattentional Amnesia", in V. Coltheart, ed., *Fleeting Memories* (Cambridge, MA: MIT Press/Bradford), pp. 71–94.

Yablo, S. (1993) "Is Conceivability a Guide to Possibility?", *Philosophy and Phenomenological Research*, 53:1–42.

Index